BIBLICAL ECONOMICS 101

LIVING UNDER GOD'S FINANCIAL BLESSING

S.R. WATKINS

NEW START
MINISTRIES

The comments and opinions expressed in this book are precisely that; "opinions" and opinions are never right or wrong; they are "opinions." It is not the intention of the author to coerce, force, or influence anyone other than to move them closer toward God. Further, it is not the intention of the author to solicit funds or donations (however, donations to this Ministry are appreciated, although tax receipts are unavailable). Suggested book reading/posters etc., are just that, "a suggestion." With a few exceptions, the author of this publication does not know the authors of the books that he is recommending.

If this book is a blessing to you, and if you have comments or suggestions, please email the author at: info@newstartministries.ca

CONTENTS

ENDORSEMENTS

"Religion and a poverty mindset are used in a powerful way to hinder Christians from receiving God's blessings for their lives! These people are often captured by the wrong use of scriptures. Believers are conditioned to believe that having finances will prevent them from being spiritual. Much of this teaching came from Greek philosophy and not from God's Word.

Dr. Stuart R. Watkins in his book, Biblical Economics 101: Living Under God's Financial Blessing, gives a Biblical understanding of God's plan for wealth. He destroys the cynicism of those who reject Kingdom prosperity. A fresh understanding of Kingdom wealth frees the reader to partner with God for transformation in the earth. Your life will be filled with the blessings of the Lord when you implement the principles found in Biblical Economics 101. Get ready to increase and multiply your finances for Kingdom purposes!"

Barbara Wentroble
President, International Breakthrough Ministries (IbM)
President, Breakthrough Business Leaders (BBL)
Author, *Becoming a Wealth Creator; Prophetic Intercession; Fighting for Your Prophetic Promises; Council Room of the Lord Series.*

"Dr. Watkins has done a great service for many of us when he compiled his book, Biblical Economics 101: Living Under God's Financial Blessing.

This has to be the most balanced and useful summary of this topic I have come across. The clarity of his thinking and explanations of what Scripture teaches is to be highly commended and needs to be used widely to educate God's people about the issue of money, wealth and the Kingdom benefits that should accrue for this wise teaching. I look forward to reports of the wide use of this book and reports of God's blessings on its use."

Selwyn Stevens, Ph.D (Bib St.); D. Min.
President, Jubilee Resources International Inc.
jubileeresources.org

"In these pages, Dr. Watkins presents us with a Scripturally sound, well-researched, and highly practical handbook on how to understand and steward the finances God entrusts to us. But this book is more than simply the handling of finances. This is an authentic explanation of money and resourcing based on a Biblical worldview that explains why there is spiritual warfare and much misunderstanding over all finances - especially when used for Kingdom purposes. God has no problem with money - we do! But to understand the history and Biblical grasp of finances and economics is essential if the use of finances and wealth is to be seen as a crucial element in fulfilling the final chapters of the Great Commission.

This book is a strategic resource for everyone in the Body of Christ. Along with pen and paper and a Bible in hand, be prepared to take notes while being challenged, informed, and prepared for a study in Biblical economics that is life-changing!"

Rev. Dr. Alistair P. Petrie
Pastor - Author
Executive Director
Partnership Ministries
www.partnershipministries.org

"Money is one of those taboo subjects most people do not want to discuss let alone explore more deeply. This subject is rarely taught on for a variety of reasons and Scriptures used are often misinterpreted. As a result, many are held back from walking in freedom in this area.

Dr. Watkins in his book, Biblical Economics 101: Living Under God's Financial Blessing, constructs a strong foundation to understand more accurately and succinctly what Scriptures have to say about money, wealth, and living with an understanding of a Kingdom economy. He provides insightful clarity to this subject, practical examples and addresses incorrect beliefs and mindsets passed along through incorrect teaching and application of the Word. Readers will find themselves on a new journey of discovery and increasing freedom as they apply the principles contained in this book and discover in new ways how they can partner with the Lord for Kingdom and eternal purposes."

Ray Borg
Ministry & Church Liaison, Financial Discipleship Canada
Compasscanada.org and notmine.ca
Co-author - "It's Not About the Money - unmasking mammon"

REVIEWS

Reviewed in Canada on February 10, 2021
5 Stars! Buy this Book!

"Biblical Economics 101, is a very easy read. I love that it is completely backed up by scripture. The writer is correct, there are so many false beliefs about what the Bible has to say about money. Thank you for writing this book and clearly letting the reader know the truth about God's views on money and how He wants to bless His people. Most importantly, a great lesson and understanding about Biblical Economics!"

Chester Henry, Halifax NS

Reviewed in the United States on September 23, 2020
4 Stars! Financially Life Changing.

"I really like this book! It is well written and opened my eyes to things I never knew. The author backs up his points with scripture, so it's hard to debate the subject. The book is an easy read and holds your attention, but if anything, may be a bit long. Nevertheless, I highly recommend BIBLICAL ECONOMICS 101, as there is nothing like it that I've seen in the market today. It will have a positive impact on your view of money and finances, and if you "put it to work," it will change your life!"

Elaine Davis, TX, USA

Reviewed in the United States on September 15, 2020
5 stars! Financial Principles Made Easy.

"This is a fresh and comfortable read, rich in biblical truths and practical life applications. Watkins does an excellent job of connecting Scriptures to illustrate life's fundamental principles. He lays out an easy to understand path to follow for the use of money, personal finances and Kingdom wealth building. He handily dispels the myth that poverty is next to godliness. I am so impressed with the truth in this book that I intend to put it into the hands of all my sons and daughters."

Alec Wade, Sparta, MS, USA

Reviewed in the United States on September 17, 2020
5 stars! Thorough.

"A lot of books will cover just one side or aspect of a topic. Dr. Watkins is very thorough in his coverage of this topic. It would do us all well to take another, deeper look at this important area of our lives and God's will. This book will give you food for thought no matter your background. Every member of the Body of Christ owes it to the body to know God's will. Have a read and see, I think you will learn some things."

John Grunewald, USA

Reviewed in the United States on September 14, 2020
5 stars! God wants you to prosper greatly!

"As someone who has spent most of his life in the church, I've always known that there is a need for the Body of Christ to come into new level of prosperity. It seems like we are always playing catch up. Most people in the church think that's where we are suppose to be. Dr Stuart Watkins gives us a clear picture of how God wants us to prosper! THIS IS A MUST READ!"

Chad Foxworth, Corinth, TX, USA

Reviewed in Canada on May 12, 2021
4 stars! What I appreciated.

"An amazing read. There is an abundance of scripture in Dr. Watkins' book dedicated to examining wealth in Christians' lives. Simply put, if you want to know what Jesus and others in the Bible taught about wealth, this book will help you.

What I appreciate about Biblical Economics 101 is that it is not specifically focused on how we can acquire wealth. It is focused on what God is up to with his wealth, and on how he is looking for servants to participate with him in managing wealth for spiritual and humanitarian benefit - a process that is intended for God's glory and others' blessing.

The book packs a compelling message that cautions persons who are looking for a way to achieve wealth merely as a personal goal. Your wealth is not about you - yes, God is able to bring prosperity into your life but he is looking for those who will both thoughtfully and compassionately use it for kingdom purposes. Don't consider that God is handing you a compliment by being blest with abundance. Consider the compliment to be that you are counted worthy to demonstrate your ability to invest it well for God's intentions.

To me Biblical Economics 101 highlights the opportunity entrusted to prospering Christians to apply their wealth (along with other persons applying their gifts and callings) to reveal God as a loving Father and faithful provider; a God who wants to be known personally, even intimately, and looks for those who will manage his wealth in a way that blesses, heals and restores people to relationship with him.

Dr. Watkins should be credited for his processing of many scriptural references that together make it clear God is for us, and desires to bless us in numerous ways if we will but recognize that the blessings we receive have an intended impact beyond our own enjoyment."

Don MacNaughton, Cochrane, AB

NOTES

I am a Canadian citizen living in sunny southern Alberta. Canadians spell a few words differently than others, as we often use British spelling practices. Examples include "colour," "favourite," "blest," "cheque," "saviour," and "centre." Out of respect for my Canadian heritage, I am retaining my Canadian culture in the writing style and the spelling of some words.

This book will undoubtedly stimulate thoughts and questions in your mind (at least, I hope so). Please feel free to email me with any queries, and I will do my utmost to answer them; before you ask, there is no charge (you already bought the book)! Feedback is always important, so please connect with me through my website or email me directly: info@newstartministries.ca. Thank you!

If you have not already noticed, you will see that I always refer to Holy Spirit as "Holy Spirit;" I never refer to Him as "the Holy Spirit." That is because Holy Spirit is not a "thing" or an "it"; Holy Spirit is a person - part of the Trinity of God (Father, Son, Holy Spirit). I do not believe that referring to Holy Spirit as "the" fits the person of God that Holy Spirit exemplifies.

I refuse to capitalize the name satan. I know that is grammatically incorrect, but satan doesn't deserve the honour; besides, it's my book. He has done everything he can to stop its publication, so this is my revenge on him.

One of the things I've learned about book publishing is that selling books is all about marketing, and the best form of marketing is the word of mouth which comes from reviews and endorsements. If you enjoy this book, please go to Amazon, Barnes & Noble or Chapters/Indigo and write a review. If you desire, an endorsement emailed to me would be greatly appreciated. A review on "Goodreads" is appreciated as well.

A prophecy was given to me by a man I trust (Allan Ainsworth), and the Lord spoke through him, and He said, *"The book will enlighten and set free and bring endurance and enlightenment to the people that read it."* I pray that this is the case. If you dear readers are one of those, I would appreciate hearing from you. Connect with me through my website. www.newstartministries.ca. Thank you!

DEDICATION

This book is dedicated to the gentlemen who have influenced my life more than any other two: Dr. C. Peter Wagner, my mentor and spiritual father for 15 years, and Dr. Peter J. Daniels, who transformed my thinking and taught me more about success than anyone else. Without these two amazing men, this book would never have been written.

I also dedicate this book to the three joys of my life, my children: Steven, Charlotte, and Janessa. Being a father has been the greatest single experience of my life. Thank you for giving me joy, purpose, and passion. Thank you for putting up with my "highs and lows" as I attempted to write my very first book.

Finally, I thank Jesus for taking me on an incredible paradigm shift. From where I was 40+ years ago to where I am today, it is nothing short of a miracle. I have been incredibly blest. Not only did He save me, but He has never forsaken me.

S. R. Watkins, Ph.D

WHO IS DOC?

Stuart R. Watkins, Ph.D was born and raised in Calgary, Alberta. He worked for two winters in the hotel industry and spent three summers as a cowboy, trail guiding in beautiful Banff National Park in the majestic Canadian Rockies. He graduated in 1981 with a Bachelor of Business Administration and began his career in entrepreneur-ship at 23, and has owned several businesses.

Returning to post-secondary education 22 years later, he completed a Bachelor of Theology, a Master's, a Doctorate of Apostolic Leadership (Practical Ministry), and finally, a Ph.D in Ministerial Studies (Economics). His passion has always been to help people, whether teaching Biblical Economics and Christian business principles or offering excellence training for marketplace ministries and businesses. An entrepreneur for 40+ years, he owns an investment company and a publishing company and serves as a financial, operational and strategic planning consultant to churches, charities and non-profit organizations. He teaches internationally and hosts conferences in Rwanda in conjunction with his work there with Compassion Canada. He is the author of: *"Biblical Economics 101: Living Under God's Financial Blessing"* (Nov. 2020, revised June 2023); *"Life is a Test - A Daily Devotional - Volume I"* (Jan. 2021); *"Life is a Test - A Daily Devotional - Volume 2"* (Dec. 2022) (Volume 3 is in the works)!

Dr. Watkins is a licensed minister of the Gospel with Eagle World-Wide Ministries in Hamilton, Ontario and commissioned by the Global Spheres Centre in Corinth, Texas, as a Business Apostle, Deliverance Minister, and Christian Author. He is a member of the Global Council of Nations, the Global Transformation Project, the Canadian and International Coalition of Apostolic Leaders, the International Society of Deliverance Ministers, and the Calgary Christian Connect Group.

At home in Alberta, he enjoys music, fine dining, skiing, fitness, gardening, and collecting Western art and antiques. Somehow, he manages to read one to two books a week! He is a Life Member and past President (5 terms) of the Trail Riders of the Canadian Rockies. For further information about his teaching classes and consulting, contact him at: info@newstartministries.ca

Written by Fred Schuman, Renewal Counselling,

WHAT'S UP WITH DOC?

I worked at a Christian summer camp in Alberta several years ago. It is customary for everyone (including staff) to be given a "nickname." Mine was "Doc" (because of my education), and they gave me no choice in the matter; the name stuck. I seldom use my first name anymore because people often do not spell it correctly and tend to shorten it (which I do not like), so "Doc" is easy to remember, pretty hard to misspell and addionally it gets rid of the formality of "Dr. Watkins."

DOC'S BOOK CLUB

An expression says that "every man has one vice." I have one; books! Out of my vast library (Would you believe I have nine bookcases? Six of which are eight feet tall), I have read over 2000 non-fiction Christian books and researched and written over 130 papers. As much as I believe that the Word of God (the Bible) is the final Word on issues and should not be "interpreted" (just read it)!, reading from good authors can educate and confirm the Word. I have made recommendations periodically throughout this book, and with a few exceptions, I do not personally know the authors, but I know their credentials and reputations.

I use the New King James Version, and for explaining issues and ease of understanding, I like the New International Version, which I often quote in this book. I enjoy reading The Living Bible as a good comparison, and the Message and Passion versions are fun too! If you are a beginner, I suggest the Living Bible for starters. Read (in this order) Ephesians, James, Romans, 1 and 2 Corinthians, Colossians, Hebrews, then John, Luke, Mark, and Matthew. Next, finish the rest of the New Testament (you can leave the Book of Revelation for a while yet), and then start at the beginning of the Old Testament. Find a gospel preaching, faith teaching, and spirit-filled church, and go!

INTRODUCTION

Having a plan is half the strategy for success. As such, in this introduction, I will explain the structure of this book and how to approach the reading.

This book is divided into twenty chapters: chapter one to five is about incorrect religious ideas regarding money and prosperity. Then, starting in chapter six, I explain the purpose of money and why God wants us to prosper. Next, we will examine several chapters on God's economy, the priestly Order of Melchizedek, Seedtime and Harvest. These chapters will study the biblical principles of wealth, success, and legitimate paths to prosperity. Finally, we will look at thirty-one ways to open the windows of Heaven upon our respective lives.

First, we have a bit of "undoing" to do. What do I mean? We have all collected false ideas and concepts over time, especially regarding money. Many of these ideas are steeped in religious doctrine, fear, and control from church organizations and governments. Romans 12:2 (NKJV) says,

> *"And do not be conformed to this world, but be transformed by the renewing of your mind, that you may prove what is that good and acceptable and perfect will of God."*

Our minds must be transformed from these errant ideas and unbiblical doctrines to the supreme truth of the Word of God. Therefore, in these first few chapters, I will ask you to allow the "bulldozer" of God's Word to knock down every mental stronghold of incorrect doctrine. I cannot overstate how necessary this is, but I promise I will base everything I teach on Scripture. As we further study the Word, we will pour a new foundation of truth, allowing revelation knowledge to come. Then you can start walking in the fullness of God's blessings, which He desires. As we know, wisdom and revelation always come through the knowledge of God and His Word (Ephesians 1:17).

I emphasize the importance of the Word of God because the Bible is an operations manual. If all else fails, just read the book of instructions! Even more than just reading it, however, Joshua 1:8 (NKJV) says,

> *"This Book of the Law shall not depart from your mouth, but you shall meditate on it day and night, that you may observe to do according to all that is written in it. For then you will make your way prosperous, and then you will have success."*

I tell the students in my seminars not to "read" the Bible but to study it. In the original translation, "meditate" means "think deeply or focus one's mind for some time." In other words, study! Memorize it. Ponder it. Let it sink in. These errant doctrines and traditions of men have gone unchecked for centuries, which has caused many people in the church (and the world) to be very perplexed about biblical principles relating to money. Further, they need clarification about whether we will be financially prosperous. People have all kinds of questions that usually stem from guilt over having material possessions:

- "Is it okay for a Christian or a non-Christian to be rich?"
- "Can we have material possessions?"
- "What is money for?"
- "Is it a sin to have wealth?"

Well, please allow me to bulldoze one giant misconception right away - I can assure you that God wants you rich, but He wants you rich for an excellent and specific reason. The Bible leaves no question about it - God's people are supposed to be rich. Not just rich in spirit, not just rich with righteousness, love, joy, peace, patience, and in fellowship with God, but also rich with money and assets. Not rich only in relationships and spiritual rewards, God's people are to be financially wealthy and prosperous in every way possible. This means plenty of money - tons of moolah. Oodles of coin, stacks of paper, substantial net worth... rich in the Bible means RICH. Again, He wants you rich for a particular reason and the right attitude in dealing with money (which I'll explain), and Scripture after Scripture confirms it:

"*The blessing of the Lord, it maketh rich, and He addeth no sorrow with it.*" (Proverbs 10:22 KJV)

"*Riches and honour are with the wisdom of God; yea durable riches and righteousness.*" (Proverbs 8:18 KJV)

"*Blessed is the man who fears the Lord, Who delights greatly in His commandments. His descendants will be mighty on earth; The generation of the upright will be blest. Wealth and riches will be in his house, And his righteousness endures forever.*" (Psalm 112:1, 3 NKJV)

"*For you know the grace of our Lord Jesus Christ, that though He was rich, yet for your sakes, He became poor, that you through His poverty might become rich.*"
(2 Corinthians 8:9 NKJV)

Ecclesiastes 10:19b (NIV) says,

"and money is the answer for everything." (meaning it solves all problems)

References to money or stewardship appear in the Bible 2,418 times. "Rich" or "riches" appears in the Bible 186 times. "Money" appears in the Bible 114 times. Jesus spoke more about money and/or stewardship than any other subject. Should we pay attention to that?

For now, please suspend your cynicism for the moment (if you have any) as you read, and please give me the benefit of the doubt. I am not trying to "get" your money, and I am not trying to sell you anything (you already bought my book)! I am trying to teach you how to expand the Kingdom of God dramatically, have the means to fulfill the call of God on your life, and have more than enough while you do that. God can do more with you if you have more means and a righteous heart toward stewardship.

With that, let's get to bulldozing!

CHAPTER 1

JESUS WAS NOT POOR.

In this chapter, I will help you bulldoze the mental strong-hold of a "poverty mentality." A sense of false humility traps so many Christians that it dramatically hinders them from accomplishing the call of God on their life

Religion (the false kind, not the James 1:27 kind) has developed an idea that spiritual maturity results from a decrease in the desire for material blessings. Jesus was obviously poor. Therefore, we must be 'poor and humble' like Him to attain His righteousness.

Now, first, let me explain what this false kind of religion is. Jesus called many of the religious leaders of His day "a brood of vipers" (Matthew 23:33) and with good reason. They did not care about the person - they cared about their power system.

The religions of the world all have one thing in common: the idea that a person must do something to pacify some superior being or so-called god. Christianity is not a religion in the sense that there is nothing you can do to impress God; there is no money you can pay Him, no gift you can give Him, nor work you can do to "get into His good books" and enter the Kingdom of Heaven. In true

Christianity, salvation is a gift that comes through His grace and your surrender. Sadly, however, the Christian church has allowed religion to taint it.

The early church worshipped God and conducted church correctly, as we see from Paul's letters and how he wrote about the church in the Book of Acts. From even the introduction and throughout this book, I will show you Scriptures that, without a doubt, prove prosperity is the will of God. Poverty, the opposite of prosperity, is logically and explicitly not the will of God. Therefore, if Paul and the Apostles wished prosperity upon the church in their letters and the early church certainly appeared prosperous, when did a poverty mindset enter the church? Well, it was under the rule of Constantine around 300 AD.

Constantine took the Greek mindset toward prosperity and added it to the Jewish or Christian mindset. The Greeks believed the whole world was divided into two equal parts - material and spiritual. These parts supposedly had a natural balance, which meant if you had more of one, you had less of the other. Therefore, to be more "spiritual," a person had to give up an equal part of the material. Wealth then was considered an enemy of the spiritual world (and by extension, according to the Greeks, Godless.) This false theology was widely spread and was further perpetuated by monks in the fourteenth century. Eventually, this pagan Greek philosophy invaded the church.

Today, we still see the devastating effects of this heretic philosophy in our churches. There are still Christians who believe poverty is next to godliness and who believe having more than an adequate amount of money or (God forbid)! wealth, is a sin. As you will discover through Scriptures and the renewing of your mind, nothing could be further from the truth!

In my decades of studying the Bible, I have concluded that many practices in the church today do not at all align with the Word of God. I would go so far as to say that about 90 percent of what I have learned about biblical economics, I did not learn in church! Why? The church does not teach it! I learned it from reading books, taking courses, attending seminars, and studying the Word of God myself.

As I'm sure you can tell by now, I am a bottom-line person, and given the vast swathes of material we must cover, I want to jump right in to show from the Bible that Jesus was in no way materially poor.

18 Points Showing Jesus Was Rich and Very Blest.

Point 1: Jesus Was Rich from Childhood.

Matthew 2:11 (NKJV) says,

> *"And when they had come into the house, they saw the young Child with Mary, His mother, and fell down and worshiped Him. And when they had opened their treasures, they presented gifts to Him: gold, frankincense, and myrrh."*

The wise men left gold because, from the signs they saw in the heavens, they correctly believed Jesus was (and is) a King so great there had been none and would be none like Him. They brought a King's treasure to honour the "King of Kings." As such, I suspect the amount of gold given was enough to provide for Him and His family for a lifetime. I won't even get into the frankincense and myrrh - both precious commodities at that time not to mention symbolic of His priesthood and anointing.

Now some might argue that Jesus gave the gold away. It is quite possible, that He probably gave some of it away; the Bible doesn't say. We do know this, however, if Jesus gave some or all of the gold away, Scriptures like Luke 6:38 tell us He would have undoubtedly received a harvest from the gifts. God's economy is based upon sowing and reaping, which you will see in great detail in a later chapter titled "The Laws of Sowing and Reaping." You can't plant into God's Kingdom without getting a return. It is a spiritual law, just like gravity is a physical law.

No matter how you look at this, Jesus was rich before He was out of diapers. Matthew 2:16-18 shows that Herod had every child under the age of two killed. This supports the idea that the wise men arrived within two years after Jesus was born. It doesn't take much thought to figure out that diplomats from a foreign nation would not travel more than a year to bring a card and a box of candy. They brought costly gifts in what is almost undoubtedly significant amounts. Myrrh, at the time, was considered more valuable than gold. If they took all that time and went to all that trouble to get there, you can bet they didn't just bring a little - they brought a lot!

During my professional and Christian life, I've had the great pleasure of meeting Dr. Peter Daniels of Adelaide, South Australia. He started his life's work as a poor, ignorant bricklayer and is now a billionaire - probably the richest Christian in the world. I have read almost all of his books and heard him speak numerous times.

The first time I heard Dr. Daniels speak, he referred to the three gifts the Magi brought to Jesus. He told the audience how curiosity had gotten the better of him and how he wanted to know the value of these three gifts. He decided to hire a theologian and a historian for an exciting project. Both had Ph.D's in their respective fields. Dr. Daniels explained that they were to have unlimited access to whatever resources they needed and the time to accomplish their task. Their task was nothing less than to find out the value of the Magi's gold, frankincense and myrrh in today's currency.

After working full-time on the project for two years, weighing all kinds of historical factors, such as what amount of gift was typical for kings of the time (let alone the King of Kings), these two experts gave Dr. Daniels the answer he was looking for. In today's currency, the value of gold, frankincense, and myrrh would equate to no less than USD 450 million! That is the minimum that would have been given. Now even if you're skeptical, regardless of the accuracy of this detective work (give or take $100 million if you like), and whether you believe it or not, the point is still made - Jesus was set for life.

Point 2: Jesus Was Born into the Royal Line of David.

In Matthew chapter one, Jesus' family tree is given, where His lineage can be traced back to King David. He was also connected to the priesthood, meaning most theologians agree that He was a Priest and a King. Both things brought higher status in ancient Israeli society. We often don't think about it due to popular contemporary imagery based on errant doctrine. However, Jesus rubbed shoulders with the wealthy and the influential from the earliest age.

Point 3: Mary and Joseph had a House in Bethlehem.

Experts calculate that the wise men arrived two years after His birth, and by then, as we saw in Matthew 2:11, the family was living in a house. This tells us that Jesus' parents owned a home, showing they could not have been poor.

Point 4: Jesus was Well Educated.

In Luke 2:41-52, we see that when Jesus was only twelve years old, He was lecturing in the local synagogue. If He were a poor peasant child, the religious leaders would never have let Him sit in on those discussions. The religious leaders were amazed at how much Jesus knew, which indicates that his family had access to a complete set of costly scrolls of the Tanakh (Old Testament). It could also suggest that His parents had the money to pay for an education from various rabbis. Money is how his family had access to Bible scrolls and how He was able to discuss theology with renowned teachers in the temple during their Passover pilgrimage.

Point 5: Jesus had a Job.

The Bible says in 2 Thessalonians 3:6-12 that we must all work. Jesus clearly set this example, as we can see from Mark 6:3a (NKJV),

> *"Is this not the carpenter, the Son of Mary, and brother of James, John, Judas, and Simon?"*

Therefore, as Jesus worked, He obviously made money, and from what we can gather by scripture, He lived a good, working-class life (despite being wealthy from the gifts of the Magi).

Point 6: Jesus had a Treasurer.

John 12:29 (NKJV) says,

> *"For some thought, because Judas had the money box, that Jesus had said to him, "Buy those things we need for the feast," or that he should give something to the poor."*

I ask you, why did a group of middle-income wage earners need a treasurer? To count and manage amounts of money that exceed a small amount, of course! Isn't that what accountants do? If you have no money, you don't need a treasurer. Jesus had one.

Point 7: Jesus had a Staff of Twelve and Later a Bigger Staff of Seventy-two Disciples.

Do you genuinely believe that when Jesus asked these people to follow Him, He required them to be destined for poverty? What about their families? The Spirit of Christ through the Apostle Paul tells us in 1 Timothy 5:8 (NIV),

> *"Anyone who does not provide for their relatives, and especially for their household, has denied the faith and is worse than an unbeliever."*

Did these men leave their jobs for three years to follow Jesus around the countryside, irresponsibly leaving their families in poverty? In those days, as Paul tells us in 2 Thessalonians 3:10, if you didn't work, you didn't eat. For His staff and their families to survive, Jesus' ministry would have had to support them financially. Consider Mark 10:29-30 (NKJV),

"Jesus answered and said, Assuredly, I say to you, there is no one who has left house or brothers or sisters or father or mother or wife or children or lands, for My sake and the gospel's, who shall not receive a hundredfold now in this time - houses and brothers and sisters and mothers and children and lands, with persecutions - and in the age to come, eternal life."

Bear in mind that there was no social welfare in those days. Perhaps the disciple's families travelled with them; we don't really know. Regardless, there had to be some source of revenue to support the staff. That is why Jesus had a treasurer; if He had a treasurer, then Jesus had a good deal of income for His ministry.

Point 8: People Financially Supported Jesus' Ministry.

Scripture clearly tells us Jesus had financial partners who put money into His ministry. Why did Jesus need money? To pay the bills, of course! Like payroll! Believe me, it was not a small amount. At first, He had 12 staff and then later, 72. Luke 8:2-3 (TLB) tells us,

"Some women went along, from whom he had cast out demons or whom he had healed; among them were Mary Magdalene (Jesus had cast out seven demons from her) Joanna, Chuza's wife (Chuza was King Herod's business manager and was in charge of his palace and domestic affairs), Susanna, and many others who were contributing from their private means to the support of Jesus and His disciples."

**Point 9: Jesus' Disciples were all Successful Business-
men.**

We can tell from the gospels and the Book of Acts that Jesus
did not call the unemployed and wanted little to do with
most well-educated religious people. Instead, He called
men who were successful in business. Four of them were
fishermen; Matthew was a tax collector (a group known
for being wealthy), while Luke was a medical doctor. Jesus
looked for men who had proven they knew how to work,
be successful, and be productive.

Think about it - if Jesus had been poor, successful men
would never have followed Him. They would have rightly
considered Him unable to support Himself adequately,
never mind a staff of 84. There is an expression about
whom people will follow, "The rich follow the rich; the
poor follow the rich; but the rich never follow the poor." If
Jesus had no credibility and no funds to look after His own
staff, even with all the divine insights in the world, I highly
doubt the disciples would have fully respected Him.

**Point 10: Jesus was so Blest that He Wore Designer
Clothes.**

Is that title mind-blowing to you? Regardless, it is true.
Jesus wore a tunic (a kind of robe) that had no seams. It
was pretty difficult in those days to weave a tunic with no
seam, and it would have had to have been custom tailored
for Him. There is no doubt that at the time, Jesus' garment
was an expensive piece of clothing. In today's culture, He
wore at least the equivalent of a custom Armani or Calvin
Klein suit. It is no wonder the soldiers wanted it so badly
when Jesus was crucified. Who would not want the costly
clothes of a rich man?

Matthew 27:35 (NKJV) tells us,

> *"Then the soldiers, when they had crucified Jesus, took His garments, and made four parts, to each soldier a part, and also the tunic. Now the tunic was without seam, woven from the top in one piece. They said therefore among themselves, "Let us not tear it, but cast lots for it, whose it shall be," that the Scripture might be fulfilled, which says: "They divided My garments among them, And for My clothing they cast lots."*

Point 11: Jesus Paid Taxes.

Matthew 17: 24 (TLB) tells us,

> *"On their arrival in Capernaum, the Temple tax collectors came to Peter and asked him, "Doesn't your master pay taxes?" "Of course, he does." Peter replied."*

Who pays taxes? People with money! They say two things in life that are guaranteed: death and taxes. This, however, is only half true. Death is guaranteed, as we know, but only people who have(earn) money pay taxes. Jesus paid taxes; therefore, we can conclude that Jesus had money.

Several years ago, my accountant told me he wanted me to pay $1 million yearly in taxes. I reacted in horror and said, "Why on Earth would I ever want to do that?" "Well," he said, "think about how much money you would be earning to pay a million dollars of tax?" I realized his point and then agreed with him. The only people who pay taxes are people that have money.

Point 12: Jesus Owned a House.

Some people mistakenly claim Jesus lived in a foxhole because of the following verse in Matthew 8:19-20 (NIV),

> *"Then a teacher of the law came to him and said, "Teacher, I will follow you wherever you go." Jesus replied, "Foxes have dens and birds have nests, but the Son of Man has nowhere to lay his head."*

If you read before this passage, however, you will see Jesus had just returned from trekking up a mountain to address the large group of people (sound carries down) more efficiently. This "ministry convention" was the famous Sermon on the Mount.

After Jesus healed His disciple, Peter's mother and many others, He needed some rest, so He commanded His disciples to cross to the other side of the lake, facing another stint of being "out on the road." Of course, He didn't have a place to sleep that night; He was out in the country and told this enthusiastic teacher of the law that He would have to do the same (sleep in a foxhole).

More compelling evidence that He owned a house is found in John 1:38-39 (KJV),

> *"Then Jesus turned and saw them following, and saith unto them, what seek ye? They said unto him, Rabbi (which is to say, being interpreted, Master), where dwellest thou? He saith unto them, Come and see. They came and saw where he dwelt, and abode with him that day: for it was about the tenth hour."*

The words dwelt and abode in this passage specifically mean ownership. They do not have any connotations of rental or temporary dwelling. Also, Matthew 4:12-13 (NIV) says,

> "When Jesus heard that John had been put in prison, he returned to Galilee. Leaving Nazareth, He went and lived in Capernaum, which was by the lake in the area of Zebulun and Naphtali...."

My question is, how do you live unless you have a place to call home? There is no description in the Bible as to what kind of a house Jesus owned, but it does mention it was near a lake. I believe it was probably a very nice home for two reasons: firstly, as we've discussed, He clearly had the money to buy it, and secondly, it would make sense that He had staff meetings and perhaps even evangelistic meetings in His house. If that were the case, He would need a large house to accommodate everyone.

I am trying to show that we can tend to deify even the practical aspects of Jesus' ministry to the point where we can't envision Him having staff meetings. We imagine Him floating around with two fingers making a peace sign, blessing His large following of disciples and huge crowds. We think everything was magically organized and flowed smoothly. Please understand that is the false kind of religious mindset, which is very destructive to a practical understanding of the Bible and spiritual growth.

Point 13: Jesus Gave to the Poor.

It isn't difficult to believe Jesus gave to people experiencing poverty, right? Of course, He did. Now follow that thinking, and we can see He could not give something away if He did not have it to give, right? Yes, you can believe Jesus blest others wherever He went, and Jesus was so blest that He could be a blessing. The following verse shows us it was Jesus' practice to give to the poor,

> *"As soon as Judas took the bread, Satan entered into him. Jesus told him, "What you are about to do, do quickly." But no one at the meal understood why Jesus said this to him. Since Judas had charge of the money, some thought Jesus was telling him to buy what was needed for the festival or to give something to the poor."*
> (John 13:27-29 NIV)

Most interesting in this passage is that the disciples had assumed that Jesus was telling Judas to give money to the poor. Considering the disciples had just spent three years with Jesus, we can assume they knew Him and His personality reasonably well. By this passage, it is clear that Jesus was a person who gave and often gave enough for the disciples to make that assumption.

Again, you cannot give what you don't have.

Point 14: Understanding the Phrase "Jesus Became Poor."

2 Corinthians 8:9 (NKJV) says,

> *"For you know the grace of our Lord Jesus Christ, that though He was rich, yet for your sakes, He became poor, that you through His poverty might become rich."*

To understand the meaning of this phrase, may I ask you, if I "become" a Doctor of Medicine does that mean I am one now? How about an astronaut? If I "become" one, am I an astronaut now? Obviously not. Therefore, if Jesus "became" poor, it means He was not poor to begin with.

This quote from a Charisma magazine article really says it all,

> *"Jesus went from riches to rags so that we could go from rags to riches (see 2 Corinthians 8:9). We can experience Kingdom blessings when we believe God's promises are for us, align with them, receive and act on God's wisdom concerning steps to take, and passionately pursue them."*
> (Jeremiah 29:13; Proverbs 8:17; Matthew 7:7)*

Looking at the culture of that time, people were divided into two social classes: the rich and the poor. There was not what we would call today a "middle class." In addition, the first part of the Scripture clearly says that He was rich; "though He was rich…." Some claim that Jesus gave up His Heavenly riches and became relatively poor on Earth, but that doesn't gel with the rest of the verse. It says, "that you through His poverty might become rich." When did we become rich? When we became joint heirs with Christ (Romans 8:17) after He completed the work of the cross.

More than this, however, is if the verse above says Jesus was rich, it pretty much summarizes all eighteen points, and frankly, the other seventeen don't matter at this point, do they? Still, I have also heard arguments that the word "rich" does not refer to money. It never ceases to amaze me how people try to manipulate Scriptures to read anything they want. The word in Greek is "rich." When you look at the root of the word, no matter how you slice and dice it, it means rich with money. Period. End of discussion.

---

* Virkler, Mark Dr. *"The Seven Prayers of Financial Freedom."* Charisma Magazine, March 2019, Pg. 48

Point 15: The First Miracle Jesus Performed was one of Extravagant, Unnecessary Luxury.

We all know the account in John 2:1-11 of Jesus turning water into wine. Just think about it; Jesus had been invited to a high society wedding. Cana was a wealthy area in that day, so this was obviously a big wedding. Even the fact that running out of wine embarrassed the host indicates it had to be a wealthy wedding. If it were a poor family, it would not have mattered much. Also, consider that if rich people were invited, and Jesus and His parents were guests, they must have been wealthy enough to have been included.

Here is what is fascinating: when you really look at this situation, this miracle was not necessary. No one was healed or delivered; the wine was entirely a luxury. If the people were genuinely thirsty, they clearly had enough pots full of water. Yet Jesus performed a miracle to keep people drinking a social, alcoholic beverage! In other words, it was a miracle of luxury and extravagance.

Obviously, Jesus had no problem with wealth or the comforts and luxuries that wealth brought. The Scripture even says the guests were astonished that the host kept the best wine until the end. Guaranteed a wedding in Cana was not serving cheap wine at the beginning either. Jesus produced some Domaine de la Romanée-Conti quality wine!

Point 16: The Disciples Did Not Question His Ability to Spend a Fortune.

In the gospels, when Jesus was with the crowd of 5,000, His disciples wanted to send the people away since it was late in the day and everyone was hungry. Jesus just told the disciples to find a way to feed the crowd. Of course, the

15

surprised disciples replied that it would take about eight months' wages to feed all the people (John 6:7). From the biblical account, we know that Jesus simply took a fish dinner from a small boy and miraculously multiplied it. However, we don't see the disciples questioning Jesus' financial ability to pay. They assumed there was enough money to buy that much food; they exclaimed that it was a lot to outlay.

Mark 6:37b (KJV) says,

> "Shall we go and buy two hundred denarii worth of bread and give them something to eat?"

If Jesus didn't have that much money on hand, the question would have never made sense. The truth is, He had plenty of money - that wasn't the issue. Why did Jesus not use His money and do exactly as the disciples had asked? I can suggest several reasons:

1. Time. They were out in the country and far from a village.
2. The logistics of going into a town to buy fish needed to be clarified. They would also assume there were enough fish in any town for 5,000 men plus their families.
3. There was no food transportation method (no trucks in those days or refrigeration).
4. The purpose of miracles is not to "impress" the saved but to impress the unsaved. Jesus also said we are to do the same miracles He did. Therefore, the true purpose of miracles is to

reach the lost. Perhaps, like the miracle of the wine in Cana, Jesus wanted to demonstrate God's ability to provide for His people and show thanksgiving and God's power of multiplication. I believe Jesus was setting an example.

Point 17: Jesus Had so Much Wealth that Apparent Waste was Not an Issue.

In Matthew's gospel, the disciples were shocked and indignant after a bottle of extremely expensive perfume was poured on Jesus as a beautiful way of worship. The perfume was worth a year's wages - likely between $30,000 and $60,000 today. This excessive display was, in their eyes, a terrible waste. They muttered that the perfume should have been sold and the money given to the poor. Even at this late juncture in their discipleship (Jesus was about to be betrayed and crucified), they did not seem to understand the idea of being blest to be a blessing. Jesus, however, didn't have a problem with such an extravagant demonstration. He knew it was a noble and prophetic gesture,

> *"But when Jesus was aware of it, He said to them, "Why do you trouble the woman? For she has done a good work for Me. For you have the poor with you always, but Me you do not have always. For in pouring this fragrant oil on My body, she did it for My burial."* (Matthew 26:10-12 NIV)

Years ago, I heard a story from a well-known pastor. He had seen a man with an extremely expensive car (I think it may have been a Rolls-Royce) come to church on Sunday and park it in the church parking lot. People in the church were very indignant about this man owning such an expensive car. Like the disciples, their thought was that he could sell the vehicle and give the money to the poor.

The pastor, however, knew otherwise. He knew of this man's "rags to riches" life story, his difficulties, and how he persevered. He also knew the man's dedication to tithing and generosity to the poor. He probably gave away more than most people in that church made in a year! In addition, this car was likely the man's reward for his faithfulness in giving.

I suspect the truth is that those people in the church were jealous, not liking that the man appeared "above" them. If that were the case, then who is guilty of sin? The rich man with a nice car or the jealous people? The man was above them in the knowledge of sowing and reaping. If you keep reading and accept this teaching, you, too, will be "above and not beneath."

In this example from Scripture, Jesus understood a basic principle: no matter how much you give to the poor, you will always have the poor with you because there will always be some who do not accept God's best for themselves. They will, therefore, never learn the principles of sowing and reaping. Don't get me wrong, some are born poor, and they learn to apply the principles of either hard work and/or sowing and reaping, (and become rich) or they don't and then stay poor. It is much better to learn both, not just work hard, because we are not to chase riches in our strength for our own corrupt ends (1 Timothy 6:9-11, Proverbs 23:4).

Some choose to remain poor rather than believe the Word of prosperity. Jesus had no problem with a woman pouring a year's wages worth of perfume on His head for His burial. He was not bound by the belief system that turns away from material possessions and their extravagant use, purely as a kneejerk reaction from some overarching (and I suspect false) guilt toward the poor. No, everything has its time and purpose, and yes, we are to give to the poor. That is clearly Scriptural. Not every blessing, however, needs to go to the poor. This Scripture shows that some have other purposes, and some can be extravagant.

Point 18: Jesus Never Lacked.

The final point is a very simple but profound: at the end of Jesus's Earthly ministry, His own disciples testified they never lacked anything. In Luke 22:35 (NIV), we read,

> *"Then Jesus asked them, when I sent you without purse, bag or sandals, did you lack anything? "Nothing," they answered."*

You can trust that Jesus wants the same for you today.

Phew, that was a lot of information and "bulldozing." Hopefully, you're still with me, and Holy Spirit is showing you what He has available to accomplish God's will for your life. The only time Jesus was only poor was when He was on the cross (and He chose to be poor for us)!

Now let's look at the next chapter. It is a much shorter read, and I address a formidable foe that has kept the church in bondage for millennia.

S.R. WATKINS

CHAPTER 2

THE SPIRIT OF RELIGION

In the last chapter, I addressed (bulldozed) the notion that Jesus was poor. Hopefully, through the many biblical proofs presented, you can understand there is no way Jesus was poor, and if not, perhaps you opened your heart to the idea. To be blunt, however, the idea that Jesus was poor is one of the most potent weapons in satan's arsenal. Why? Because if he can limit the church's resources, he can determine the church's effectiveness. The key to overcoming this problem is understanding the root of this fallacy. In this chapter, I will address why many people have an errant notion of biblical prosperity. I believe if there is any residual doubt concerning God's will for your prosperity, it will be removed entirely by the end of this chapter.

One of the observations I have made in my study of biblical economics is that people who are against the concept of Christians (or Jesus) being wealthy literally cannot even comprehend the thought of wealth. It is one thing to consider an idea you may disagree with at first rationally, but I have met people who are completely dead set against Christians having any form of wealth and who view Jesus as, in their words, "poor and humble."

The first question you should ask of someone who holds a belief so emphatically are, "Why do you believe that?" and, "Can you show me scriptural support for your belief?" I'll quickly answer that for you - they cannot answer either question. These concepts are based on complete ignorance and a lack of understanding of God's Word. Additionally, I think such beliefs are rooted in envy, which has given place to deception by an evil spirit of religion. It is also interesting to note that the people against wealth and the idea that Jesus was wealthy always seem to be in dire financial straits.

What exactly is a "spirit of religion?" According to Dr. Peter Wagner, who was a leading authority in church growth and spiritual warfare, a "spirit of religion" is:

> "...an agent of satan assigned to prevent change and maintain the status quo by using religious devices. Many people are not familiar with this term as it is not biblical. However, the words "Trinity" or "abortion," "Christmas," or "ministry" are not in the Bible either." *

Let us not get legalistic in understanding this concept simply because the specific word is not directly stated in the Bible.

To be clear, I am not talking about the pure and undefiled form of religion that James mentions:

> "Religion that God our Father accepts as pure and faultless is this: to look after orphans and widows in their distress and to keep oneself from being polluted by the world." (James 1:27)

* Wagner, C. Peter, **"Freedom from the Religious Spirit."** Chosen Books, 2002, Pg. 12.

This oppressive spirit seeks to enslave mankind through meaningless rituals and ideas that are not from God. This is the type of spirit Jesus addresses in Luke 11:46 (NIV),

> *"Jesus replied, And you experts in the law, woe to you because you load people down with burdens they can hardly carry, and you will not lift one finger to help them."*

Characteristics of the Spirit of Religion.

This spirit of religion is one of satan's most potent deceptions to keep people from salvation, from experiencing the fullness of salvation, and from fulfilling their call from God. Some common characteristics of this demonic spirit are:

1. It is a very high-ranking demon like that of Beelzebub (see Luke 11:15), the Prince of Greece (see Daniel 10:20), and the Queen of Heaven (see Jeremiah 7:18).

2. It is a corporate spirit, meaning it invades groups of people instead of individuals. It can cast a spell over the leaders of all segments of God's people if allowed. This, for example, is reflected in Galatians 3:1 (NKJV),

   > *"O foolish Galatians! Who has bewitched you that you should not obey the truth...?"*

3. The spirit (demon) of religion is highly subtle and does not speak out loud of itself; people under its influence usually have no clue of its presence or existence. The corporate spirit of

religion is cunning - it succeeds in making people think they are doing God's will! Again, an excellent example of this is many of the Pharisees opposing Jesus. They were so caught up with rules, regulations, and laws to the extreme that they missed the Messiah when He appeared to them, even though many details of His life were prophesied in the book of Isaiah.

4. This spirit manipulates leaders into opposing God's plan for new times and seasons. Jesus said to not put new wine into old wineskins (Matthew 9:14-17, Mark 2:18-22 and Luke 5:33-39). This is a metaphor for the work and power of Holy Spirit. Sometimes pastors and leaders can be so stuck in their ways that they miss changes Holy Spirit is implementing in the body of Christ. I have been in churches where the style of service and worship has not changed in 40 years...

Peter Wagner explains this very well when he says:
"In order to accomplish its purpose, the corporate spirit of religion administers what could be described as an intravenous injection of fear. Old wineskins leaders fear losing their positions of power. They fear being pulled out of their comfort zones. Their typical question is, "What am I going to lose by moving into God's new times and seasons?" They rarely ask, "What is the Kingdom of God going to gain?" They are hesitant to risk the possibility of either losing control or losing money. So, they capitulate to the religious spirit and do whatever it takes to preserve the status quo, while honestly thinking that they are doing God's will." *
*IBID Pg. 21

5. A spirit of religion says, "who is right, and who is wrong," then adamantly defends either position. Conversely, God works in and through life and what produces death.

Traditions of Men.

This insidious spirit of religion keeps people closed-minded, married to ungodly traditions of men, critical of anything fresh and different, and consequently not open to learning anything new. This demon blinds people's eyes to the truth to the point that they can be easily misled and even become victims of cults. Examples of this spirit in action include Mormonism, Jehovah's Witnesses, the New Age movement, Freemasonry, Buddhism, and Hinduism. You don't, however, need to look further than your own church to see the activity of a spirit of religion. When people argue about doctrine, procedure, and tradition, it is often the root cause of church splits and is most certainly the devil's work.

In the case of biblical economics, I see people wholly bound with this spirit to the point that they will argue living in poverty over living without lack. It is not unlike the person who will (contrary to scripture) argue Jesus doesn't heal anymore, taking that concept to their grave. The Bible is clear that we are to be,

> *"transformed by the renewing of your mind, that you may prove what is that good and acceptable and perfect will of God."* (Romans 12:2 NKJV)

The question in this verse, of course, is transformed from what? The short answer is that we must be converted from any ideology, emotion, education, thinking, and will that does not align with God's Word. In short, get rid of your "stinkin' thinkin'." Every single part of your life is to be entrenched in God and His Word. If anything does not line up with the Word of God, have nothing to do with it!

Fear and Guilt.

Two more critical traits of the spirit of religion are fear and guilt. They seem to motivate many Christians and non-Christians alike. This is not productive and not in line with the Word of God.

Now there is the fear of God, which is a Holy reverence (Proverbs 9:10), but this ungodly fear or guilt will deaden our sensitivity toward our Father and make us tailor the truth from our message so it doesn't offend anyone. For example, many pastors will not discuss the subject of money in church for fear of offending people. Instead of trusting God to provide for the church's needs when he speaks the truth, the pastor fears these people will leave the church, decreasing the church's income. Many pastors will not allow me to speak in their church for this reason, even going as far as to claim I am speaking blasphemy. The truth is that they fear I can back up my statements with Scripture, and they fear getting into trouble as some of the congregation tend to be "seeker sensitive" instead of "God sensitive." That religiosity leads us to try to fit true to our desire and preconceived ideas rather than what God desires, which is demonic. The Bible is banned in 52 countries, meanwhile, Disney and their products are not. Go figure...

Anemic Faith.

The spirit of religion also seeks to blind us to the fact that we have been legally delegated power over the enemy. We should never tolerate his attempts to destroy our life, finances, or health. We tend to live "bound up," justifying how we are, rather than pursuing the truth of God's abundance and healing for us. The spirit of religion hates that God has made provision for His children to be physically well and financially blest.

In Luke 6, we read how Jesus healed a man. The Pharisees - instead of rejoicing in the man's healing - were actually,

> *"filled with rage and discussed together what they might do to Jesus."* (Luke 6:11 NKJV)

Have you ever noticed the number of "religious" things people do inside a church that is not in the Bible? Why are they doing them? The answer is the ungodly traditions of men, usually crafted by spirits of religion. Reflecting on my days as a staunch Anglican, I can now see all the kooky religious rites, rituals, and observances I so piously participated in and supported. It benefitted me nothing because it had no foundation in the Word of God and could not be mixed with any faith to produce results. What a waste of time!

In Mark 7:13 (NASB), Jesus said,

> *"thus invalidating the Word of God by your tradition which you have handed down, and you do many things such as that."*

The spirit of religion will cause us to be influenced to a point where it develops into an entrenched attitude that obstinately cries, "But we've always done it this way so that we will continue."

Tradition tends to put God in a box and leave Him there. Revelation, on the other hand, brings knowledge, wisdom, and change that produces results. Suppose you allow the spirit of religion to go unchecked for too long. In that case, it becomes a legally controlling spirit, rendering everything around you impossible to deal with in a manner that glorifies God (technically this is refered to as a spiritual stronghold). In the Book of James 1:6-8, he warns us not to be double-minded, believing something first, then questioning God later. Look, I get it - the actual circumstances of life can afflict believers, but they become double-minded when they read one thing in the Word, then believe another thing by focusing on their worldly affairs. Tradition causes them to doubt and act on their doubt, subsequently never solidifying their foundation in God.

Therefore, the question stands, "How do we set ourselves free of the spirit of religion?"

Years ago, I read a book by a great teacher named Craig Hill titled, *"Deceived? Who Me?"* The book's point was, yes, we can all be deceived about certain things in our life. We can also be very ignorant and, consequently, deceived. As I mentioned, the answer is to study the Word of God for yourself and remain humble before Him. Constantly nurture your relationship with Him; then, you will discern what is from God and what is of the spirit of religion.

In my daily devotions, I pray the following prayer:

"Lord, break me, mould me, make me. You are the potter; I am the clay. Forgive me for my selfishness. I consecrate my life to You afresh this day. I give You permission to

Doc's Book Club: Read *"Deceived? Who Me?"* by Craig Hill.

break, mould, and make me according to Your will. This is all the work of Your grace. I choose to embrace whatever circumstances you send into my life to rid me of pride and self-will. I prefer to live on Your altar and by faith. As I empty myself, I ask You to fill me with Your Holy Spirit. Here I am, Lord; send me to do the assignments you have for me. Lord, am I deceived? If so, in what way, and about what? Please send me the wisdom to know and to grow in your Word. Help me not to be contemptuous but rather to be a servant to everyone and respond to all people always in love."

The key to resisting the spirit of religion is to look in the mirror regularly and consistently and ask yourself if your thoughts, words, and actions are lining up with the perfect will of God as found in His Word. Or have you been deceived in any way by a spirit of religion? The more honest you are, the freer you can become.

I had to address this spirit of religion to show you how dangerous it is. This wicked spirit has robbed countless believers of their resources, health, and life. I do not want the devil to steal from you, my friend; I want you to prosper and fulfil God's call for your life! When you are free from the influence of the spirit of religion, God will reveal mind-boggling things to you. Things like Jesus wasn't just wealthy - He was beyond wealth.

Let's look at some more fascinating truths now.

S.R. WATKINS

CHAPTER 3

CHRISTIANS, WEALTH, AND BEYOND WEALTH

What is a Christian?

You can tell by now that I like to get to the bottom line of a point as quickly and effectively as possible. The reason I communicate this way is that clear definitions make strong foundations. The strongest foundation you can have is the Word of God, so correctly understanding the Word of God is crucial to life. It makes sense that precise definitions are critical to understanding the Bible.

As such, the thought has occurred to me that if a reader of this book does not clearly understand what a "Christian" is, most of what is written here about God's desire for His children to prosper will not be understood. The task is not small, so in this age of fake news and false understanding, I think it is appropriate to "wipe the slate clean." This is so you, the reader, will clearly understand what the word "Christian" means and can subsequently frame the rest of the chapters on this sound foundation.

Let's take a quick history lesson on the roots of Christianity. If we go back to the time of Abraham, we will see that almost all people on this planet had completely fallen away from God. Abraham was the only God-fearing man left in his time, so God told him to leave his family and go to a different land where He would make him,

"The father of many nations." (Genesis 17:4)

God then established what is known as the "Abrahamic covenant," and fourteen generations later, God Himself was born in the flesh from the womb of a young girl named Mary. Jesus arrived precisely how the book of Isaiah prophesied He would. The family God established through Abraham were and are known as Hebrews or Jews. Jesus, therefore, was born, raised and was Jewish. The word "Christian" did not exist at the time Jesus lived. The followers of God and the followers of Jesus were known simply as "Hebrews."

Born Again.

In John 3:3, a Pharisee named Nicodemus came to Jesus at night and asked Him what he must do to believe and be a part of what Jesus taught. Jesus' famous response was, *"You must be born again,"* indicating that a person must be born of God's Spirit to be made alive unto God. Later, on the day of Pentecost, another 3000 people received Holy Spirit (Acts 2), and for the rest of the Book of Acts, these Hebrews who believed in Jesus were known as "Followers of the Way." This was to differentiate themselves from the Jews who did not believe in Jesus.

In 300 AD, everything changed when the Roman Emperor Constantine saw a flash in the sky, convinced himself it was a sign from God, and decided to believe in Him. He did not like the Jews, however, nor the "Followers of the

Way sect," as they were also known. Part of the reason he did not like either group was that Constantine wanted to maintain control over the empire. He subsequently labelled the "Followers of the Way" "little Christs," as they appeared to demonstrate the power Jesus had. Before I go any further, I must clarify what "Christ" means. It is necessary to understand that "Christ" means "anointed One." The best analogy for this phrase is when you baste a turkey with butter before you put it in the oven. The butter drenches the turkey in flavour completely and even serves to seal the turkey so it doesn't dry out. Essentially, you are anointing the turkey.

When Jesus is referred to as "Jesus Christ," it means "Jesus, who is the anointed One." The word Christ is not so much a name as a title. It would be far more accurate to call him "Christ Jesus" in the way you would call a knight of the round table, "Sir Arthur" (the Anglican Church is very accurate when calling Him "Christ Jesus.")

If a person is born again and filled with Holy Spirit (more on that later), then they are anointed with "the Christ," or perhaps worded differently, they are anointed with Holy Spirit, who is the Spirit of Christ (Romans 8:9). Therefore, saying a Christian is a "little Christ" is accurate. Constantine was correct with his label of "little Christs," which then evolved into the word "Christian."

To summarize large swaths of history (which you can verify if you are interested), the Christian church at that time was almost destroyed and then rebuilt according to power-hungry Constantine's design since he wanted to control his new religion. Constantine copied a demonic cult called Mithraism and brought in all types of religious protocols that were not biblical and had nothing to do with

Jesus or God. In fact, for a very enlightening and thorough examination of this, I strongly recommend a book called *"Rome's Anathemas; Insights into the Papal Pantheon"* by Dr. Selwyn Stevens, Ph.D. This book will give you an insight into what the highest levels of the Roman Catholic Church are really about. Unfortunately, many demonic Mithraic practices are widespread in many churches today, particularly in the Roman Catholic, Anglican, Orthodox, and Coptic Christian denominations.

What is the true definition of a "Christian" today? Simply put, a Christian is someone who has done three things found in the Bible:

1. They have chosen to be "born again" (John 3:3).
2. They have been born again by following Romans 10:9 (NIV), which says,

"If you declare with your mouth, 'Jesus is Lord,' and believe in your heart that God raised him from the dead, you will be saved."

3. They have asked God to forgive their sins and turned away from their old life. When leading someone to Christ, ministers often use a prayer known as the "Sinner's Prayer," which walks a person through the above three requirements. Ironically, this prayer is nowhere to be found in the Bible, but my experience is that it still works! No one would be better proof and an example of this than evangelist Billy Graham!

Doc's Book Club: Read *"Rome's Anathemas; Insights into the Papal Pantheon"* by Dr. Selwyn Stevens, Ph.D
Published by Jubilee Resources International Inc.
www.jubileeresources.org

Note: There is a problem with this prayer. Too many pastors/evangelists use the "sinner's prayer," and people are praying it, but they are missing a part; a VERY important part of the whole package of salvation. Repentance! The standard sinner's prayer asks people to confess their sins, and they ask Jesus to forgive them. Fine, and we need to do that, but we must also renounce the sin! That is the repentance part! Change! Stop doing it, and we must then live our lives for Jesus! If you are using/saying the sinner's prayer, make sure this sentence is in it: "I confess my sins, repent and turn from them." Then do that very thing, and Jesus said you would be saved. (Copied from my book, *"Life is a Test: Hope in a Confusing World Volume 3,"* publishing in 2024).

Unfortunately, what we see in our world are people who call themselves "Christians" because they "believe in God" (or some self-contrived idea of God) but were never actually born of Holy Spirit. The bottom line? You can call yourself anything you want, but you are not a Christian unless you have followed those steps sincerely and honestly. Millions of people world-wide and many going to church on Sunday, have never been born again and erroneously believe they are Christians. They are no more a Christian than someone who sat in a garage for a year is a car! If you think I am being harsh, this is not my doctrine-Jesus said,

> *"Truly, truly, I say to you, unless one is born of water and the Spirit, he cannot enter the kingdom of God."* (John 3:3 ESV)

I remember years ago hearing a testimony from a pastor. He had graduated from seminary and pastored churches for forty years. Wanting to advance his education as he enjoyed his retirement, he enrolled at Rhema Bible College in Tulsa, Oklahoma. For the first time in his life, he heard the gospel message. To his shock, he discovered that despite his education and pastoral credentials, he was not "born again" and, therefore, not a Christian! He quickly rectified the situation.

This dilemma has developed to a point where, in our modern-day language, two expressions are used for a supposed believer in Christ: "Christian" and "born-again Christian." The term "born-again Christian" is an oxymoron; it is terrible grammar because you cannot be a Christian unless you are born again. For this reason, I wish people would stop using the term "born-again Christian." If you have been born again, you are a Christian (a "little Christ"). If you have not been born again, you are not a Christian, despite what you may call yourself, think or believe.

In John 20:22, we see the New Testament's first example of Jesus anointing His disciples with Holy Spirit. This is duplicated with a larger group in Acts 2. Today we refer to this as "being filled with Holy Spirit," which, in my opinion, is inaccurate. The Bible clearly states that we are born dead into sin and made alive when we are born again by Holy Spirit (read Romans 6). Therefore, we are already filled with Holy Spirit at the new birth. A more accurate way to word the "filling" experience of Holy Spirit would be to say, "The activation of Holy Spirit in a person." To use the expression "a Spirit-filled, born-again Christian" is a double oxymoron!

If you have never made Jesus the Lord of your life and therefore are not a Christian, you can change that right now before we go any further. Believe me, it is the most valuable and critically necessary gift you will ever receive. God loves you and wants to adopt you into His family. I urge you to accept this invitation today. Believe this in your heart, confess your sin, and decree and declare the following:

"O God, in the Name of Jesus, I believe with all my heart that Jesus died for my sins and was raised from the dead. Jesus, I ask you to come into my heart. I receive you as my Lord and Saviour. Thank you for doing that. Satan, I renounce you! I renounce the past and repent of my sins. You are not my God or Lord, and I turn from you. You will have no part in my life for the rest of my life. I now belong to Jesus. He is my Lord and Saviour, and I will tell whoever wants to know that I am a believer. I believe every Word of it! I believe it and receive it.

Fill me, Lord, to overflowing with your precious Holy Spirit. I am now baptized in the Spirit of the living God, and I fully expect all His manifestations. I expect power! Jesus said I would receive power when Holy Spirit comes upon me. Power to witness for Him. Power to live and walk in the Word of the living God. I fully expect a supernatural prayer language that I can speak to God. I expect it now! In the Name of Jesus, I pray. Amen."

Congratulations, my new brother or sister in the Lord! Welcome to the Kingdom of God! I wish I were there to hug you and help you grow in the Lord. One of the most important things you need to do right now is find yourself a Spirit-filled church which believes in and practices the Gifts of Holy Spirit. The work of Holy Spirit never ceased; in fact, we are seeing greater results than the Apostles and even Jesus did on Earth today! If you are attending a church that is not spirit-filled, well, it is time to leave. Start learning, and grow, grow, and grow some more.

Can a Christian Have a Demon?

Moving on to another foundational topic related to this chapter and the last, another bone of contention in the church is the entire subject of spiritual warfare and whether a Christian can have a demon. I fail to see the controversy. Christians can have anything they want! The whole issue can be explained quite easily.

As humans, we consist of three parts: spirit, soul, and body. It is interesting to note that God is a "Trinity," and so, are we. Further, our souls are divided into three parts: our mind, will, and emotions (another "trinity.") When we become a Christian, our dead spirit is then made alive by the power of Holy Spirit (i.e., we are born again). As a Christian, no demon can now enter and possess our spirit. That, however, does not stop him from harassing our souls, and there are three levels of a demonic attack against a Christian:

1. The first level can be equated to mosquitoes buzzing around and inflicting annoying, sometimes painful bites. Another example would be a snake bite. This is just the daily harassment that all Christians face (at least if you allow demons to do so).

2. The second level would be when a demon attaches itself to the person's soul (due to sin, often from unforgiveness), much like a leech that attaches to your skin and sucks your blood. This attack results from a trauma or a persistent sin (e.g., an addiction) and manifests in mood and personality problems.

3. The third level would be an infestation, like tapeworms inside your body (for example, when satan entered Judas in Luke 22:3). Historically, this type of harassment has not been overly common. However, with the increase of sin in our world - from pornography to horror movies to sexual immorality and, yes, even Harry Potter - those in deliverance ministry and counselling are busier than ever.

In 2008 I joined the International Society of Deliverance Ministers (founded by Peter and Doris Wagner, (www.isdmministers.org), the largest and most accredited organization in the world that deals with the controversial subject of deliverance. After over ten years of training, I have concluded that not only can a Christian have a demon, but my experience has been that Christians tend to have more demons than non-Christians! (Note: Deliverance is not to be confused with "exorcism," a Roman Catholic rite. The Roman Catholics have it half right (no pun intended), but most of their actions are not biblically based and, consequently, completely ineffective).

Think about it... satan does not need to harass unsaved people in any way. I am not saying he doesn't; I'm just saying he doesn't have to. Why? He already has nonbelievers in his clutches, as they have not been born again. Have you ever met a married couple with a good marriage and several normal and healthy children? They have a good income, enjoy a rewarding, happy lifestyle, and never seem to have too many problems. They may or may not believe in God, but overall, they regard themselves as good people. If there is a God, they know they would go to Heaven because they live a good moral life. Sadly, they have not been born again, and satan knows it. He, therefore, never has to harass them; he already has them!

Once a person has been born again, satan is not a happy camper. The newly-born Christian has just entered boot camp for the Kingdom of God, and satan now sees that person as a significant threat. He will do everything he can to make their life miserable and ultimately try to pressure them to give up their faith. The sad truth is that satan is very good at his job. This explains why many Christians have just as many divorces, pornography problems, addictions, etc., as unsaved people do. Demons still get into a Christian's life, brainwashing them so severely that they do not even know they are being severely influenced by evil.

Make no mistake, the devil's greatest power is to deceive you into thinking he does not exist, or he is not constantly trying to exert power over you just because you are "saved." That is just naivety to the point of complete stupidity.

As you might have guessed, I have never been a person to shy away from controversy (on the contrary, I tend to jump into it with both feet)! I do not know of a more controversial subject in the church than spiritual warfare. Consequently, the devil is laughing all the way to the bank because of the naiveté of Christians. Not only can Christians be oppressed by a demon in their flesh or mind, but spiritual strongholds can develop over a person, a community, a province/state and even an entire country. Evil spirits can bewitch people (Jezebel being a prime example) and not even know it. Without sound teaching on spiritual warfare, much of the church lives utterly ignorant of the demonic oppression from which they could be set free. Case in point: Canada, not unlike many other nations, has a political agenda that is quite liberal and, therefore, mainly against the Word of God. Our country supported abortion and gay rights long before the USA did. The spirit of Jezebel controls these issues and many others. Satan can control whole geographic areas and even people groups, and they don't even know it! That is how a cult operates. If people knew that they were in a cult, would they stay? Of course not. People are in cults like Freemasonry, Mormonism and Jehovah's Witness and don't even know they are!

Getting Demons Out.

(Note: We in deliverance ministry will not minister to anyone who is not a Christian.)

1. Crowd them out! Fill your life with things that demons don't like. Learning about Jesus is a great example! Read your Bible, attend a Spirit-filled church, get involved in ministry, etc. The bottom line is you can't be at home on the internet, looking at pornography, if you are out helping at the church's soup kitchen.

2. Starve them out! Demons feed on the works of the flesh and love it when you sin. Stop sinning! It's called discipline. Walk in love and purity.

3. Command them out! Be very diligent about steps one and two, and if that's not working for you, decree and declare the following:

    In the Name of Jesus, I come against your demonic spirits satan, and bind your activity in my life. I declare that I have confessed and repented of every known sin and that Jesus has forgiven me. I declare that Jesus is my Lord. My life belongs to Him! I confess that I am redeemed by the blood of the Lamb and out of the hands of the enemy! Spirit of _____(name it), I speak directly to you. The blood of the Lord Jesus Christ has set me free from your oppression. You have no legal right to touch me. I drive you out of my life now and command you to leave in the Name of Jesus! Go now! Do not return! Thank you, Jesus, for setting me free! Amen!"

Praise God! I believe if you are being harassed or oppressed by anything demonic, you are now free! Walk in that freedom and continue to step into and walk in what God has called you to (and stop sinning)!

Now that we have covered what it means to be a Christian, I want to close the first three chapters with a revelation that has been such a blessing to me. The list below shows an entirely different perspective on how God approaches wealth.

Doc's Book Club: Read *"Set Yourself Free: A Deliverance Manual"* by Dr. Robert Heidler.

Beyond Wealth.

I have established several points in previous chapters, which I will reiterate and summarize now with the help of the following excerpt from Dr. Peter J. Daniel's book, Jesus and Wealth. More importantly, this excerpt shows that Jesus was not just wealthy; He was in fact, beyond wealth. This means He was not limited to wealth - wealth served and obeyed Him for His Father's purposes. This is very pertinent. The value of the wealth that Jesus received in the form of gold, frankincense, and myrrh that was given to Jesus after His birth in today's currency was worth USD $450 million.

The extraordinary power of Jesus was beyond imagination, as He stopped the wind, calmed the seas, walked on water, raised the dead, healed the sick, and restored severed body parts. It has been easy and convenient to overlook the fact that Jesus was above and beyond wealth because He could turn water into wine and multiply the loaves and fishes and actually produce money from the fish's mouth.

The definition of wealthy, is "one who is able to obtain what is immediately required." This would have to be the ultimate in luxury and would put one well beyond wealth as we know it. Could there possibly exist a level of wealth beyond our traditional definitions? Could this wealth, if it existed, be demonstrated by a man of Hebrew descent who was a common carpenter? Jesus is the only person in history who qualified for the status of "wealthy."

Jesus Was Beyond Wealth: 15 points.

1. Beyond wealth, because without the liability and obligations of managing a vineyard or the need to own a winery, Jesus turned water into wine, and it wasn't even His water! Not just wine, but "the best wine" without even paying for it (John 2:10)! He was able to obtain what was immediately required. He was beyond wealth.

2. Beyond wealth, because as an inside trader in the fishing industry, He had prior knowledge in respect to the location and volume of catch that would make any futures trader on the New York stock exchange a millionaire in thirty days (John 21:6). He was beyond wealth.

3. Beyond wealth, because of the twelve businessmen He dined with on one occasion, Jesus
could predict which one could not be trusted,
right down to the time that the betrayal took
place (Matthew 26:21), and which of the twelve
would deny Him even after publicly confirming
a vote of confidence in favour of Jesus' leadership (Matthew 26:34). Any executive demonstrating such insight into people's character as
Jesus possessed could easily demand of any
multinational conglomerate corporation a
"mega salary" to chair their board meetings, and
they would willingly pay. Jesus was beyond
wealth. How often have you said, "If only I
knew that was going to happen, I could've made
a fortune!" That "knowing the future" was a
normal experience for Jesus. He knew the
headlines for tomorrow morning's newspaper;
for next year's stock prices for that matter. He
was beyond wealth.

4. Beyond wealth, because when it came to paying
taxes, He was able to extinguish His liability
simply by having a fish pay the tax for him
(Matthew 17:27)! Jesus even picked up the tab
on His associates' tax obligation courtesy of the
same fish! In short, He was able to obtain what
was immediately required. He was beyond
wealth.

5. Beyond wealth, as there is no evidence that Jesus
ever paid civil taxes! The approach to collect tax
from Jesus (Mark 12:14) by the civil government
agents came to an end, as Jesus was able to
negotiate a "nil tax liability" status within the
state. How much wealthier would your family

be today if you had no tax encumbrance on your family assets or income? Jesus was beyond wealth.

6. Beyond wealth, because He could heal the incurable diseases of His day with just a touch (Luke 5:13). No need for years of laboratory research at the cost of millions of dollars, or doctors and expensive medicines.... just one touch. He was beyond wealth.

7. Beyond wealth, because when He wanted to travel into town, without so much as a phone call, He had a donkey waiting that He had never bred, never fed, never stabled, never trained, and He never had to worry about parking when He arrived at his destination! He received a voluntary "red carpet" reception (Matthew 21:7). Jesus was beyond wealth.

8. If "knowledge is wealth," Jesus tops the list again as surely as His intellect was beyond any known measure of knowledge in the then known world. The intellectuals of His day in open debate marveled at His knowledge (and this happened when He was just a kid)! (Luke 20:26, John 7: 14, 15). His reservoir of knowledge clearly silenced His would-be critics and put Him far beyond any wealth of knowledge they could muster!

9. Beyond wealth, because His Father owns the largest cow ranch on the planet ("He owns the cattle on 1000 hills" Psalm 50:10), and the mineral reserves beyond the biggest publicly traded mining company on Wall Street. ("The

earth is the LORD's and everything in it." Psalm 24:1)

10. Beyond wealth, because although many of the world's richest people live in a mansion, Jesus' neighbourhood contains many mansions, and the main street is not constructed of asphalt or even stylish cobblestones, but with gold (Revelation 21:21).

11. Beyond wealth, because just a cursory glance at His miracles confirms that He was able to multiply assets exponentially! In the case of the feeding of the 5,000, if we conclude that one person would have eaten half a loaf of bread and one fish, then Jesus' "food fund" showed a capital growth rate of 50,000 percent per day (bread) and over 250,000 percent per day (fish)! No capital growth fund in history can come close to that. At that rate of return, you could give Jesus one dollar on Friday night, and over the weekend He would turn you into a multimillionaire! He was clearly beyond wealth. To top it off, Jesus gave it all away, and it didn't diminish His asset base one bit!

12. Beyond wealth, because Jesus was a unique dresser, as one discovers He wore the clothes of one who shopped in the finest stores. So much so that after his assassination, rather than cut up His coat and divide it four ways as a souvenir, the soldiers decided to draw straws for this trophy and keep this quality seamless garment as one piece, as such a masterpiece of tailoring demanded (John 19: 23, 24).

13. Beyond wealth, as His burial was that reserved for the very, very, rich. In this case, the mega rich merchant, Joseph from the town of Arimathea, donated the tomb that Jesus was buried in. Jesus didn't even have to pay a dime for the tomb! (Matthew 27:60) He had the ability to obtain that which was immediately required, even after He breathed His last breath! Jesus was clearly beyond wealth.

14. Beyond wealth, because "what shall it profit a man if he gains the whole world and loses his soul?" Jesus conquered death.

15. Beyond wealth, because you clearly can't give what you haven't got, and you can't lead from behind, so when Jesus' Father promises to give wealth, He could only do so if He first possessed wealth, (Ecclesiastes 5:19 "Furthermore, as for every man to whom God has given riches and wealth, He has also empowered him to eat from them and to receive His reward and rejoice in his labour; this is the gift of God.") which He clearly does. You would therefore not be surprised to discover that this same Jesus is able to teach His wealth techniques and multiply wealth to the "apprentices" that follow Him. Deuteronomy 8:18 says, "And you shall remember the LORD your God, for it is He who gives you power to get wealth, that He may establish His covenant which He swore to your fathers, as it is this day.") Jesus was clearly, beyond wealth! (And He is willing to teach it to us)! *

---

* Daniels, Dr. Peter J. *"Jesus and Wealth."* Vanuatu, South West Pacific. World Centre for Entrepreneurial Studies Foundation.

(The author is very grateful to his mentor, Dr. Peter J. Daniels, who gave him permission to reprint this wealth essay.)

Review of the Last Three Chapters.

These first few chapters have, at the very least, made you aware that there is more to this Christian walk than many realize. More provision, more joy, and more power. In closing, I will summarize the last three chapters:

1. Have you been born again? If not, pray the prayer in this chapter.

2. Are you filled with Holy Spirit? If not, ask Him to fill you now.

3. Conduct a self-analysis and see if you are deceived about anything classified as a spirit of religion. If you find something, cast it out. Ask God to forgive you, and repent (repentance means permanently turning away from your old ways).

4. Do you need deliverance? The truth of the matter is that we all need deliverance every day! It is called "confession of sin." The word "deliverance" means to be set free, which is what happened when you were born again and what you do when you confess your sin every day. Therefore, "deliverance" should be a daily occurrence.

5. God wants you rich because Jesus was rich when He walked the Earth, and we are to be like Him.

6. Jesus was beyond wealth. He superseded it and used it as a tool.

We have covered much material, but hopefully, the foundation is set for more extensive and brighter revelations. One of the most powerful is having a biblical understanding of money. Let's have a look.

S.R. WATKINS

CHAPTER 4

FALSE IDEAS ABOUT MONEY - PART 1

Now that we understand what it means to be a Christian and why the Word of God - the Bible - is critical to our understanding of money, we can continue eradicating false ideas about money. In the following chapters, you will see even more clearly that God has a plan for using money. An excellent example of this is found in 1 Timothy. Perhaps the most misquoted scripture in the Bible is this one:

> *"For the love of money is a root of all kinds of evil. Some people, eager for money, have wandered from the faith and pierced themselves with many griefs."* (1 Timothy 6:9-10 NIV)

The misquote, of course, is, "Money is the root of all evil." No, reread it. The Bible says the "love" of money is the root of all kinds of evil. Money itself is neutral. It is not a living, breathing entity. It cannot be good or evil. Just one chapter earlier in 1 Timothy 5:8 (KJV) the Apostle Paul says,

> *"if any provide not for his own, he hath denied the faith and is worse than an infidel."*

How can you provide for your own (doing good) without money?

Money is typically viewed as evil by people indoctrinated with the aforementioned pagan mindset Constantine adopted from the Greeks; that is until a need for money arises. A man who lacks the five necessities of life, because he doesn't have enough money to supply them does not think for one minute that money is evil. He knows money will save his life. Does a poor, starving child in a third-world country believe money is evil? If money were evil, why did Jesus have so much of it or, at least, why was He given so much of it at His birth? No, money is neither inherently good nor evil; it is a wrong desire for money to use it wickedly - that is evil. The lack of money usually causes this desire. I could even say, "The lack of money is the root of all kinds of evil!"

Understand this key: money is a measurement of a person's heart and one's obedience. It is a tool to pay for the cost of preaching the gospel. That is a righteous desire for money. God is not against wealth; He is against sin. So, what is wealth? What is prosperity? As Peter Daniels says in his book *"Jesus and Wealth,"* wealth is the ability "to obtain what is immediately required." *

I agree wholeheartedly with this sentiment and my own quote: "prosperity is having enough provision to complete God's instructions." Even so, as powerfully as money can be used in the right hands, we must remember that it is the lowest form of power. Money does not destroy yolks nor cause miracles. Money is simply a tool to obtain the power to accomplish God's will, but it is not power itself.

*IBID

The Story of the Rich Young Ruler.

I do not know of a passage of scripture that has caused more strife about biblical prosperity than the one I'm about to share. I have seen people hold onto an incorrect understanding of this passage with such vigour that they are bound (no pun intended) and determined to remain poor to prove their point. It is not unlike the infamous account of Paul's "thorn in the flesh" in 2 Corinthians 12:7-9. People would rather die of sickness, holding onto the wrong notion that Jesus doesn't heal any longer, by claiming that Paul's thorn in the flesh was sickness. Study it for yourself - it was persecution, not sickness.

Likewise, according to the unbelievers, the following scripture is supposed to prove their point that a rich man can never enter the Kingdom of God. For them, the issue is closed. They are wrong, and I'll explain why once you've read the passage:

> "Now as He was going out on the road, one came running, knelt before Him, and asked Him, "Good Teacher, what shall I do that I may inherit eternal life?" Jesus said to him, "Why do you call Me good? No one is good but One, that is, God. You know the command-ments: 'Do not commit adultery,' 'Do not murder,' 'Do not steal,' 'Do not bear false witness,' 'Do not defraud,' 'Honour your father and your mother.'
> And he answered and said to Him, "Teacher, all these things I have kept from my youth."
> Then Jesus, looking at him, loved him, and said to him, "One thing you lack: Go your way, sell whatever you have and give to the poor, and you will have treasure in heaven; and come, take up the cross, and follow Me. But he was sad at this word, and went away sorrowful, for he had great possessions.

*Then Jesus looked around and said to His disciples,
"How hard it is for those who have riches to enter the
kingdom of God!" And the disciples were astonished at
His words. But Jesus answered again and said to them,
"Children, how hard it is for those who trust in riches
to enter the kingdom of God! It is easier for a camel to
go through the eye of a needle than for a rich man to
enter the kingdom of God." And they were greatly
astonished, saying among themselves, "Who then can be
saved?" But Jesus looked at them and said, "With men
it is impossible, but not with God; for with God all things
are possible" Then Peter said, "See, we have left all and
followed You."*

*So, He said to them, "Assuredly, I say to you, there is
no one who has left house or parents or brothers or wife
or children, for the sake of the kingdom of God, who shall
not receive many times more in this present time, and in
the age to come eternal life."* (Luke 18: 18-29 NKJV)

The key to understanding this passage is knowing that a
bit of knowledge can sometimes be dangerous knowledge.
Jesus spoke many times using parables to make His point.
In this passage, we can plainly see Jesus doing exactly that
using a parable. When reading a parable, first, you must
read the verses before and after the parable. Second, read
the scripture in a variety of translations and paraphrases.
Additional help can also be found by using a Greek
concordance, or as I like to use, the Dake Anointed
Reference Bible. Here you will find an explanation of the
metaphor of a camel going through the eye of the needle.
To understand this, we must understand the context of the
passage - specifically, how cities were built in the time of
Jesus, and also the culture of that time.

When Jesus walked the Earth, cities had large walls to protect the inhabitants from invaders. How, then, did anyone gain access to the city? Obviously, through a gate. Although wide gates with wooden doors are familiar to us (used in castles, for example), these doors can be rammed or lit on fire and burned to the ground, giving access to the enemy. The Israelite cities used a more ingenious method: building a very tall, narrow gate appropriately called "The eye of the needle." The gate was so tall and so extremely narrow that a camel, fully loaded with a pack or even a rider, could not fit through, as it was too wide. So how did man and beast get into the city? The camel had to be stripped of the loads it was carrying on either side and then be led through the gate. The gate was so narrow that there were just a few inches of clearance between the camel's side and the entrance wall (like a ship in a canal lock).

So, what is the parable's meaning, then?

Jesus was making the point that a rich man (or any other man for that matter) cannot enter the Kingdom of Heaven unless he strips himself of what he values more than God, thus surrendering himself to God. Isn't that how we become a Christian? We deprive ourselves of our life and give it to Him. Didn't Jesus say,

> *"For whosoever will save his life shall lose it: and who-soever will lose his life for my sake shall find it"?*
> (Matthew 16:25 KJV)

The point is that it is about something other than the money. It is about our heart's desire to spend the money that is the issue. If we are going to spend it all on our own lusts, then that is a separate issue (one of sin), as opposed to using the money to feed the poor and send Bibles to third-world countries, for example.

In the second part of the scripture, you will notice how astonished the disciples were with His parable. So much so that they asked, "Who then can be saved?" I want you to ask yourself a question: if the disciples were poor, why would they have been astonished by Jesus' response? On the contrary, if they were poor and believed they were doing the will of God by being poor, indeed, they would have been overjoyed, saying, "See, I told you, it's better to be poor because a rich man can't get into the Kingdom of God." Of course, that was not their reaction. They were undoubtedly astonished because they thought they could not be saved. After all, they were rich.

How do we Know the Disciples were Rich?

1. They hung around Jesus for three years and were provided for, as I have shown through scripture in previous chapters.

2. When Jesus sent them out on their own to teach, He said,

"Take nothing for the journey, neither staffs nor bag nor bread nor money; and do not have two tunics apiece." (Luke 9: 3-5 KJV)

Then when they returned, He asked them how they were doing financially. Their response?

"Then Jesus asked them, when I sent you without purse, bag or sandals, did you lack anything? 'Nothing,' they answered." (Luke 22:35 NIV)

Again, in that society, you were either rich or poor. Here the disciples were saying they lacked nothing.

The point is that insight and wisdom are needed to determine whether riches hinder a person from entering the Kingdom of Heaven. Mark 4:19 talks about the deceitfulness of riches, but it does not say we are not to have riches. All the rich man needed was to use faith in God to meet his needs. Jesus loved him and saw the hold that money had on his life. The young man, however, did not trust the love of God coming from Jesus. Jesus was literally calling him into the ministry as an Apostle, and this young ruler traded his apostleship for money.

As Christians, we are to define ourselves in terms of our relationship with Jesus. You can be successful and not wealthy; conversely, you can be wealthy but not successful. To be a successful businessman, however, is to be wealthy and know Jesus. Never measure success by how much money you have; measure success by how intimate your relationship is with Jesus.

This concept is best illustrated in Matthew 6:24 (NKJV) where Jesus said,

> *"No one can serve two masters; for either he will hate the one and love the other, or else he will be loyal to the one and despise the other. You cannot serve God and mammon."*

The difference is in whom you serve. You can be rich and serve God with a pure heart, or poor and serve mammon (money) with impure motives. I put it this way: greed desires everything and is satisfied with nothing; grace desires nothing but is satisfied with everything.

It can be very difficult if you take what we call a "self-made millionaire" and try to preach the Kingdom to him. He has made his money independently and feels he doesn't need God. There is, however, always an emptiness inside of such a man. An emptiness he tries to fill with another drink and/or more drugs, another business deal, a bigger boat, a bigger house and more cars, another marriage... the list goes on and on. He doesn't realize that he can only fill that void through a relationship with God. God doesn't make sense to him. He has an "I can do it on my own" mentality. He may keep his conscience at bay by being generous and giving to charity as "fire insurance," but he knows - as did the rich young ruler who went away sad - something massive is missing.

Indeed, it is very hard for a rich man to get into the Kingdom of Heaven if he is a "self-made" man. I have met many so-called "self-made" millionaires in my life, and as a rule, I find them to be ignorant of God and very shallow people. The point is, never trust in money or yourself; trust in God - rather use money to further the gospel. The more money you have, the more of the gospel you can spread.

It has been said that money if it does not bring you happiness, will at least help you be miserable in comfort. I agree, but you don't have to be miserable - you can have money and be happy IF you know Jesus and follow His will.

You don't have to be poor to be in the will of God. As I will show you in the next chapter, it is certainly not God's will for you to be poor. In fact, poverty is a curse, and I am about to expose the evil nature of poverty and show you how to be totally free from its slavery.

CHAPTER 5

FALSE IDEAS ABOUT MONEY - PART 2

As I've already shown, possibly the leading false idea about money is that poverty equates to humility. In this chapter, I want to blow that myth out of the water. I want to destroy that yoke of bondage so entirely that it never rears its ugly head in your life again. Let it sink in: Poverty and humility are unrelated; poverty is a curse.

In Deuteronomy 28, God describes in detail the curses that will come upon people not obedient to His Word. Although the chapter does not explicitly use the word "poor," this list of curses accurately describes the state of poverty and total lack in all areas of life. The same chapter lists abundant blessings that will flow in the life of a person who obeys God's will. It is interesting to note that there are fifteen verses of blessing and fifty-two verses of cursing. I think God is trying to get our attention with these numbers - to me, it seems to be a caution that there is more availability to mess up.

Logic dictates that if a person is not walking in blessing, they must be walking in cursing. Does it not make sense to find out what we are missing (i.e., in what way are we being disobedient) that brings on the curses and blocks the blessing? These fifty-two verses describe in nauseating detail the horrible things that will happen to a person disobedient to the Word of God, rejecting redemption, with several of those verses directly relating to poverty. Therefore, saying that Jesus was "poor and humble" is not true. "Humble" yes; "poor" no. Deuteronomy 15:4 (KJV) says,

> "...there shall be no poor among you."

I'm not sure of a scripture that is clearer than that one.

Do you remember the teaching about the spirit of religion a few chapters back? I mentioned that people oppressed by this spirit will fight to remain in poverty. The spirit of religion and the spirit of poverty are almost twins! Poverty is a demonic curse.

Five Signs of Oppression by a Spirit of Poverty.

1. If a person is missing any of the five necessities of life: food, clothing, shelter, money, health, and spiritual and/or mental peace consistently, they may be suffering under some level of the influence of a spirit of poverty. If a person has constant money problems (debt, needing credit, etc.), a spirit of poverty may keep them from correctly managing the money. People often think that more money is the solution to their problems, yet often that is not the case.

    I remember reading in the newspaper several years ago a story about a poor man who won two million dollars in a lottery. He had no clue how to manage his money, so in less than two years, he had spent all of it and was back in poverty. In desperation to get his lifestyle back, he robbed a bank, was caught, and went to prison. He then felt so ashamed that he committed suicide. Had he placed half of the money in a mutual fund, he would have earned enough interest to live comfortably for the rest of his life.

Another example is that sometimes, we read about a person who lived the life of a pauper and died homeless on the street. Strangely, his family then discovers the man is a multimillionaire. How can that be? This is a spirit of poverty gloating from that newspaper story; a demonic spirit who successfully destroyed a person's life, despite their wealth. If you're confused, remember this; very wealthy people can still be oppressed by a spirit of poverty as stinginess completely controls their life. The attitude of the heart defines a sinful approach to money.

2. Believe it or not, obesity can be another sign of oppression by a spirit of poverty. Rich people tend to develop "rich habits." One example is that rich people tend to read more books (more on this later). Conversely, poor people develop poor habits. A poor person manages to read very few books or none at all. Instead, they spend their time watching television, valuing being passively entertained instead of actively engaging their mind in a book. They become the classic couch potato, and what do they usually do when they sit on the couch? They eat. Generally, they eat what is known as "junk food." Additionally, poor people tend to buy

lower-quality food because of budget con-
straints, and this food often has the most
calories. This doesn't mean they can't afford
good food - a bunch of organic bananas is a little
over a dollar. Yet, poor people lack the incentive
to look after their bodies (i.e., go to the gym, jog
or even walk each night), and ironically, in first-
world nations, many impoverished people
become obese. Such is not the case in third-
world countries; they don't have the money to
buy food in the first place.

Further, often but not always, people who suffer
from depression issues and/or self-esteem
issues are poor. They frequently raid the refrigerator with little willpower to eat in a manner
that would reduce their symptoms. Food is to be
used for fuel, but in our culture, it is tied to our
emotions. This is a clear symptom of oppression
by a spirit of poverty.

How does a person beat the "battle of the
bulge?" Smaller meals, no snacks, avoid calorie-
dense foods like pizza, watch your intake of
"junk food," commit to regular, weekly exercise,
and commit to two to three periods of fasting per
year.

Please understand that the purpose of fasting is
not to lose weight. That is not the biblical form
of fasting; that's diet reduction. The purpose of
fasting is to dominate the flesh so you can be
more in tune with God. On a side note, fasting
is not about you trying to get God to do something. The sole purpose of fasting is to bring
yourself closer to God, strengthening your faith.

You will, however, rarely see an obese person fasting. Jesus said, *"When you give..."* (Matthew 6:2), *"When you pray..."* (Matthew 6:5), and *"When you fast..."* (Matthew 6:16). He did not say, "IF you want to fast...."

I usually fast from one to three weeks, taking only juice, water and electrolytes. I highly recommend Jentezen Franklin's wonderful books on the subject, complete with journals.

An observation I've made is the epidemic of obesity in the USA. When I travel there, I can see why. Every US city I go into has a significant proliferation of restaurants. The food portions are enormous there, and I have learned to order just a salad or appetizer because that will be a meal within itself. I've also noticed that so much food is not eaten and ends up being wasted, while over 60 percent of the world's population has insufficient food. I believe this is the sin of gluttony. (I am not suggesting that Canada does not have the same problem, but the percentage is a bit lower.)

3. A person's appearance can be another sign of oppression by a spirit of poverty. An old expression says, "If it looks like a duck, walks like a duck, and talks like a duck, then it must be a duck!" A spirit of poverty will keep a person dressed very poorly. Whenever I mention this subject in my seminars, well-meaning people are all over me saying, "Clothes don't make a person!" I could not agree more; however, they certainly introduce you! Case in point, if I were to stand at the podium in front of a large

audience during one of my teaching contracts, would I have any credibility as a speaker if I had not shaved in a week, my hair was a mess, I was wearing baggy sweat pants, a T-shirt, and a backwards baseball cap? Compare that with my $4,000 suit, complete with a French-cuff shirt, gold cufflinks, gold rings, a gold and diamond watch, a silk tie, and shined black cowboy boots. Again, people will listen to a rich man but not a poor man, or more accurately worded, whom they perceive to be rich.

I agree that clothes don't make a person, but there is something about wearing really nice clothes and "feeling rich" that makes a person feel good and commands the audience's attention. "Success breeds success," and I like to look successful!

"For as he thinks in his heart, so is he."
(Proverbs 23:7 KJV)

I think "success," and I become what I believe. I remember years ago, when I was enrolled in a Toastmasters program, one of the things that they taught me was to "take command" of the room when you are a public speaker. You do that through establishing eye contact with your audience, posturing and body language, relevancy on the topic of which you are speaking, and last but not least, dress and appearance. Thinking on biblical principles (*"be the head and not the tail"* - Deut. 28:13) will rapidly drive a spirit of poverty away.

One of the many businesses I've owned was a manufacturing plant. For the entire eighteen years I owned it, I never once went to work without a tie and jacket or tie with a suit. There were people in the community who laughed behind my back, but the joke was on them because my company was making a full 10 percent higher profit margin than the industry average for that type of business. We looked professional, and we were professional, and I made more money because of it! (BTW, our competitor filed for bankruptcy...)

When my youngest daughter went to high school, the standard was that the teachers were all very casually dressed, and the students were instructed to address their teachers by their first names. One teacher refused to accept those standards and maintained his own, which was to be addressed by his last name, and he wore a tie and jacket. One day I complimented him on this practice, and he told me he had more discipline and respect in his classroom than any other teacher. The moral of the story? If you look good and act professionally, you will command respect, and people will listen.

At this stage in life, I always introduce myself as "Dr. Watkins." I have been accused of being a "stuck-up old prune" and/or on an ego trip. I do not look at it that way at all. I see it as professional and respectful; I respect others, and I trust they will respect me. If they don't, that's their problem (or their lack of manners). All I know is when I am introduced as "Dr. Watkins" and then walk in front of an audience "dressed to the hilt," I "take command" of the room, and people listen and pay attention. Isn't that what they are there to do?

4. Untidiness is the fourth sign of oppression by a spirit of poverty. Closely related to obesity but not quite the same, sloppiness is a sure sign of this spirit's influence. Years ago, I lived in a small town. Close to my house, two families lived in homes with government-subsidized rent. Both families were impoverished. You could easily spot which two houses they lived in. Both houses needed paint and repair; both houses had a collection of toys, garden tools, bicycles, etc., scattered all over the front yard. If you entered either house, you would see junk strewn from one end of the house to the other. It costs nothing to keep one's home orderly, yet succumbing to a spirit of poverty will cause people to be slobs.

5. Poverty is also an institutionalized curse. This does not mean it is a financial problem; on the contrary, it is a spiritual one. Poor decisions are made by people under the control of a demonic spirit. People often talk about getting wealth without first addressing why they are experiencing poverty. Keep in mind that the spirit of poverty has nothing to do with the amount of money a person has. Wealthy people can be so stingy and fear losing their money that a spirit of poverty controls them. Conversely, poor people think the solution to the problem is more money. Such is not the case. The answer to the

problem is spiritual deliverance, and deliverance begins with hearing the Word and implementing it.

One thing is undeniable: poverty-stricken people are highly limited in their ability to fulfill the Great Commission. Without funds, you will have difficulty going into the world to preach the gospel. You can't even help send someone else to do it. If God requires every believer to carry out this mission, does it not make sense that it is His will and plan for His people to prosper and have the money to do so? It is really that simple. Conversely, wealthy people oppressed by a spirit of poverty will spend their money on themselves, never wanting to part with a cent of their money to help others.

My daughter was an employee with Youth with a Mission (YWAM) and was unpaid as a full-time missionary. It is expected that the church, family and friends will support her, so she can do the work the rest of us either can't or won't do. It amazes me the number of people that cannot grasp that concept. Even my own family...

Eight Steps to Poverty.

I have explained several false ideas about money, and hopefully, you agree (or at least admit that the scriptures I present are compelling). Even so, if anyone still insists on living in poverty, here are eight easy steps to do so (or you can run in the opposite direction if you want to receive blessings). Here goes:

1. Be lazy and work half-heartedly for yourself and/or your boss; you have an ironclad guarantee that poverty awaits you. Success in life is the result of working hard, as shown in Thessalonians 3:10 (NASB),

"if anyone is not willing to work, then he is not to eat, either."

Obviously, exceptions must be made for widows, orphans, disabled people, etc. There is, however, no place in the Bible that says governments should give out social welfare to people who don't want to work. It is the church that is to help society, not the government. (Socialism is demonic; but that is another book to write...)

"How long will you slumber, O sluggard? When will you rise from your sleep? A little sleep, a little slumber, A little folding of the hands to sleep. So, shall your poverty come on you like a prowler, And your need like an armed man." (Proverbs 6:9-11 NKJV)

Sometimes a spirit of poverty can be so firmly entrenched over so many people that it becomes a stronghold in a geographic area. An example is the Island of Hispaniola in the Caribbean. The island is divided into two countries: the Dominican Republic and Haiti. The Dominican Republic is relatively stable, with a per capita gross domestic product of $18,164. The country is 95 percent Christian. Haiti, on the other hand, has a per capita gross domestic product of $1,819, and although it claims that 54 percent of the population is Roman Catholic, their Catholicism is primarily mixed with Voodoo and superstition.

Haiti, of course, has a tremendously higher poverty rate and terrible problems with soil erosion, and a few years ago, when a massive earthquake struck the island, it curiously centred in Haiti, not the Dominican Republic. It is not difficult to see demonic spirits of poverty, witchcraft, and religion active on the Haitian side of the island, but far less so on the Dominican Republic side. These demonic strongholds are what cause Haiti to continue to have economic problems. Billions of financial aid dollars have been poured into the country, which hasn't solved too much and it won't until the spiritual issues are addressed.

2. In the Bible, foolishness is often associated with drunkards, gluttons, and wasteful people. Anyone who embraces these things and other foolish behaviours are embracing poverty.

"Why should fools have money in hand to buy wisdom, when they are not able to understand it?" (Proverbs 17:16 NIV)

"Whoever loves pleasure will become poor; whoever loves wine and olive oil will never be rich." (Proverbs 21:17 NIV)

3. If you have pride in times of prosperity, and subsequently forget God, it will undoubtedly lead you to poverty.

"Because you did not serve the Lord your God joyfully and gladly in the time of prosperity, therefore in hunger and thirst, in nakedness and dire poverty, you will serve the enemies the Lord sends against you. He will put an iron yoke on your neck until He has destroyed you."
(Deut. 28: 47-48 NIV)

4. Hiding your sins will eventually bring you to poverty.

"If you ignore criticism, you will end in poverty and disgrace; if you accept correction, you will be honoured."
(Proverbs 13:18 TLB)

5. The love of money, otherwise known as greed, will bring poverty. If you desire money more than anything else - more than God, your children, and your spouse - guess what? Poverty will show up on your doorstep. You will always lust for more money, and it will slip through your fingers one way or another.

"Whoever loves money never has money enough..."
(Ecclesiastes 5:10 NIV)

"For the love of money is the root of all evil: which while some coveted after, they have erred from the faith, and pierced themselves through with many sorrows."
(1 Timothy 6:10 NIV)

6. Being selfish and stingy is another absolute formula for poverty. People who do not learn to give will be impoverished.

"A stingy man is eager to get rich and is unaware that poverty awaits him." (Proverbs 28:27)

"Those who give to the poor will lack nothing, but those who close their eyes to them receive many curses." (Proverbs 28:27 NIV)

7. Being fearful will lead you to poverty. Remember the twelve spies in the Book of Numbers? Ten were afraid, and two were not. The Ten were never permitted to enter the promised land because of fear. This fear led to another sin that eventually led to their deaths and the deaths of many others who followed them. Romans 14:23b (NIV) says,

"Everything that does not come from faith is sin. Since fear is the opposite of faith, we can conclude fear (doubt in God's promises) is sin and will result in poverty."

8. Generational curses will keep you in poverty. In Exodus 4:6-7, God makes it very clear that if one generation of a family or group of people is consistently sinful, curses will be brought upon them and their descendants for up to four generations. If your great-grandfather was involved in some demonic sin, you could feel its consequences today. It may not be your fault, but it is your responsibility to confess the sin and repent on behalf of your forefathers. Poverty is one of the many generational curses, and I have seen it passed down from generation to generation in some families. Derek Prince likened a curse to a dam which holds back waters of blessing - all you get is just a trickle of

71

gifts plus many problems. God expects Christians to live according to Biblical principles. No demon or curse may take hold of us when we do that.

Christians must know that curses are not the only cause of human problems. Problems may arise because of our own choice to sin. For example, sexual sins reap a harvest of viral and bacterial diseases, and abortions often result in emotional and spiritual problems. So many people have told me they don't believe in "generational curses." (I mean curses in a family that are being passed on from one generation to the next.) However, whether we accept it or not, they do exist. These are not just "bad habits" kids have learned from their parents. They are actually "legal contracts" on a person's life, supported by demonic spirits that will not give up their legal right to be there. Most often, they are the only explanation for a person's problems. It holds as well that people in an entire nation can be held in bondage with a familiar evil spirit. This causes people to have a common view, even if it is against the will of God.

The Bible says these curses will go for at least four generations and sexual sins can last for ten generations. Satan uses this not just to destroy individuals but to destroy generations of families. It is a brilliant plan - to keep his hold on individuals that have not yet been born! The Lord says that He blesses the generations of the righteous up in a thousand generations. Your children's children will be blest if YOU serve the Lord. Regardless of whether you are a new

Christian or a long-time one, you may be drawn to all sorts of practices that are against the will of God, regardless of whether you understand them or agree with them. Sin is sin!

An obvious example from Scripture would include David's immorality with Bathsheba, with the resulting murder of her first husband and the birth and death of the baby conceived in iniquity. Then one of David's sons, Amnon, raped his stepsister, Tamar. Amnon was then killed by the stepsister's brother, Absalom (see 2 Samuel 13). This same Absalom tried to usurp David's throne later. This is a sin repeated by the subsequent generation.

The Power of Generational Curses.

A Cursed Family	A Blessed Family
Max Jukes (Atheist) Wife (Godless woman)	Jonathan Edwards (Christian) Wife (Christian)
560 Descendants	**1394 Descendents**
310 died paupers 150 Criminals 100 Alcoholics 7 Murders Over 50% of women were Prostitutes	294 College Graduates 13 College Presidents 30 Judges 1 Dean of Law School 80 held public office 65 College Professors 75 Officers in the military 100 well-known missionaries 3 State Governors 3 Mayors of large cities 1 Comptroller of the U.S. Treasury 1 Vice President of the U.S.A.
Descendants of Max Jukes cost the U.S. taxpayers more than $1.25 million in 19th Century dollars.	**Not one descendant of Jonathan Edwards was a liability to U.S. taxpayers.**

Many thanks to Jubilee Resources for the reprinting of this chart.
https://jubileeresources.org

Doc's Book Club: For a complete understanding of this subject, read Derek Prince's international bestseller, *"Blessing or Curse."*

You Have to Recognize the Deception of Poverty.

It seems so easy. But getting back to the "spirit of religion" lesson, many Christians get by, remaining in that rut because deep down, they cannot shake the misconception that it is somehow spiritual to be poor. It is this battle within us that keeps us there. We want change, but as we think, so we are. Jesus said in Luke 6:45b (NKJV),

> *"For out of the abundance of the heart his mouth speaks."*

If poverty is in you, guess what will come out of you? If "just get by" is in you, imagine what emerges. At this point, satan has rendered you powerless, robbing you of your divine destiny and robbing those millions of salvations who would have received life through your obedience in finances and Kingdom prosperity. Or, at the other end of the spectrum, who have so much money that they are blind to the purpose of it, the needs of others and their calling in life.

Deep down inside of you in your subconscious is your belief system. Your belief system makes 90 percent of the decisions throughout your day. It determines how you respond to your spouse when they come home. You don't think it through; it just comes out of you. Someone cuts you off in traffic, and you don't think twice about giving them the one-finger peace symbol. It just happened. Until we change our thinking, we will be stuck with "just getting by." The biggest bondage holding the church back from doing so much more - the problem of keeping the wealth of the wicked in the hands of the wicked is this idea that has been passed down from generation to generation: the idea that it is spiritual to be poor. Remember 2 Corinthians 8:9 (NLT),

"For you know the grace of our Lord Jesus Christ, that though He was rich, yet for our sakes He became poor, that you through his poverty might become rich."

Continued in the next chapter in 9:8 (NLT) it says,

"And God is able to make all grace abound toward you, that you, always having all sufficiency in all things, may have an abundance for every good work."

Imagine what the body of Christ could do if we controlled the world's wealth! We could do what we were called to do - change the world! I'm sure you do not want to live under the oppression of a spirit of poverty, so since I believe you ran from the previous list, please allow me to present you with a better list.

Steps to Be Free of a Spirit of Poverty.

1. Step one is a scripture,

"Believe His prophets, so shall ye prosper."
(2 Chronicles 20:20 KJV)

> (Note: I find it interesting that the verse is "20:20," as in "strong and clear vision.")

> I subscribe to several prophetic online news-letters that keep me abreast of what God is saying to the body of Christ through His prophets. We live in world of fake and/or

manipulated news, so what is the point in watching and using social media? In addition, I constantly stay in tune to hear what the Lord is saying to me in prayer time. Where I can, I also receive prophetic Words from those with the Gift of Prophecy. Lastly, I also attend a prophetic church. Many prophetic words I have received have caused me to avoid bad financial decisions, and some have caused me to make wise financial decisions.

2. Operate in the Spirit, which is opposite to the spirit of poverty - that is Holy Spirit, the Spirit of abundance and wealth. Remember, the devil is always the opposite of God.

3. Confess your sins. Proverbs 28:13 (NIV) says,

"Whoever conceals their sins does not prosper, but the one who confesses and renounces them finds mercy."

4. Follow what John Wesley said:

"Earn all you can.
Save all you can.
Give all you can."

5. Use the binding keys found in Matthew 18:18 and lose the devil's grip on you. Also, bind your mind to the mind of Christ (daily).

6. Watch what you think, speak, wear, and how you look after your possessions (remember the duck story)!

Practical Thoughts on Escaping Poverty.

God has many new ways of getting wealth to His people. When it comes, however, some people will not receive it because they are not ruled by what Jesus said:

"From everyone who has been given much, much will be demanded; and from the one who has been entrusted with much, much more will be asked." (Luke 28:12 NIV)

If Christians cannot handle money well, God will not transfer wealth into their hands. Think about it; they will spend it foolishly instead of building the Kingdom, which is what money is meant for.

Please believe I am not trying to convince you of anything for my benefit. I want to help you be completely free of the bondage of poverty, even if you live a middle-class life or higher. The point is that you can do more for the Kingdom of God with a biblical prosperity mindset. That is my goal.

Ask yourself these questions honestly:

1. How do we glorify God in poverty?
2. If God wants us to live in poverty, why do we struggle with a desire to have more?
3. Are we carnal Christians because we desire to accumulate wealth?
4. How can people in poverty be used to change the world?

Unfortunately, many Christians live in poverty, waiting for Jesus to rescue them. Their focus is on getting out of this world (i.e., The Rapture) while God wants us free from poverty so we have the wealth to fulfill the Great Commission, which makes disciples of all men.

Christians desperately need a revelation of biblical economics. Unregenerate man believes that God delegated everything to the State, which has led to the formation of and belief in the system of socialism. There is, however, no provision for that in the Bible! Biblically shared property is always voluntary (from the heart) and never forced by God. Our tithes and offerings are biblical responses to God in our personal economic life. That is not due to any form of socialism; it is a personal decision.

Doc's Book Club: Read *"Compassionate Capitalism: A Judeo-Christian Value"* by Harold Eberle.

Humility

Humility is a significant marker of freedom from poverty. Humility is "not proud; having or showing a low or modest estimate of one's own importance." This does not infer humility means being meek, mild-mannered, or some doormat wimp. As Christians, we need not esteem ourselves more highly than we should but be firm and assertive in the Lord. An interesting thing I have noticed about most of the great preachers in the world is that their power in God to heal and evangelize is directly proportionate to their humility.

Andrew Murray in his excellent and aptly titled book, Humility, * defines humility as: "Humility - the place of entire dependence upon God, is the secret of blessing."

* Doc's Book Club: Read *"Humility"* by Andrew Murray, Whitaker House; Updated edition (Feb. 1 2005)

Here are some brief notes from the same book:

"Pride must die in you or nothing of God can live in you. Pride makes faith impossible.

Humility - the insignificances of daily life are the tests of humility, as they prove what really is the spirit that possesses us (i.e., don't sweat the small stuff; and it's all small stuff).

The humble man feels no jealousy or envy.

Being occupied with self can never free us from self.

The deeper you sink in humility before Him, the nearer He is to fulfill every desire of your faith.

Look upon every man who tries or vexes you as a means of grace to humble you.

Take every opportunity to humble yourself before man and God."

Here are a few other quotes I have collected over the years:

"Wisdom is the result of humility."

"Those who refuse to embrace humility will face the furnace of humiliation."

"When we speak without restraint, pride is the motivating factor."

"Doing God's work your way, is wicked."

"The best way to humble yourself is to not take yourself too seriously."

"Humility is the one thing that attracts God."

"The centre of our vision should be to attain the character and power of Jesus Christ. Humility helps us see what we lack; prayer helps us appropriate God's provision for that need."

"Pride closes the heart; humility opens the heart."

"Truth sounds like hate to those who hate the truth."

"Pride is doing your thing instead of God's."

In conclusion, false ideas about money can enslave you into forfeiting your divine destiny if allowed to continue unchecked. I have found that the surest way to revelation is to humble myself under the mighty hand of God. He is always faithful to reveal the truth when I genuinely seek it.

If you lack discernment or wisdom, you can ask Him for it, and He will show you the truth of His plan of prosperity for your life. If you feel you lack humility, please pray the following prayer:

Humility Prayer.

"God, of your great goodness, make known to me, and take from my heart every kind and form and degree of pride, whether it be from evil spirits or my own corrupt nature; awaken in me the deepest depth and truth of the humility which can make me capable of Your light and Holy Spirit. In Jesus' name, I pray. Amen.

That concludes these two chapters on false ideas about money. We know now what some false statements are about money, but what are some right ideas about money? More specifically, the following fascinating chapters are where we take a deep dive into the purpose of money.

Before we go onto the next section, let's quickly review the following:

1. Spiritual maturity does not come from poverty.
2. Jesus was not poor. He was rich; He became poor so that we might become rich through Him.
3. Poverty is a curse and is not related to humility.
4. Humility is complete dependence upon God.

Let's now take a look at the true purpose of money.

CHAPTER 6

THE PURPOSE OF MONEY - PART 1

To correctly use money the way God intends, it is only logical that we must understand the purpose of money. The current dilemma is that what can be used for good - what God intended - has primarily been twisted and distorted from God's original intent. Remember, God created everything in the heavens and on Earth for the benefit of mankind; that includes money. It seems, however, that with everything He makes, the devil gets in there and warps it to the opposite of God's intended use.

Think for a moment of several opposites you see in everyday life. Whenever you see the "twist" (and it is usually 180 degrees), you know the devil is involved:

1. Prophecy is twisted into fortune-telling, bio-rhythms, astrology, etc.
2. Saint Nicholas is twisted into Santa Claus.
3. Legitimate herbal remedies (God made the plants for our use) are twisted into a whole host of new-age medicine, including acupuncture.
4. All Saints Day is twisted into Halloween, an event that we should have nothing to do with.
5. The beauty of sex between a man and a woman after the marriage has been twisted into a host

of sins, including pornography, fornication, adultery, homosexuality, and ad infinitum.

6. Children's literature's creativity, beauty, and fine quality have been twisted into Harry Potter etc.

7. Although God calls us to be blest, that has been turned into an orgy of narcissistic materialism. And the list goes on....

The real tragedy in any list we make is that you can easily see the devil at work, but Christians are often involved in many of these activities and see no harm in them. Again, it is not my intent to write a book about spiritual warfare and deliverance, but here are a few examples of how Christians can get involved with the devil without even knowing it:

1. There is no such thing as "Christian yoga." The roots of yoga ("Christian" or otherwise) are anchored in Hinduism, which is traced back to Baal worship. I'll go so far as to say yoga is one of the most demonic practices I know of.

2. It amazes me the number of demonic symbols today, and Christians happily buy them, display them in their homes, or wear them around their neck, giving no second thought to them. These are things like dream catchers, Buddha statues, ritual masks, and carved idols brought home from foreign countries. Many naïve tourists fail to realize that it is not uncommon for witch doctors to place curses on these objects.

3. The Bible is obvious in the book of Leviticus not to cut or mark the skin, yet tragically, tattooing is very much "in vogue" these days. Tattoos, like many unclean things, can open doors to the demonic. Not always, but it can. What do you

do if you have one and can't get rid of it? Pray, ask God to forgive you and move on.

Doc's Book Club: *"What's Behind the Ink?"* by Rev. William Sudduth. (www.ramministry.org)

4. Christians become involved with cults and don't even realize it. Freemasonry, Mormonism, and Jehovah's Witness are some of the worst. In addition, many organizations in our society may not fit the technical definition of "occult" but have a very cultish attitude about them. Years ago, I belonged to a Rotary club. Now let me be clear, Rotary is an outstanding organization and not a cult in the true sense of the word (although there are some similar "overtones" to Free Masonry). I would agree that Rotary exists primarily to solve problems in local communities. It is, however, customary with all Rotary clubs to meet for a meal and have a meeting once a week, and the organization is powerful on consistent weekly attendance. So much so, there is an expectation that if a club member is out of town, they should visit another Rotary club somewhere in the world (at the time I was a member, there were 22,000 clubs in every corner of the earth).

My club was in Banff, Alberta, the world-famous tourist town, and consequently, our weekly meetings would always entertain many foreign guests. It never ceased to amaze me the number of guests who, when introduced, would stand and boast they had "Twenty-five years of perfect attendance," for example, at Rotary meetings.

I found that to be simply shocking! I thought, "If these Rotarians were as diligent about going to church as they are attending Rotary, we would have a revival!" The issue is that people's attitude becomes "cultish" in nature.

Although not biblical, a wise expression says, "Anything that keeps you from God is sin." You can take that further and say, "Anything (outside of God) with which you are obsessed is sin." As another example, I remember several years ago when the NHL (National Hockey League) went on strike. When the media broke the story, our local station interviewed a young lady in a sports bar, asking her opinion. She was utterly distraught and said she didn't know what she would do with herself. My response was that she should get a life! * There is nothing wrong with watching hockey, but your priorities are seriously mixed up if it becomes such an obsession. I often joke that hockey is Canada's national religion!

If you are confused about which organizations are cultish, what is of the devil, and what is not, a good source of information is www.jubileeresources.org

I remember a friend being utterly distressed for over a week because his favourite football team lost the Super Bowl. He was in such a foul mood that he could not even be around others. Frankly, I find that to be incredibly immature. My problem with this is that two-thirds of the world's population are missing one or more of the five basic necessities of life. All I can say to anyone obsessed with a sport is simply this, "It's just entertainment; get a life!*"

---

* I say this in jest. It's a cute expression, but you should not be "getting a life" you should be losing your life to Jesus!

The list of examples is endless, but my point has been made. What Christians need to question is the root and origins of any subject at hand. People have told me, "Yes, but acupuncture works!" Of course, it works; if it didn't work to some degree, the devil would never be able to make you believe in it! Whether it works or not is not the question to ask; the question should always be, "What is the source?"

Christians must have a clear understanding of the foundation of the world. It consists of two forces: one called "The Christ" and the other, "The antichrist." As I have previously mentioned, the word "Christ" means "anointing" or "anointed." Anointed with what? Holy Spirit, of course. That is whom satan is raging against. Therefore, to be "anti-anointed" would be "anti-Christ," which is satan himself. I don't question that acupuncture, can work for many people, but what is the source? I don't doubt that psychics have telekinetic powers to make objects move, to see into the spirit realm, or even to tell people things they could not humanly know. Pharaoh's sorcerers imitated God's power to a degree (Exodus 7:11). The question remains, "What is the source?" Everything in this world is either Christ or the antichrist. So how do we know if something is of God or satan?

People who are newborn Christians will not have the spiritual discernment or skills to differentiate. Therefore all Christians must learn how to grow in the Spirit and be taught the difference between good and evil. Your best source, of course, is the Bible, and as you increase in your walk in the Lord, you build communication with Holy Spirit. At this point, you ask God to guide and direct you to what is good and not evil. Much of this comes down to common sense, however. Do you think a Christian should be watching horror movies? Do you think a Christian should be reading Harry Potter? Unfortunately, we live in a world where common sense is uncommon!

I said all that to say this: the same holds for money. There was a time when money was pieces of gold or silver. Then it became ink on paper. In many countries, including New Zealand, the UK, and here in Canada, paper money has been replaced with plastic bills to foil counter-fitting. Now it has gone a step further, and money has become the transfer of numbers from one account to another. (I can't remember the last time I wrote a cheque...) Most people in first-world nations live in a cashless society, rarely seeing their own money. As we now know, "money" is neither good nor evil. It is simply a substance, whether a silver coin, ink on paper, or your credit card statement. Again, well-meaning Christians will say, "Money is the root of all evil." A piece of paper with printed ink on your desk (in the form of a $20 bill) is neither good nor evil. How you spend that $20, however, will either be good or evil as a result. Simply put, spending $20 on pornography is not good, whereas spending $20 on food for your family or a Bible for a new Christian would be very good.

To understand the true purpose of money, all you must do is ask, "What does God say to do with money?" Let us look at scripture:

> *"And you shall remember the LORD your God, for it is He who gives you power to get wealth, that He may establish His covenant which He swore to your fathers, as it is this day."* (Deuteronomy 8:18 NKJV)

Notice that this scripture says God gives us "power to get wealth," He does not just magically drop wealth out of the sky onto our collective heads. In other words, He has given you a brain and abilities; He has told you to work hard (Thessalonians 3:10), and He even gives us clever ideas for employment or self-employment,

> *"wisdom dwell with prudence, and find out knowledge of witty inventions."* (Proverbs 8:12 KJV)

You need this power to get wealth, but He will not hand it to you on a silver platter. It would be best if you worked for it.

This was a primer on the true purpose of money. Now let us look at the meat of the matter. You're going to love this.

S.R. WATKINS

CHAPTER 7

THE PURPOSE OF MONEY - PART 2

Hopefully, something dawned on you between the end of the last chapter and this one. Think about it for a moment... if God did not want us to be wealthy, why would He give us the power to get wealth on Earth? If He gives us the power to get wealth, then it seems apparent that He wants us to be wealthy. Again, we can logically conclude that wealth is not sinful, but rather it is the misuse of wealth contrary to the will of God that constitutes sin.

The key is to remember our purpose - why we are here. God commanded Adam and Eve to take dominion over the land, multiply, and replenish the Earth. Jesus commanded us to go into the world and make disciples of all men (Matthew 28:19). The bottom line is straightforward: we cannot do any of what Jesus has asked if we don't have the money to do it! Yes, the gospel is free, but it does take money to preach it. For example, a Muslim (or adherent to any other of the half-a-dozen other major religions) will be separated from God in hell when he dies because no one has told him about Jesus.

Why? The reason no one told him about Jesus is because there needs to be more people funding missionaries.

Why isn't there? Because people either don't have enough money, misuse the money they have, or don't know that is what they are supposed to do! They neglect to pour it into the Kingdom of God, which is the true purpose of money, as we saw in Deuteronomy 8:18.

The bottom line? The loss of, or saving of, souls is dependent upon money! It isn't a difficult concept; the more money spent on evangelism, the more resulting salvations. That is why money solves all problems (Ecclesiastes 10:19). Also, the more money, the more blessings we can give to others; the more blessings, the more the gospel is preached. Only two things in life are free: God and the weather; everything else in life has a price attached to it. Some may suggest water is free, for example, and argue it doesn't cost anything; perhaps, but it costs somebody something to get it to you. There is a cost to everything in life for someone, but God and the weather are both free.

Still, so many people are caught up in the lust for money. James 4:3 (NKJV) says,

> *"You ask and do not receive, because you ask amiss, that you may spend it on your pleasures."*

The King James translation uses "lust" instead of pleasures. The Dakes reference Bible lists several reasons for unanswered prayer: lusts, murder, covetousness, fighting and war, adultery, pride, rebellion against God, backsliding and sin, double-mindedness or doubt, misuse of the tongue (i.e., speaking wrong words), and more.

Lust is considered any unhealthy obsession inconsistent with the will of God, and it will steal your power to get wealth. As with the example I mentioned in a previous chapter, when people win a lottery, all they talk about is how they will spend it, and it is usually on themselves. Just once, I would like to hear someone say they're going to tithe, give some offerings, donate to charity, pay off debt, and invest the rest! What a testimony that would be! (not that I support the purchase of lottery tickets. I don't. People are placing their "faith" in the wrong thing.).

This happens because when someone does not know something's purpose, they will abuse it. Therefore so many people have so many problems with money; they are clueless about its purpose and don't know how to handle it. This is true of even Christians, as Hosea 4:6 (NKJV) tells us,

"My people are destroyed for lack of knowledge."

It Is Not About You.

When tempted to spend what is God's money selfishly, remember the first sentence of the first chapter of Rick Warren's book *"The Purpose Driven Life"* (which has sold over 60 million copies) says, *"It's not about you."* Plain and simple. Pastor Warren is entirely "right on" (If you have not read this book, you need to...)

This is the trouble with money; we think it belongs to us, believing we can spend it however we wish. "But I earned it," people will argue. They forget, however, some very fundamentals of life: you and I are nothing without God. We are only here because He created us. He has given each of us an assignment to fulfil the Great Commission

Doc's Book Club: Read *"The Purpose Driven Life"* by Pastor Rick Warren. Zondervan 2013

uniquely. He has also given us the power to get wealth to the same end. Not only do all our possessions and money belong to Him but our bodies and lives are His. The one thing He has given us to control is the power to choose whether we will live for Him or live selfishly. That is why in Deuteronomy 30 (NIV), He says, *"Now choose life...."* In other words, He has given us freedom of choice and a limited time on Earth to complete the tasks He has given us. Heaven forbid we choose to live in complete disobedience. Women who argue it is their right to have an abortion because it is "their" body are completely confused. They did not create their body and do not own it; it belongs to God, and they have no right to commit murder.

Then there are the people that don't believe in God but instead some fantasy about "the big bang" and evolution. Right... I believe in the big bang theory. "God said bang! And it happened!" I am most amused by a definition of Atheism that I saw on the internet one day: "The belief that there was nothing and nothing happened to nothing and then nothing magically exploded for no reason, creating everything and then a bunch of everything magically rearranged itself for no reason whatsoever into self-replicating bits which then turned into dinosaurs and from there you evolved and were born." Right...makes perfect sense. Look, you cannot have creation without a creator. His name is Jehovah (in Hebrew), and His son is Jesus, who said no one comes to the Father except through Me (John 14:6). Not through Buddha or Mohammed or some other weird conjured fantasy like New Age. Unlike Buddha and Mohammed, and all the Hindu gods that don't even exist, Jesus is not dead but alive and comes to take up residency inside you when you are born again. But I digress....

Please understand that God does not need our money. He is God! He can make a way where there seems to be no way (Is. 43:16-19). He would, however, prefer that we act obediently in using the money we earned or were given to us. Too many people ask, "Why doesn't God do something about Africa's poor, starving people?" Well, He is sitting in Heaven asking us when we will do something about it! He gave us the planet Earth, He gave us life, He gave us His commandments to live by, He gave us the power to get wealth, and He gave us an assignment, including witty inventions and ideas that will make us money (Proverbs 8:12). The reason there are poor people in Africa (and everywhere else in the world) is that we haven't done anything to solve the problem. We have been too busy fighting wars, being greedy, not living for Jesus, etc.

Would there be war and poverty if everyone on the planet was a faithful Christian? And I don't mean someone who calls himself a Christian but doesn't live a Christian life. If everyone on Earth were sold-out for Jesus, we wouldn't have any of these problems. The solution, therefore, is obvious; we need to win everybody to Christ! That takes money, which makes Pastor Warren's statement absolutely correct: "It is not about you." It is about what you do to fulfil the Great Commission and solve the world's problems!

We need to send Bibles to India. Money answers that. We need food for those starving in Africa. Money answers that. We have single moms in our local churches who are homeless. Money answers that. We have a dying world that needs to hear the gospel. Money answers that. We need to build churches and send missionaries out into the world. Money answers that. We need to look after people in our own neighbourhood. Money answers that. We need to buy medicines and build schools for those in need. Money answers all of that.

Money really is the answer to everything (Ecclesiastes 10:18). As my father used to say, "Whether you are rich or poor, it's nice to have money."

Understanding the Engine Behind the Seven Cultural Mountains of Influence.

Having been an entrepreneur for over forty years, I know a businessman always looks for a return on investment. Whether it be a return on investment of time, labour, resources or money, that is just how a businessman thinks; it is how God made him.

When looking at the ROI of allegedly well-meaning government solutions to poverty, I see the billions of dollars they, and genuinely well-meaning charities, have given in foreign aid to third-world countries. I can't help but believe so much of it has been wasted, and the rest has not accomplished much since most of the problems in these countries remain. As a businessman, what kind of a return is that? No wonder some people are tired of the endless demands for charity funds. What people want is results; a return on their investment. The problem eventually must be solved.

A few years ago, Bill Bright, the founder of Campus Crusade for Christ, developed what is now known as the Seven Cultural Mountains of Influence in society. He then had lunch with his friend Loren Cunningham, the founder of YWAM, and they discovered that Loren had been given the same "download" from God. These cultural mountains are government, education, media, arts and entertainment,

religion, family, and business. Now consider that God gave
Adam dominion over the entire world, which included
these seven "mountains." The church has been charged
with controlling these Seven Cultural Mountains yet failed
miserably. Consequently, in the West, we have just about
lost our entire Christian-based culture, and the progression
of the Kingdom of God appears to be stagnant (Note: Peter
Wagner, Lance Walnau and Johnny Endlow have all taught
the "Seven Mountain message").

How did this happen? I'll tell you: the Christian church is
guilty of four things which have contributed to the loss of
power and influence, which has in turn, resulted in the
degradation of our society:

1. Disobedience (Deuteronomy 8 and 18: worship-
    ing idols, meaning anything that takes God's
    place in your life).
2. The church teaches salvation but does not teach
    Kingdom authority and dominion.
3. The church has historically had a biblical view
    of work and ministry, but no longer. Only 19
    percent of Christians hold a biblical view of the
    world.
4. The church has not had the economic power to
    exercise power and influence because the church
    has given up on tithing. Did you know that less
    than 10% of the body of Christ tithes? No
    wonder the church is powerless; it has no money
    to do anything!

Along with the degradation of society has come the
inability of the church to directly solve world problems like
famine, sickness, disease, war, crime, etc. We have also lost
our influence on the world to do so. Billions of people

suffer daily from inadequate food, water, shelter, clothing, employment, and sanitation. Yet, in some areas like North America and Europe, some of the world remains enormously wealthy. The United Nations has spent billions of dollars attempting to help impoverished nations, but much of it is wasted, and that will continue until the spiritual issues are addressed.

Of the Seven Cultural Mountains in society, the business mountain supports all the rest because this is where money is generated, and money is the engine or "fuel" for everything else. The problem is that the church has still not come to terms with the fact that money is not inherently evil, wrong, or a sign of greed. Further, the church needs to operate more like a business. As I said, people will never listen to a poor man, only to a rich man. Why? Because the rich man has influence, while a poor man does not.

Kingdom-driven Churches.

Ask yourself, who has the money and wealth of the world? Three groups: governments, who get theirs primarily by stealing it in the form of taxes; criminals, terrorists, and warmongers (many would lump this group in with governments)!; and then, businessmen. Of the three, only the businessman can truly solve problems. Give a problem to an entrepreneur, and he will solve it. That creates wealth, and believe me, Christian-dominated wealth is what solves the world's problems Case in point, when hurricane Katrina hit New Orleans, the Samaritan's Purse organization - a Christian charity operated by Franklin Graham - was far more effective than the government's "FEMA" relief organization was.

Ephesians 2 says the church is to be built upon the foundations of apostles and prophets; however, such is not usually the case. Churches are typically established and constructed by pastors. Although faithful pastors are obviously needed and very anointed, they are often not skilled at the creative process of building a church. This process is not unlike a business. Consider that Jesus said He was about His Father's "business;" notice He did not say "ministry."

Pastors are gifted in shepherding people, which does not necessarily mean solving church financial and vision issues. This is what the apostle does. Consequently, pastor-founded churches tend to be mercy-driven as opposed to Kingdom-driven. A Kingdom-based church driven by an apostle can influence the businessman, who in turn affects the Business Cultural Mountain, which controls, changes, and dominates the other six Cultural Mountains to build the Kingdom of God. If pastors with exclusively mercy-driven agendas head churches, they will " feed a man for a day." The next day, the man needs to be fed again. And again. And again. This explains why 80 percent of North American churches have less than 200 people; they are run by pastors instead of "apostles and prophets," as Ephesians 2 states. The apostles will, with the business-man, teach the poor man how to feed himself. That is what a micro-loan can do.

The Power of Micro-loans.

The question then stands, "How do we, as Christians receive a return on our investment?" How do we take our influence, answer the world's problems by making money, then sow it into people and countries in need? The best opportunity I have personally seen is a concept called "micro-loans." Millions of people in third-world countries live in a state of mere subsistence. Each day is a struggle to find food, water, cooking fuel, a job, etc. Most of the time, if they only had a small helping hand, they could overcome this vicious cycle and be on their way to self-sufficiency. In time, this can even generate wealth and eliminate systemic poverty.

Most third-world poor are willing to work to make money; they just lack the opportunity. A micro-loan often is a small helping hand that can change people's lives forever.

The best example of micro-loan success is in an organization called Kiva (kiva.org).* How does it work? Simple: businesspeople lend a small amount of money, even as low as $100. The money is lent to a third party in need, who then starts a business. How do you start a business with only $100? Not so easy in a first-world nation, but in a third-world country, a hundred dollars can buy a sewing machine, for example. A simple sewing machine could quickly start a single mother on her way to making a living and providing for her family.

A hundred dollars can buy a popcorn machine and start a man on his way to entrepreneurship. After a few months, the loan is paid back, the man makes a living independently, and the money is reused for another loan. A micro-loan is the proverbial gift that keeps on giving. With a default rate of about 10 percent, I don't know of a better return on investment than this idea!

Micro-loans, combined with Christian businessmen willing to instruct people in the basics of business and model and teach the example of Christ, can change a nation by

* I also recommend micro loans through www.homeofhope.ca

advancing its people from subsistence living to personal growth and development, eventually lifting them out of systemic poverty. Further, they will understand that the help came from a place of true love, and they can receive the most crucial gift of all - the gospel.

Another good example is a foreign investment: a wealthy Christian businessman can build a manufacturing plant in a third-world country, hiring local contractors to build the plant and residents to work in it. Problem solved. One form of charity helping I joined a few years ago was sponsoring six children in Rwanda through Compassion Canada. www.compassion.ca. For $55 a month per child, I can change not only one child's entire life but their whole family! What a bargain! And it is tax deductible!

To finish these two chapters, what is the moral of the story? Get yourself delivered from sin, spirits of poverty and generational curses, learn how to manage money, and make more of it! Some people have an anointing for this (like a businessman), while others do not. Regardless, all are required to be good stewards of what God has blest them with and to make it grow.

The key to being blest, however, is knowing God wants you blest. Wait until you read the next chapter!

Review

The purpose of money is to build up the Kingdom of God.

CHAPTER 8

DOES GOD WANT US TO BE BLEST? (YES, AND OUT OF DEBT TOO)! PART 1

If you are still not convinced that God wants you financially blest, the best way to persuade you should be with the Word of God. In this chapter, I won't add any of my own commentary; I'll simply present scriptures for you to read and decide whether God wants you blest.

> "I will make you a great nation; I will bless you and make your name great; And you shall be a blessing. I will bless those who bless you, And I will curse him who curses you; And in you all the families of the earth shall be blest." (Genesis 12:2-3 NKJV)

> "So, you shall serve the Lord your God, and He will bless your bread and your water. And I will take sickness away from the midst of you." (Exodus 23:25 NKJV)

> "May the Lord God of your fathers make you a thousand times more numerous than you are, and bless you as He has promised you!" (Deuteronomy 1:11 NKJV)

> "Both riches and honour come from You, And You reign over-all. In Your hand is power and might; In Your hand it is to make great And to give strength to all."
> (1 Chronicles 29:12 NKJV)

"If My people who are called by My name will humble themselves, and pray and seek My face, and turn from their wicked ways, then I will hear from heaven, and will forgive their sin and heal their land." (2 Chronicles 7:14 NKJV)

"Blessed is the man, who walks not in the counsel of the ungodly, Nor stands in the path of sinners, nor sits in the seat of the scornful; But his delight is in the law of the Lord, And in His law, he meditates day and night, He shall be like a tree, planted by the rivers of water, That brings forth its fruit in its season, Whose leaf also shall not wither; And whatever he does shall prosper." (Psalms 1:1-3 NKJV)

"The Lord is my shepherd; I shall not want." (Psalms 23:1 NKJV)

"The Lord has been mindful of us; He will bless us; He will bless the house of Israel; He will bless the house of Aaron. He will bless those who fear the Lord, Both small and great. May the Lord give you increase more and more, You and your children. May you be blest by the Lord, who made heaven and earth." (Psalms 115:12-15 NKJV)

"Let them shout for joy and be glad, Who favour my righteous cause; And let them say continually, 'Let the Lord be magnified, Who has pleasure in the prosperity of His servant.'" (Psalms 35:27 NKJV)

"Blessed is he who considers the poor; The Lord will deliver him in time of trouble." (Psalms 41:1-2 NKJV)

"Blessed is the man who fears the Lord, Who delights greatly in His commandments. His descendants will be mighty on earth; The generation of the upright will be

blest. Wealth and riches will be in his house, And his righteousness endures forever. Unto the upright there arises light in the darkness; He is gracious, and full of compassion, and righteous. A good man deals graciously and lends; He will guide his affairs with discretion. Surely, he will never be shaken; The righteous will be in everlasting remembrance." (Psalms 112:1-6 NKJV)

"He who tills his land will be satisfied with bread, But he who follows frivolity is devoid of understanding." (Proverbs 12:11 NKJV)

"Wealth gained by dishonesty will be diminished, But he who gathers by labour will increase." (Proverbs 13:11 NKJV)

"A good man leaves an inheritance to his children's children, But the wealth of the sinner is stored up for the righteous." (Proverbs 13:22 NKJV) (Note: you cannot leave an inheritance if you don't have one.)

"Commit your works to the Lord, and your thoughts will be established." (Proverbs 16:3 NKJV)

"By humility and the fear of the Lord, Are riches and honour and life." (Proverbs 22:4 NKJV)

"He who has a generous eye will be blest, For he gives of his bread to the poor." (Proverbs 22:9 NKJV)

"He who covers his sins will not prosper, but whoever confesses and forsakes them will have mercy." (Proverbs 28:13 NKJV)

"I know that nothing is better for them than to rejoice, and to do good in their lives, and also that every man

*should eat and drink and enjoy the good of all his labour-
it is the gift of God."* (Ecclesiastes 3:12-13 NKJV)

*"As for every man to whom God has given riches and
wealth, and given him power to eat of it, to receive his
heritage and rejoice in his labour - this is the gift of God.
For he will not dwell unduly on the days of his life,
because God keeps him busy with the joy of his heart."*
(Ecclesiastes 5:19-20 NKJV)

*"Thus, says the Lord, your Redeemer, The Holy One of
Israel: "I am the Lord your God, Who teaches you to
profit, Who leads you by the way you should go."*
(Isaiah 48:17 NKJV)

*"For I know the plans I have for you," declares the Lord,
"plans to prosper you and not to harm you, plans to give
you hope and a future."* (Jeremiah 29:11-13 NIV)

*"For you know the grace of our Lord Jesus Christ, that
though He was rich, yet for your sakes He became poor,
that you through His poverty might become rich."*
(2 Corinthians 8:9 NKJV)

*"Christ has redeemed us from the curse of the law,
having become a curse for us (for it is written, 'Cursed
is everyone who hangs on a tree'), that the blessing of
Abraham might come upon the Gentiles in Christ Jesus,
that we might receive the promise of the Spirit through
faith."* (Galatians 3:13-14 NKJV)
(Note: A gentile is not a non-Jewish person; it
means to be absent from God).

*"And my God shall supply all your need according to
His riches in glory by Christ Jesus. The Lord will
preserve him and keep him alive, and he will be blest on*

the earth; You will not deliver him to the will of his enemies." (Philippians 4:19 NKJV)

"Command those who are rich in this present world not to be arrogant nor to put their hope in wealth, which is so uncertain, but to put their hope in God, who richly provides us with everything for our enjoyment."
(1 Timothy 6:17-18 KJV)

"Beloved, I pray that you may prosper in all things and be in health, just as your soul prospers." (3 John 2 NKJV)

The Blessing Verses and the Cursing Verses.

Blessings

"Now it shall come to pass, if you diligently obey the voice of the Lord your God, to observe carefully all His commandments which I command you today, that the Lord your God will set you high above all nations of the earth. And all these blessings shall come upon you and overtake you, because you obey the voice of the Lord your God:

"Blessed shall you be in the city, and blessed shall you be in the country.

"Blessed shall be the fruit of your body, the produce of your ground and the increase of your herds, the increase of your cattle and the offspring of your flocks.

"Blessed shall be your basket and your kneading bowl.
"Blessed shall you be when you come in, and blessed shall you be when you go out.

"The Lord will cause your enemies who rise against you to be defeated before your face; they shall come out

*against you one way and flee before you seven ways.
The Lord will command the blessing on you in your
storehouses and in all to which you set your hand, and
He will bless you in the land which the Lord your God
is giving you.*

*"The Lord will establish you as a holy people to Himself,
just as He has sworn to you, if you keep the commandments of the Lord your God and walk in His ways.
Then all peoples of the earth shall see that you are called
by the name of the Lord, and they shall be afraid of you.
And the Lord will grant you plenty of goods, in the fruit
of your body, in the increase of your livestock, and in the
produce of your ground, in the land of which the Lord
swore to your fathers to give you. The Lord will open to
you His good treasure, the heavens, to give the rain to
your land in its season, and to bless all the work of your
hand. You shall lend to many nations, but you shall not
borrow. And the Lord will make you the head and not
the tail; you shall be above only, and not be beneath, if
you heed the commandments of the Lord your God,
which I command you today, and are careful to observe
them. So, you shall not turn aside from any of the words
which I command you this day, to the right or the left,
to go after other gods to serve them."*
(Deuteronomy 28:1-14 NKJV)

Choose Life

*"I call heaven and earth as witnesses today against you,
that I have set before you, life and death, blessing and
cursing; therefore, choose life, that both you and your
descendants may live; that you may love the Lord your
God, that you may obey His voice, and that you may
cling to Him, for He is your life and the length of your
days; and that you may dwell in the land which the Lord*

swore to your fathers, to Abraham, Isaac, and Jacob, to give them." (Deuteronomy 30:19-20 NKJV)

Cursings

"But it shall come to pass, if you do not obey the voice of the Lord your God, to observe carefully all His commandments and His statutes which I command you today, that all these curses will come upon you and overtake you:

"Cursed shall you be in the city, and cursed shall you be in the country. Cursed shall be your basket and your kneading bowl. Cursed shall be the fruit of your body and the produce of your land, the increase of your cattle and the offspring of your flocks. Cursed shall you be when you come in, and cursed shall you be when you go out.

"The Lord will send on you cursing, confusion, and rebuke in all that you set your hand to do, until you are destroyed and until you perish quickly, because of the wickedness of your doings in which you have forsaken Me. The Lord will make the plague cling to you until He has consumed you from the land which you are going to possess. The Lord will strike you with consumption, with fever, with inflammation, with severe burning fever, with the sword, with scorching, and with mildew; they shall pursue you until you perish. And your heavens which are over your head shall be bronze, and the earth which is under you shall be iron. The Lord will change the rain of your land to powder and dust; from the heaven it shall come down on you until you are destroyed.

"The Lord will cause you to be defeated before your enemies; you shall go out one way against them and flee seven ways before them; and you shall become trouble-

some to all the kingdoms of the earth. Your carcasses shall be food for all the birds of the air and the beasts of the earth, and no one shall frighten them away. The Lord will strike you with the boils of Egypt, with tumours, with the scab, and with the itch, from which you cannot be healed. The Lord will strike you with madness and blindness and confusion of heart. And you shall grope at noonday, as a blind man gropes in darkness; you shall not prosper in your ways; you shall be only oppressed and plundered continually, and no one shall save you.

"You shall betroth a wife, but another man shall lie with her; you shall build a house, but you shall not dwell in it; you shall plant a vineyard, but shall not gather its grapes. Your ox shall be slaughtered before your eyes, but you shall not eat of it; your donkey shall be violently taken away from before you, and shall not be restored to you; your sheep shall be given to your enemies, and you shall have no one to rescue them. Your sons and your daughters shall be given to another people, and your eyes shall look and fail with longing for them all day long; and there shall be no strength in your hand. A nation whom you have not known shall eat the fruit of your land and the produce of your labour, and you shall be only oppressed and crushed continually. So, you shall be driven mad because of the sight which your eyes see. The Lord will strike you in the knees and on the legs with severe boils which cannot be healed, and from the sole of your foot to the top of your head.

"The Lord will bring you and the king whom you set over you to a nation which neither you nor your fathers have known, and there you shall serve other gods - wood and stone. And you shall become an astonishment, a proverb, and a byword among all nations where the Lord will drive you.

"You shall carry much seed out to the field but gather little in, for the locust shall consume it. You shall plant vineyards and tend them, but you shall neither drink of the wine nor gather the grapes; for the worms shall eat them. You shall have olive trees throughout all your territory, but you shall not anoint yourself with the oil; for your olives shall drop off. You shall beget sons and daughters, but they shall not be yours; for they shall go into captivity. Locusts shall consume all your trees and the produce of your land.

"The alien who is among you shall rise higher and higher above you, and you shall come down lower and lower. He shall lend to you, but you shall not lend to him; he shall be the head, and you shall be the tail.

"Moreover, all these curses shall come upon you and pursue and overtake you, until you are destroyed, because you did not obey the voice of the Lord your God, to keep His commandments and His statutes which He commanded you. And they shall be upon you for a sign and a wonder, and on your descendants forever.

"Because you did not serve the Lord your God with joy and gladness of heart, for the abundance of everything, therefore you shall serve your enemies, whom the Lord will send against you, in hunger, in thirst, in nakedness, and in need of everything; and He will put a yoke of iron on your neck until He has destroyed you. The Lord will bring a nation against you from afar, from the end of the earth, as swift as the eagle flies, a nation whose language you will not understand, a nation of fierce countenance, which does not respect the elderly nor show favor to the young. And they shall eat the increase of your livestock and the produce of your land, until you are destroyed; they shall not leave you grain or new wine or oil, or the

*increase of your cattle or the offspring of your flocks,
until they have destroyed you.*

*"They shall besiege you at all your gates until your high
and fortified walls, in which you trust, come down
throughout all your land; and they shall besiege you at
all your gates throughout all your land which the Lord
your God has given you. You shall eat the fruit of your
own body, the flesh of your sons and your daughters
whom the Lord your God has given you, in the siege and
desperate straits in which your enemy shall distress you.
The sensitive and very refined man among you will be
hostile toward his brother, toward the wife of his bosom,
and toward the rest of his children whom he leaves
behind, so that he will not give any of them the flesh of
his children whom he will eat, because he has nothing
left in the siege and desperate straits in which your
enemy shall distress you at all your gates. The tender
and delicate woman among you, who would not venture
to set the sole of her foot on the ground because of her
delicateness and sensitivity, will refuse to the husband
of her bosom, and to her son and her daughter, her
placenta which comes out from between her feet and her
children whom she bears; for she will eat them secretly
for lack of everything in the siege and desperate straits
in which your enemy shall distress you at all your gates.
"If you do not carefully observe all the words of this law
that are written in this book, that you may fear this
glorious and awesome name, THE LORD YOUR GOD,
then the Lord will bring upon you and your descendants
extraordinary plagues - great and prolonged plagues -
and serious and prolonged sicknesses. Moreover, He will
bring back on you all the diseases of Egypt, of which you
were afraid, and they shall cling to you. Also, every
sickness and every plague, which is not written in this
Book of the Law, will the Lord bring upon you until you*

are destroyed. You shall be left few in number, whereas you were as the stars of heaven in multitude, because you would not obey the voice of the Lord your God. And it shall be, that just as the Lord rejoiced over you to do you good and multiply you, so the Lord will rejoice over you to destroy you and bring you to nothing; and you shall be plucked from off the land which you go to possess.

"Then the Lord will scatter you among all peoples, from one end of the earth to the other, and there you shall serve other gods, which neither you nor your fathers have known - wood and stone. And among those nations you shall find no rest, nor shall the sole of your foot have a resting place; but there the Lord will give you a trembling heart, failing eyes, and anguish of soul. Your life shall hang in doubt before you; you shall fear day and night, and have no assurance of life. In the morning you shall say, 'Oh, that it was evening!' And at evening you shall say, 'Oh, that it was morning!' because of the fear which terrifies your heart, and because of the sight which your eyes see.
"And the Lord will take you back to Egypt in ships, by the way of which I said to you, 'You shall never see it again.' And there you shall be offered for sale to your enemies as male and female slaves, but no one will buy you." (Deuteronomy 28:15-68 NKJV)

If you did your due diligence and read through those verses, the choice should be simple; the option of course is yours. Which do you wish to have? The blessings or the curses?

If you choose the blessings, I have more good news for you. It is revealed in the next chapter, in the first section titled, When Do You Get Your Reward?

CHAPTER 9

DOES GOD WANT US TO BE BLEST? PART 2
WHEN DO YOU GET YOUR REWARD?

People have argued adamantly with me, saying, "You will get your reward in Heaven!" This is partially true, but let us take a look at Mark 10:29-30,

> "So Jesus answered and said, "Assuredly, I say to you, there is no one who has left house or brothers or sisters or father or mother or wife or children or lands, for My sake and the gospel's, who shall not receive a hundredfold now in this time - houses and brothers and sisters and mothers and children and lands, with persecutions - and in the age to come, eternal life. But many who are first will be last, and the last first."

You can't miss it! The NKJV says in red ink, "Now in this time," and other translations say, "In this age." You do not have to die to enter the Kingdom of Heaven. You are already in the Kingdom of Heaven if you are a Christian. Let me explain...

There are three parts or levels of Heaven. The first one is "the heavens" from our Earthly perspective. This heaven is what we know as the skies, stretching from the clouds to the outer stratosphere. Next is what is known as "the second heaven" or the "heavenly realms." This area around the Earth operates at the speed of light and is a place where demons and angels exist. Last but certainly not least, "Heaven," or the "third Heaven," is the place where God abides - the place you (your spirit and soul) will go when your body dies (assuming you are a Christian).

The Kingdom of Heaven is God's form of government in the heavenly realms. We can access all the power and benefits within that governmental system once we are saved.

Unfortunately, many Christians do not know of the second Heaven's existence and/or do not know how to access it. Hosea 4:6 (NKJV) says,

> *"My people are destroyed for lack of knowledge"*

and many people are perishing because of a lack of understanding about how to operate in the Kingdom of Heaven.

However,

> *"If any of you lacks wisdom, let him ask God, who gives generously to all without reproach, and it will be given him."* (James 1:5 NKJV)

Sometimes just reading the Bible (a form of "asking") can give a person the wisdom and understanding they lack. John 10:10 (NKJV) says,

> *"The thief does not come except to steal, kill, and destroy. I have come that they may have life and have it abundantly."*

That is truly wonderful news, but having this "abundant life" and operating in the Kingdom of God involves several critical steps for application:

1. Search the scriptures to find a reference to what you want. For example, if you need healing, search for healing scriptures. If you need wisdom, search for wisdom scriptures, and so on. Whatever it is you need, find the answers in the Bible. They are there. Consult with a pastor or Christian teacher if necessary.

2. Make a list of these scriptures and meditate on them repeatedly during the day (see Joshua 1:8). You must believe the Word of God deep in your heart, and the way to do that is to meditate on scriptures. Memorize them. Ponder them. Make sure they sink deep into your heart.

3. The Bible says we are to believe in our heart and speak with our mouths (Romans 9:10). This is the basic foundation of the Christian faith. "Christianity" is known as "the Great Confession" which, in this usage is defined as, "a statement of one's principles." In Genesis 1, the entire planet and universe were created by God making a "confession." Nine times He spoke, and different elements of creation and the world came to be. Further, numerous passages in the Bible tell us to do the same thing: decree or speak out what it is that we want according to the Word of God. Furthermore, Jesus said,

"...and greater works than these he will do, because I go to My Father." (John 14:12)

Now think about that! Jesus is telling us that we will do greater works, and this is coming from a guy who raised people from the dead and walked on water! Get your head around that one! Raised anyone from the dead lately? Why not???

4. Use faith when you speak what it is for which you believe. The truth is that we control our destiny by the words of our mouths. It works negatively as well. If you say, "I am poor, and I never get anywhere in life," that's precisely what you will have! People will say, "I think I'm catching a cold," which is exactly what happens. When I experience cold symptoms, I first keep my mouth shut and confess nothing. Next, I reach for vitamin C and echinacea, then I get all my healing scriptures and decree them. There is nothing wrong with taking medicine or seeking professional medical help; what is coming from your mouth? (Note: I have had one cold in the last 25 years that put me to bed sick. Last time I had the flu I was 8 years old and no, I do not take flu shots or covid shots).

Each morning, as part of my one-hour daily devotions, I have a list of confessions and decrees (based on scriptures), which are prophetic statements. I speak them over myself daily, and I've been doing this for years and years and will continue to do so till my last breath. It has amazed me over the years how many of these confessions have come to pass. Don't start speaking to them today; expect your whole life to change by Tuesday of next week. This procedure is a dedicated, regular lifestyle that takes years to develop and often takes years to see the results. If you are consistent, however, you will see results. (Note: sin must be confessed and repented from first, and a lifestyle of living for and with Jesus must be established).

The Lord has given me the idea of taking these daily decree devotionals I have collected over the years and making them into what I will call a "Prayer Pilot." That is another book idea "down the road." I also have a secular business book to write, and I have written three daily devotionals. I have also produced ten "success" posters as well (what I am calling "The Christian Life Manifesto Series"). Check my website for more details.

God Is a Debt Cancelling God.

Did you know the Bible has at least two stories about debt cancellation? I have paraphrased them both, but you can read the original text in 2 Kings 4 and 6.

One day the wife of one of the prophets came to Elisha to tell him of her husband's death. "He was a man who had loved God," she said, "but he owed some money when he died, and now the creditor is demanding it back. If I don't pay, the creditor said he will take my two sons as his slaves. What shall I do, prophet Elisha?" she asked.
Elisha replied, "How much food do you have in the house?"
"Nothing at all, except a jar of olive oil."
"Okay. Borrow as many pots and pans as you can find from your friends and neighbors," Elijah instructed. "Go into your house with your sons and shut the door behind you. Then pour olive oil from your jar into the pots and pans, setting them aside as they are filled!"
The widow did as she was told. Her sons brought the pots and pans to her, and she filled one after another. Soon every container was full to the brim.

Finally, she said to her sons, "Bring me another jar."

"There aren't any more!" they told her, after which the oil stopped flowing.

When she told the prophet what had happened, he said to her, "Go and sell the oil and pay your debt, and there will be enough money left for you and your sons to live on!" It was a tremendous miracle.

One day after that, the seminary students came to Elisha and told him, "As you can see, our dormitory is too small. Tell us, as our president, can we build a new one down beside the Jordan River, where there are plenty of logs?" "All right," he told them. "Go ahead."

"Please, sir, come with us," a student begged.

"Okay, I will," he agreed.

When they arrived at the Jordan River, they began cutting down trees, but as one of them was chopping, his axe-head fell into the river.

"Oh, sir," he cried, "My axe-head was borrowed!"

"Where did it fall?" the prophet asked. The youth showed him the place, and Elisha cut a stick and threw it into the water. The students looked on puzzled, but soon the axe-head floated to the surface! "Grab it," Elisha said to the student, so he did and the students were amazed and rejoiced. God showed Himself faithful in both of these situations, to cancel the widow's debt, as well as the student's. The lesson? God takes care of His children if they only believe. Yes, it is God's will for you to be debt free, as the following scriptures show:

"For the LORD your God will bless you just as He promised you; you shall lend to many nations, but you shall not borrow; you shall reign over many nations, but they shall not reign over you." (Deuteronomy 15:6, NKJV)

Doc's Book Club: Read *"Five Wealth Secrets 96% of Us Don't Know"* by Craig Hill and books by John Avanzini.

"The LORD will open to you His good treasure, the heavens, to give the rain to your land in its season, and to bless all the work of your hand. You shall lend to many nations, but you shall not borrow. And the LORD will make you the head and not the tail; you shall be above only, and not be beneath, if you heed the commandments of the LORD your God, which I command you today, and are careful to observe them." (Deuteronomy 28:12-13a NKJV)

"The rich rules over the poor, And the borrower is servant to the lender." (Proverbs 22:7 NKJV)

Who is the boss when you borrow from the bank? The bank, of course! If you have a mortgage on your house, you do not own it; the bank does. If you are carrying credit card debt, then you are in debt. The bank owns your future income. Granted, it can be challenging for the average person to buy a house without a mortgage, but there are ways to reduce that burden..

The debt culture in which we live is not how God intended it to be. He intended us to be so blest we would never have to borrow money. Let me run down a small list of the debt we expose to our children daily.

1. They live in houses with a thirty-year mortgage.
2. They wear clothes purchased with credit cards.

3. Those same clothes are washed in washing machines purchased on monthly payment plans.
4. They study from mortgaged computers.
5. They watch mortgaged televisions.
6. They sleep on mortgaged beds.
7. They are born into a family up to its eyeballs in debt.
8. They live eighteen to twenty-five years in this debt-ridden environment.
9. When they are old enough to drive, we usually co-sign a bank loan to purchase their first automobile.

By so doing, we launch them into their own ocean of debt, never to be debt free again.

What is our position in Christ? We are to be healed, sanctified, blest, anointed, praised, prosperous, and debt free! We are to be blest going in and blest going out (Deuteronomy 28:6). Our work is to be so blest that we are lending money instead of borrowing it (i.e., obviously not in debt). Then we will be the head and not the tail (Deuteronomy 28:12-13). We are entitled to and are to take money from the wicked, which has been saved for us because we are the just and righteous (Ecclesiastes 2:26). We are to be wealthy, prosperous, enjoy the fruits of our labour (Ecclesiastes 3:13), and establish God's covenant (Deuteronomy 8:18), and finally go into the world and make disciples of all men (Matthew 28:19). (if you can't do the last one, pay someone else, like sponsoring a young person in YWAM.www.ywam.org.)

That is your purpose in life - to be blest to be a blessing.

People say, "Money doesn't bring happiness." That's right; it doesn't (in itself). It does, however, bring more happiness than poverty ever did!

CHAPTER 10

GOD'S ECONOMY - PART 1, TITHING

Now that you are (hopefully) assured God wants you to be blest, I will show you how to do so in this and the following two chapters. I am sure you will agree that our natural world has an economic system based on receiving. Common mantras are:

"Work hard, make lots of money, and spend it on yourself."

"The difference between men and boys is the price of their toys."

"He who dies with the most toys wins the game."

The world's economic system is based solely on consumption, i.e., receiving. We are inundated daily with advertisements and financial spam on how to get more money. People buy lottery tickets hoping for the big one, relying on their "luck." What is really tragic in this case is how people misuse the word "luck." Did you know the word's origin is "Lucifer" - the name given to satan? Therefore, when you wish someone "luck," you are putting a curse on them. In addition, the word "luck" is nowhere to be found in the Bible. It does, however, say,

> *"For by your words you are justified and by your words you are condemned."* (Matthew 12:37 NKJV)

Therefore, the next time you want to bless someone, use the word "blessing" and refrain from using the word "luck." When someone wishes me luck, I correct them if they are saved, or if not, I smile politely, and under my breath, I bind their words off me. Christians even have a nasty habit of using luck when referring to "potluck" lunches! It should be a "pot-bless" lunch, shouldn't it?

God's economy is 180 degrees different; contrary to the world's system of consumption or receiving, God's economy is based upon giving and uses the Law of Seedtime and Harvest. God has three ways of financially blessing His people through three different seeds. However, before we look at those types of seed planting, we must start with the basic foundation of tithing. Please remember that the seed comes before the blessing, but before that comes tithing!

Tithing

The word "tithe" means 10 percent. Well, 10 percent of what? The term "tithe" merely calculates the minimum of your gross income to be returned to God. Why? Because according to the Bible, although everything on this planet belongs to God, He allows us to control 90 percent of what we have. The remaining 10 percent (or, more accurately worded, the first 10 percent) will be returned to God.

Notice I said "returned" to God; I did not say "given." You cannot give what is not yours, and the Bible is clear that the tithe belongs to the Lord. We are stewards of His possessions while we are on Earth. We are to return 10 percent of our gross income to our local church, after which we can keep 90 percent. This is not optional.

> *"And all the tithe of the land, whether of the seed of the land or of the fruit of the tree, is the LORD's. It is holy to the LORD. And concerning the tithe of the herd or the flock, of whatever passes under the rod, the tenth one shall be holy to the LORD."* (Leviticus 27:30, 32 NKJV)

> *"And this stone which I have set as a pillar shall be God's house, and of all that You give me I will surely give a tenth to You."* (Genesis 28:22 NKJV)

> *"You shall truly tithe all the increase of your grain that the field produces year by year."* (Deuteronomy 14:22 NKJV)

You may ask, "Where did this practice start?" Well, it started at the beginning of Genesis in the story of Abram (later, God changed his name to Abraham). In the following chapters, I'll explain this in more detail, but Abram had gone to rescue his nephew Lot, whom a foreign king had captured. On his way home, in the Valley of Shaveh, he ran into the King of Salem (ancient Jerusalem), whose name was Melchizedek. Melchizedek was a fascinating figure, as you'll learn in an upcoming chapter, but for now, we'll say he was the high priest of God. The King brought bread and wine and blest Abram. In return, Abram gave him a tithe of all he had (Genesis 14:18-20). Note that this practice of tithing occurred before God made His covenant with the people of Israel. The tithe continues today, and Jesus said we must give our tithes.

"But woe to you Pharisees! For though you are careful to tithe even the smallest part of your income, you completely forget about justice and the love of God. You should tithe, yes, but you should not leave these other things undone (Luke 11:42 LB).

Three Purposes of Tithing.

1. The tithe is essential; the first question is, "Why does God ask us to do this?" The answer is easy. First and foremost, it tests our hearts. It is a test of obedience to see if we will obey. God wants to know where our hearts are.

2. God may not need your money, but the church does, and God wants to use you to pay the bills and build His Kingdom. You are His chosen vessel, and as we have discussed already, this is the purpose of money.

3. Tithing is not a method of getting money from you; it is a method of earning money for you. This principle is entirely accurate, and it is based on spiritual law. This law will work for the believer and the non-believer. I'll prove it. Have you ever met a poor Mormon? Although the Latter-Day Saints "church" is not a Christian church but is, in fact, a cult (see Jubilee Resources International Inc., www.jubileeresources.org. for more information about cults), the Mormon "church" insists their members tithe and make offerings to their church. Mormon people, as a general rule, are pretty financially successful. How can this be if they are not Christian, despite thinking they are?

Very simply because tithing is a spiritual law and applies to anyone that uses the law.

"The rain falls on the just and the unjust." (Matthew 5:45 NKJV)

I have met people who are not Christian in any way, nor do they attend any kind of church, nor even believe in God, but they do believe in tithing or giving and are exceptionally prosperous.

To grasp these concepts, it is essential to understand that tithing is not an act of giving. We worship the Lord by returning to Him what is His. You cannot give what is not yours. Christians have a terrible habit of saying they are "giving" their tithe. You cannot give what does not belong to you, and since the tithe belongs to the Lord, you are returning to Him what is already His in the first place.

Tithing Is an Act of Worship.

Hopefully, you are a cheerful giver (actually a "returner"), but maybe without thinking about it, you've allowed tithing to become a religious ritual. You write the cheque and put it in the bucket - end of story. Perhaps you may even resent the whole process of offering your tithe before the Lord. If you do, you must ask for forgiveness, change your attitude, and repent. Worse yet, less than 10 percent of the body of Christ tithes! Think of how quickly the entire world could be transformed if ALL Christians tithed! The act of tithing is a sacred act of honour; it is an act of worship!

Under the Old Covenant, the people were to take their tithe to the priest declaring,

"With this gift I acknowledge to the Lord your God that I have entered the land He swore to our ancestors He would give us." (Deuteronomy 26:3 NKJV)

Then the priest would place the tithe in a basket and present it on the altar before God as the people declared their redemption before the Lord (verses 5-10, 13-15).

The procedure in most churches on a Sunday is not biblical; that is, the passing of the offering plate (bucket or whatever). The correct approach is to have an altar somewhere in the church or gathering place where the people present their tithes. The people should then return the tithe to the Lord, either giving it to a priest to put at the altar on their behalf or placing it on the altar themselves.

Here is how I recommend people return their tithes: the tithe is a simple mathematical calculation - 10 percent of your combined household gross income. That includes earnings, bonuses, inheritances, gifts, winnings - everything. It does not need to include income tax returns. Why? Because you've already tithed on your income and paid that tax in the first place.

The next step is for you (and your spouse, family, etc.) to lay hands on the cheque and pray over it by thanking God for His provision. You are now separating (sanctifying) this money from the rest of your money. By doing so, you are making it Holy. The word "Holy" means to separate something from everything else. Make sure you pray with a humble, thankful, and grateful heart, praising God for His excellent provision. When you get to church, walk up to the altar of God and place it on the altar. Then you should continue to praise God for His wonderful blessings in your life.

If your church does not have an altar with an opportunity for you to bring your tithes to that altar, suggest to your pastor that you get one! Show him Deuteronomy 23. An "altar" does not have to be anything fancy. It can be a simple stand or table, or you can even use the steps to the stage. If you like, you can decorate your altar with a theme reflective of the time or season of God's calendar (which people errantly call the "Hebrew calendar"). Perhaps you can even use the theme of the pastor's sermon. Have fun with it!

Take Communion over Your Tithe.

You must understand that the tithe is consecrated (sacred) and Holy to God. The attitude and condition of your heart are crucial. You're throwing a blessing away if you have been giving ritually out of religious obligation, not mixing your tithe with faith. Tithing is heartfelt, deliberate, and intentional. Mostly, it should be joyful! The person who gives cheerfully, revering and fearing the Lord is a true tither before the Lord.

I strongly recommend taking communion when you return your tithe. This changes the entire focus of your tithe and moves you away from a ritualistic routine to an act of worship, respect, and awe. It also allows you to meditate on God's goodness, considering your tithe Holy and dedicated to God. All of this will make you sure your heart is right before God, and that is when you open the door for God's blessing.

On communion, the Lord's Supper symbolizes the entire work Jesus did when He died for us; it is far more than a ritual or tradition. When you drink the wine/juice (representing His blood), meditate on the fact that Jesus' blood is what has cleansed you from sin. When you partake of the bread (representing His body), meditate on the physical torture and spiritual anguish Jesus suffered to save you from every part of sin's curse - fear, poverty, lack, danger, temptation, addiction and more. Partaking of the Lord's Supper is an act of worship and should be done in faith and love.

Further, you don't have to receive Communion in church - you can partake of Communion in your own home, or fact, anytime, anywhere. If you haven't practiced taking Communion regularly, it is high time to start! The Communion table is also the table of healing, the table of deliverance, and the table of confession. It is like God's spiritual central power station.

Think of it this way, whenever you receive Communion, it deepens your faith. Further, it makes God's covenant far more accurate; we realize the value of Jesus' sacrifice and the payment He made with His body and blood. Receiving Communion requires faith, so it is essential to do so with determination.

Return your tithe to God and receive Communion simultaneously by following these steps: Buy a Communion set of a cup and plate to be used only for that purpose. If you prefer pre-made kits, you can buy individual juice and wafer packs that last a long time on the shelf. I break off a piece of bread I have on hand. I have a tiny sherry glass that belonged to my mother, and I fill it about half-full with whatever wine I have available in the house. You can use whatever is available. I remember being on a wilderness backcountry trip on horses, and we had a Sunday service. The only thing we had for Communion was a dried bagel and a can of pop. Guess what? It worked!

The point is, don't get religious about it.

Again, feel free to receive Communion any time. Receiving Communion is claiming the blood of Jesus over your life and worshiping Him for everything He has done for you. Don't think of it as a religious ceremony. This means you can forget about requiring a priest, pastor or minister to serve it to you; that is just a spirit of religion that makes all those silly rules. Before you partake, you must examine your heart (1 Corinthians 11:28-29). Repent for anything in your life that you know does not please God, and ask Him for forgiveness. To reiterate, be sure you are not simply performing a religious exercise but receiving all the blessings Jesus' sacrifice has provided.

Next, come to the Lord presenting your tithe; have the cheque ready. If you tithe by credit card, text message or automatic withdrawal, that is not a problem, but offer a receipt before the Lord, showing what you are returning to Him.

Present the tithe to Him. The following is a suggestion of what to say:

"Lord, I present my tithe before You today, offering it before You. Thank you for providing for me, blessing me, and ministering life to me. I accept the blessing of Abraham in faith as a joint heir with Christ."

Then eat the bread, which symbolizes the physical torture and spiritual anguish Jesus suffered to redeem you from the entire curse of the law. Make the following confession:

"Heavenly Father, thank you for all Your provision through Christ Jesus by Your New Covenant. I partake of all your good promises now! I am redeemed from poverty. I am the head and not the tail. I am above and not beneath. I present this tithe to You as an act of worship and obedience on behalf of my entire family and household, and all these blessings also apply to them."

Thank you for Your promises to us who tithe. Thank you for rebuking the devourer for our sake. Thank you for opening the windows of Heaven and pouring blessings to the point of superabundant overflowing. Thank you for making all the works of our hands prosper.
In Jesus' mighty Name, Amen."

Once you have done this, you have situated yourself and your family for an overwhelming harvest of God's abundance. I will share an observation which I cannot prove biblically. Still, anecdotally in my own life and from the testimonies of others, this is a conclusion I have reached: don't expect a great harvest or blessing from a tithe alone. Remember, you are just returning what is God's. This protects you from the devourer (satan), but you have not "given" God anything other than your obedience. Even though He is good and blesses us anyway, why should God bless you for returning the tithe that belongs to Him regardless?

That being said, why tithe? Again, it is about obedience, testing your heart, and not being a thief! Here is what happens: once the tithe has been returned, you are now in a position to receive the harvest. You don't owe God anything because you returned to Him what is His. He recognizes your obedience and tells you to plant your seed and watch Him bless you with an abundant harvest.

Jesus, being our High Priest, receives our tithe as we present it to Him, and He rejoices in our liberation from satan's kingdom and our granted entrance into God's Kingdom (Colossians 1:13). Jesus then presents our tithes to the Father, Who in turn blesses us (read Hebrews 7).

The scriptural place to return your tithe is the storehouse, meaning the place you get your spiritual food. This is according to Malachi 3:10. This brings up a controversial question: What is the definition of God's storehouse? I interpret this scripture as you should return your tithe to your local church. The church needs to be the place where you are primarily fed spiritually. Justification for this can be found in Ephesians 4:16 (AMP),

> "For because of Him the whole body (the church, in all its various parts), closely joined and firmly knit together by the joints and ligaments with which it is supplied, when each part [with power adapted to its need] is working properly [in all its functions], grows to full maturity, building itself up in love."

If you are not being provided in your local church, change churches and find one that provides you.

Some claim they tithe to televangelists, their local Salvation Army chapter, and other charities. Those are all good places to give and may be considered giving offerings, but once again, tithing is not giving. You are to return your tithe to the site at which you are fed spiritually.

Think of it this way: who will you call at 2:00 a.m. during a family crisis? Your favourite televangelist or your pastor? Whom will you call when one of your family members is in the hospital, and you need meals cooked? The charity you support, or your brothers and sisters from your congregation? It is simple; return your tithe to your local church.

Some people have argued, saying they don't attend a local church for various reasons (they were hurt, the pastor ran off with the secretary, etc.). Instead, they gather with a few friends on a Tuesday night and have their prayer meeting. That may sound peachy, but it is not biblical. If that is your rationale, I suggest you thoroughly study the Book of Acts to understand the biblical model of how the New Covenant Believer should approach worship and church.

If you asked how many people had been hurt in any church service across North America this Sunday, I guarantee at least 80 percent of the hands will go up! I do not know of any institution with more history of abusing its members than the Christian church. However, you cannot find a place in the Bible that says hurt or even persecution by fellow brethren should hinder you from regular attendance. If you've been hurt, you must approach the offender, work it out, and forgive them. Then it would be best if you moved forward.

Now, some situations in a church may be so severe that switching churches is the only answer, but if that becomes necessary, you must meet with your pastor and ask for his blessing to leave and attend the new church. Never meet with the new church pastor until you have done your utmost to leave your current church peacefully and lovingly. Most importantly, do not cause a church split! Remember what happened to Miriam when she opposed Moses and started murmuring in Numbers 12. (She was instantly stricken with leprosy)! The tithe goes to your local church. Case closed.

One final point: I have had people tell me that they don't "financially tithe" but tithe their "good works" that they do in the church. In other words they call their volunteerism their tithe. Nada! No go! That is not in the Bible. The truth is that they are in fear and don't tithe.

In the next chapter, let's take an even deeper and more fascinating dive into tithing.

S.R. WATKINS

CHAPTER 11

GOD'S ECONOMY - PART 2, TITHING CONTINUED

Continuing to discuss the importance of tithing and the blessings it will release in your life when you take the time to stop and honour the Lord with your tithe - that is, returning it to Him with prayer, thanksgiving, and honour - you will see a powerful change in both your relationship with the Lord and your faith for finances. I encourage you never to allow the devil to rob you of the blessing from tithing. When you tithe, the windows of Heaven are open over you in Jesus' Name!

Watch Your Confession.

The first lesson you must learn when tithing is that what you confess over your tithe is vital to your blessing. Tithing is an ordinance of God, and we are to confess, according to Deuteronomy 26, what the Word states. Don't just toss your tithe onto the altar or into a basket and talk about never having enough to pay your bills. Tithing is a step of obedience but must be mixed with faith. When you talk about lacking finances, you are planting weeds on top of all the tithes and/or seeds you have just sown (Mark 4:7). Always make a confession of praise and thanksgiving over your tithe as you return it to God. Yet again, the tithe is not a gift from you; you are returning to God what is His from what He has given you. Praise Him for it.

Besides the wrong confession, many people don't see the blessings outlined in Malachi 3:10 because they are inconsistent in their tithing. They tithe for a while; then because they don't see an immediate harvest, they withhold their tithes and become ensnared by the enemy. The devil doesn't want you to tithe because he does not wish for you to be blest. If he can convince you to tithe only when you have enough left over, he will ensure you never have any money left over. Tithing puts you in a position to receive, and the scripture says God rebukes the devourer for your sake, but the tithe itself does not bring forth a harvest. You are simply returning to God what is His. It opens the door to blessing. God will put "bread and butter" on your table if you put it on His.

To Tithe or Not to Tithe: That Is the Question.

To tithe or not to tithe? Gross or net? Old Covenant or New Covenant? The tithing debate has raged on for decades, yet there isn't a debate like so many other biblical truths. You might say, "Well, I tried tithing, and it didn't work." Tithing isn't something you "try;" it's something you live. Tithing opens the door to blessing, so why would you not want to do it? The real reason people don't tithe is because of fear or out of ignorance. Fear they will not have enough money left over at the end of the month and ignorance of the blessing it will bring.

In 1998, I received a phone call from a pastor who wanted to plant a church in Canmore, Alberta, where I lived. I was his primary contact, so with our spouses and several other people, we went ahead and, with no money, planted a church. Within a year, he moved to Kelowna, in British Columbia, to plant another church. From there, the head office in Calgary replaced him with a kid, fresh out of a Bible college. He was so broke; he was almost an example of what I've heard Charles Capps say more than once, "He was so poor that he couldn't pay attention!" However, he and his young wife had heard about tithing, seedtime, and harvest, so they faithfully tithed through thick and thin.

Fast forward to twenty five years later, and I have observed two things about this couple: first, they have not had as many of the "normal" financial problems everyone else seems to have. So many people don't tithe out of fear that they won't make it through to the end of the month, but guess what happens to them about the third week of every month? The roof leaks, the water heater breaks down, the dishwasher needs repair, etc. This pastor and his wife never seemed to have any of those problems, and they always seemed to have a little bit extra at the end of every month. As Malachi 3:11 (NKJV) says,

"And I will rebuke the devourer for your sakes."

The second thing I've observed about this pastor is that he has been promoted two or three times and now leads a congregation of nearly a thousand people. Furthermore, he lives in an eight-bedroom house, has six children, two cars and a motorcycle, and I suspect he probably has a reasonably substantial paycheque from his position. This is just one of the dozens of testimonies (including my own) I know from people that have been faithful tithers.

Some people get defensive when a pastor or minister talks about the tithe. "All they want is my money," they cry. Well, I will tell you that opinion results from a spirit of fear which is the opposite of faith and not of God. Most pastors are trying to teach you the principles of God. Granted, there are fakes and charlatans out there, but they are very much a small group.

The question is, "Are you placing God first in your life?" If He is first, there won't be such strong opposition to giving Him your first and best. Leviticus 27:30 (NIV) says,

> *"A tithe of everything from the land, whether grain from the soil or fruit from the trees, belongs to the Lord; it is holy to the Lord."*

There's no way around it; if we don't return to God the first and best of what He provides us, we're robbing Him (Malachi 3:8).

God looks at the heart. A person who puts their tithe on the altar with a bad attitude will not be blest in any way. If you want to live in the benefits of a tither, you must first become a real tither - one who returns consistently, year after year, no matter the circumstances, and most importantly, with a tither's joyful heart.

Nine Tithing Truths to Be Blest.

These truths will only strengthen your resolve if you're already a tither. If you're not and feel like you need to have a revelation in this area to embrace the concept, these truths are for you. No matter which way you slice it, tithers are blest. The Bible is chock full of benefits, rights and privileges for tithers, and trust me; you don't want to miss them! You can live the life of a tither - a blest life - with the following top seven Biblical tithing truths:

1. Our Tithes are Presented to Jesus.
    In the Old Covenant, the people would present
    their tithes to the high priest. Today, Jesus is our
    High Priest, so our tithes are presented to Him
    (Hebrews 4:14-16). Tithing is about honour, not
    money. We honour God when we present our
    tithes to Jesus. How do we do this? First, we do
    it joyfully, without complaining. Then, we make
    it a deliberate act of worship.

2. Tithe in Faith - Not Fear.
    If you're tithing in the fear that you won't have
    enough left over, you won't be able to make ends
    meet, or you fear you won't get a return; you're
    not tithing in faith and, therefore, not eligible to
    receive the benefits. Remember:

*"But without faith, it is impossible to please Him, for he
who comes to God must believe that He is and that He
is a rewarder of those who diligently seek Him."*
(Hebrews 11:6 NKJV)

Therefore, when you tithe, tithe in faith! Do it
believing God will rebuke the devourer (satan)
for your sake (Malachi 3:11) and that He will
open the windows of heaven over your life
(Malachi 3:10). The simple truth of the matter is
that your priorities are in the wrong place if you
aren't tithing faithfully. You prioritize in the
natural realm instead of in the spiritual realm,
and what's in the spiritual realm will deliver you
out of trouble and result in you being
abundantly blest. Faith declares, "We're going to
tithe first." Faith is the knowledge that God will
super-naturally care for you.

3. Tithing Protects the Other Ninety percent.
   Have you ever heard or said these words?
   "I can't afford to tithe." The reality is that you
   can't afford not to tithe! You may have even
   thought, "I'll tithe when I can afford it." Yet,
   some have been thinking about that for ten years
   and still don't think they can afford it. Now, that
   ought to tell you something; what you're doing
   is not working! Here is a fundamental truth
   about tithing: return to God what is His, and He
   will protect what is yours - everything we have
   is protected: our finances, our home, our possessions. As you honour God with the 10 percent
   that belongs to Him, He'll get involved with the
   other 90 percent, and it will go further than ever
   before because you have the supernatural power
   of God involved with your finances. If you're
   not a tither, look back on your life, and I
   guarantee you will see where your fruit was
   destroyed, a situation didn't work out well
   financially, a job didn't come to full fruition, or
   you weren't able to do what you set out to do.
   This is what happens when people don't tithe.
   The blessing is missed!

4. God says, "Try Me."
   In Malachi 3:10-11 (NKJV), God Himself speaks,
   saying, *Try Me now in this.* This is the only time
   in the Bible where God instructs us to try Him;
   it is the one area where most people shrink away
   from trying Him. He tells us He will rebuke the
   devourer for our sakes and open the floodgates
   of blessing over us. Does God mean tithe one
   week and see what happens? No. It isn't an
   experiment or a hobby - it's a lifestyle. A tither

tithes from the heart consistently; if you're not a tither, you're not entitled to a harvest.

5. Our Covenant Connection.
   Tithing grants God the legal right to intervene in your financial affairs, to bless you richly, and to defend you against the devastation the devil brings. Refusing to tithe disconnects you from the covenant of blessing.

6. Begin Now.
   Don't wait until you're in a corner to tap into the blessings. Start right away. Meditate on God's Words, His blessings, and promises as a tither. Stand firm on the promises of God, and then the devil will have no place in your life. Tithing is the most foundational part of prosperity - it's where it begins. God reinvests our tithe back into our life for our benefit. Your tithe protects your harvest. You can't sow unless you're tithing - tithing comes first. The benefits are beyond anything you could imagine. This is illustrated in the Word,

"Then you... shall rejoice in all the good things the Lord your God has given to you and your household."
(Deuteronomy 26:11 NIV)

7. Tithing Opens the Door of Blessing.
   Administering someone else's money is the testing ground - the qualifier, for Kingdom promotion and being entrusted with true riches. This all starts with the proper handling of what belongs to God - the tithe; this opens the door to the blessing God says is the way He is going to

meet your needs, bless you, and keep you prosperous is tithing.

In Deuteronomy 26, God talked to the Israelites
about letting Him in on their finances through
the tithe. Then, in Deuteronomy 28, He spoke
to them about the curse and the blessing. Why
did God do this? Not because He needed the
money but because they needed help. They
were about to enter the Promised Land, where
they would encounter many challenges. In that
order, God told them about tithing, the curse,
and the blessing.

8. Don't quit.
   As my Dad used to say, "Keep-a-goin'."

9. Focus on God and Your Church.
   Don't get focused on false charlatans. Focus on
   the Word! This is Biblical Economics 101! Let
   these Bible truths become a revelation to you,
   then put them to work. If you've been hesitant
   to live the life of a tither, commit and take the
   plunge. Look up tithing scriptures and act on
   them. Then, the very next paycheque you get,
   tithe!

The Rights Tithers Have.

Tithing not only opens the door for blessings and privileges in your life, it more importantly, grants you specific
rights in the Kingdom of God. These rights are yours to
claim when you tithe joyfully, with a heart of gratitude,
and in faith. Here are three of the rights you have as a
faithful tither:

1. God Rebukes the Devourer for Your Sake - Finances.

   One of your rights as a tither is protection from the devourer. He comes to steal your money, seed, job, and possessions; he will often get away with it, too, unless you put a stop to it.

"And I will rebuke the devourer for your sakes, and he shall not destroy the fruits of your ground; neither shall your vine cast her fruit before the time in the field, saith the LORD of hosts." (Malachi 3:11 KJV)

If you're not actively operating in the Word of God regarding tithing, you're missing out on the devourer being rebuked for your sake. It won't matter how loud you holler and scream at the devil; if you refuse to tithe, God is not obligated to rebuke the devourer on your behalf. Tithe money that isn't devoted to the Lord will blow up in your pocket. It will be spent on one crisis after another until it's all used up. Right after the car breaks down, the refrigerator will need repairs, or there will be unexpected medical bills... and on and on it goes. When lack attempts to enter your life, you say, "No, I don't lack!" If you are laid off, you say, "Lord, I claim a better job. Please show me where to find a better job. I never go without. I am prosperous. I am blest. I am a tither. The windows of Heaven are open to me."

Your tither's rights cover every economic situation - they put you above and not beneath the economy. No recession will close the tither's windows of Heaven - not even something as severe as the Great Depression.

2. God Rebukes the Devourer for Your Sake - Family.

Are you aware that when God says He will rebuke the devourer for your sake, it includes more than money? As a tither, you have rights that extend beyond the financial realm; you have the promise that God will rebuke the devil from devouring anything in your life. When the devil tries to steal anything in your life, you enforce your rights and shout, "You're not taking my healing, my family's healing, or my finances from me! I'm a tither, satan, and I rebuke you. Healing belongs to me, the windows of Heaven are open to me, and I receive all Heaven has to offer, in Jesus' Name!"

3. Receive an Outpouring of Blessings.

Do you want to know how to receive a super-abundant outpouring of blessings?

Malachi 3:10 (NKJV) shows us how,

"And try Me now in this," says the Lord of hosts, "If I will not open for you the windows of heaven and pour out for you such blessing that there will not be room enough to receive it.'"

The verse above opens with "Bring all the tithes..." so we can see God is talking specifically to tithers in this verse. The windows of Heaven are open over tithers, and God says He will pour out such a blessing that you won't have room for it all! That is the purpose of abundance - to be living in such overflow that you can keep giving it away to further the Kingdom of God. This is why it is so perplexing that some Christians will fight tooth and nail against the principle of tithing. Tithing is for their benefit! Don't let satan's deceptive arguments keep you from honouring God with your tithes. The "windows of heaven" represent an outflow of God's blessings, showering every part of your life. The blessings are God's response to our obedience to His Word.

These three tithers' rights are significant and powerful, and every Christian should know them and, more importantly, operate in them! If you haven't been claiming your tither's rights, meditate on these truths and begin to make them part of your daily life. If you aren't a tither, you can change that today! There is no faster or surer way to break the curse of lack and poverty than tithing because when you get God involved, He'll multiply every good thing in your life.

Don't ever settle for second best, don't settle for financial setbacks or your possessions breaking, and don't settle for attacks on your family. You are a tither, and you have rights!

Once you have become a faithful tither by returning 10 percent of what God has provided you, you will be so blest you can begin giving to expand the Kingdom of God. Remember, tithing is not giving; it is returning to God part of what He has given you.

There are various methods of giving, and they have their principles, as you will discover in the following fascinating chapter. This is where we kick our biblical economics into high gear!

S.R. WATKINS

CHAPTER 12

GOD'S ECONOMY PART 3 - GIVING

As we have seen, faithful tithing grants us fundamental rights in the Kingdom of God and opens the windows of Heaven over our lives. I can't explain how important this is to the life of a believer. After you have tithed, there are three types of giving into God's Kingdom. These are the gifts that bring your harvest to the next level. There is, however, a critical condition to these three ways of giving, and that condition is that you must tithe to God before you provide any additional money to His work. In other words, your giving starts after you have tithed. The tithe is to go to the local church you attend and giving should go where God directs you.

Let's have a look at the three types of giving and how they operate:

1. Seed Offering.

This is where you become like a farmer and plant your seed with the expectation of a harvest. God says His Kingdom is about seedtime and harvest. Do what the farmer does; plant good seed - not "corrupt" money from illegal gain and plant it into good soil. This would be ministries that are well grounded in the Word, have reasonable administration costs, operate ethically, have abundant fruit from their charitable efforts, etc.

Next, the farmer waters, fertilizes and weeds his crop. For you, this means praising God, praying over your seed, blessing it, calling it forth into a harvest, using faith, (i.e., *"call things that be not as though they were"* Romans 4:17, KJV), and do not speak negatively over your seed. Finally, the farmer goes and reaps his harvest. For you, be prepared to receive, just as you would for the birth of a child, by getting his or her room ready and buying clothes and a crib. Keep standing in faith and believe in your harvest. An excellent way to think about it is to do what you would do as if the harvest had already been received. I suggest reading the following foundational scriptures that support the principles of sowing: Genesis 8:22, Galatians 6:7, 2 Corinthians 9:6, and 2 Corinthians 9:10.

Remember, attaining "things" is not the motivation of your life and not to be the inner drive of your existence. Jesus said we are to receive, not pursue, the blessings of God. You are to follow God and Him only. When He is first and foremost in your life, and your whole existence consists of being His instrument and vessel, you will live in divine prosperity.

So, where do we plant our seed? We plant it where God tells us. Spend time in prayer; ask Him for guidance in this area. What burdens your heart? Missions? Widows in your church? Youth ministry? Paying off someone's debt? Ask God in faith; Holy Spirit will direct you where to plant your seed.

2. Giving Alms.

This charitable deed of giving to people experiencing poverty must be done quietly and, if possible, anonymously to protect the receiver's dignity,

> *"But when you do a charitable deed, do not let your left hand know what your right hand is doing, that your charitable deed may be in secret, and your Father who sees in secret will Himself reward you openly."*
> (Matthew 6:3-4 NKJV)

Proverbs 19:17 tells us that helping the poor is like lending to God and that He will pay you back what you have given. Do not expect a harvest from this type of giving because the Word says God will reimburse you. Being a loan, does it mean God pays it back with interest? The Bible does not say, and I have often wondered what interest He pays, (if He does) but I can only imagine God would look very favourably upon us for helping the poor.

3. Firstfruits.

Giving God our firstfruits means that at every new beginning, we honour God by giving Him the first of that income. Of the three types of giving, fristfruits seem to return more blessings and harvest than the other two types of giving combined. I am not sure why, but after listening to testimony after testimony, it appears to be that way. Your tithe, being ten percent, is a large amount of money regardless of what your actual dollar income is. Ten percent of any sum is a lot of money. Firstfruits, however, can be small or large, and it's not the amount that matters. Firstfruits are keys to God's blessing!

> *"Honour the Lord with your wealth, with the firstfruits of all of your crops; then your barns will be filled to overflowing, and vats will brim over with new wine."* (Proverbs 3:9-10 NIV)

> *"Seek first His Kingdom and all his righteousness, and all these things shall be added to you."* (Matthew 6:33 NKJV)

Firstfruits are one of the foundational principles of the Kingdom of God. Some people assume that the concept of firstfruits is just in the Old Testament, but it is not; it is all through the Bible. In Paul's letter to the Corinthians, we see that Jesus is the "firstfruits" of a new creation (1 Corinthians 15:20). Then, in his letter to the Romans, he says,

> *"For if the first fruit is holy, the lump is also holy..."* (Romans 11:16 NKJV)

We go through life with mundane things consuming our time; then, we try to figure out how to fit God into our life. We have this all backwards; we need to give God the first of everything we do, including our time and money.

In every new beginning, we must honour God first! Start each new day in devotional time spent with Him and prioritize God during the day. When I reap a new harvest, I give the first "sheaf of wheat" to God. When I get new income, I offer a portion to God before I spend any of it. In a new month and a new year, the first thing I do is honour God. That is the principle of firstfruits. God promised that our barns would overflow, as we saw in Proverbs 3:9-10, and the Lord honours His promises. Understand that it is not the size of the gift we're giving to God that makes the difference.

Here is a suggested prayer you can use after you've written your first, firstfruit cheque. You can also give a firstfruit by debit or credit card, although the church must pay a fee. There are also several modern ways in which we transfer money. I am using the word "cheque" simply for terminology purposes:

"God, I was a sinner, and I called upon the Name of Jesus, and You heard me and lifted me out of spiritual darkness. You forgave me and put me into your Kingdom. I am now yours and have the power of Your son Jesus to use for authority over satan.

I am now bringing the firstfruits which You gave to me. Thank you for blessing me and my family. All of this is according to Your will. Thank-you God.

Jesus, as my Lord and High Priest, I bring the firstfruits of my income, which You have given me. I expect You to set it before the Father and worship Him with it. I rejoice in all the good You have given me and my household. I have listened to the voice of the Lord my God and have done according to all You have commanded me."

Here you have the theory; let's go over the principle of firstfruits giving and the practical application of it in our lives:

What Does Firstfruits Mean?

1. Firstfruits means to give God the first of your increase or profit. In Deuteronomy 18:4 (ESV), we are told to give *"the firstfruits of your grain, of your wine and your oil, and the first fleece of your sheep."* When you get additional income or a

new source of income, you give a portion of it to
God first; examples would be a raise or a bonus.
Also, you give to God first in a new season, like
a new month or year.

2. Your gift should be the best portion. Don't give
used or unwanted stuff, like what would be
given to a church rummage sale; that is not a
firstfruit.

*"Bring the best of the firstfruits of your soil to the
house of the Lord."* (Exodus 23:19 NIV)

In the agricultural days of the Bible, crops
ripened all through the year - barley early in the
spring, wheat in early summer, grapes in late
summer, olives in the fall, and lambs were born
in the spring. Each harvest was like a paycheque;
it was a reward for a person's labour. They gave
God the first portion of their "paycheque at each
harvest." Giving firstfruits doesn't mean giving
your whole paycheque! It means that whatever
you get paid, you honour God by giving something to Him first!

What Is the Significance of Firstfruits Giving?

1. It honours God as your source; it is a declaration
that blessing comes from God.
2. It sanctifies the rest of the harvest. If the first-
ruits are Holy, the whole batch is Holy (Romans
11:16).
3. It releases blessings. Give the first portion... so
a blessing may rest on your household (Ezekiel
44:30).

4. Firstfruits giving opens us to receive God's overflowing provision. (Prov. 3:9-10)

God promises abundant blessings for those who give firstfruits, but how much is appropriate to give as firstfruits? The key here is that it's not about the amount you give; it's about showing honour to God by putting Him first! At the start of every new beginning, ask the Lord, "What can I give to honour you?"

A Warning About Murmuring Against God.

God's Word tells us He blesses those who are obedient and joyful in their giving, but I want to offer a word of caution. I have seen people in the church and at crusades get excited about the Word and immediately begin to plant good seeds. However, when they don't see their harvest right away, they get discouraged and lazy. Before you know it, they are sowing among thorns again. Their zeal and diligence have left, and they can't understand why they are not reaping a harvest. You can't let your field grow in thorns and expect a harvest. Farming requires much work, and an idle soul will suffer hunger.

> "The soul of a lazy man desires and has nothing, But the soul of the diligent shall be made rich." (Proverbs 13:4 NKJV)

Slothfulness is an enemy of faith, and laziness will steal your harvest. The Bible tells us,

> "the thoughts of the diligent tend only to plenteousness." (Proverbs 21:5 KJV)

The diligent see only abundance. A diligent man will look beyond the problem, know the solution, and steadily try to accomplish it. He is patient and doesn't even think of quitting because all he can see is victory.

According to the Cambridge English Dictionary, being patient means *"the ability to accept delay, suffering, or annoyance without complaining or becoming angry."* Don't become discouraged when it doesn't seem like you are reaping a harvest. A farmer doesn't plant his seed one day, then go out and reap his harvest the next morning.

> *"To everything there is a season, A time for every purpose under heaven: A time to be born, and a time to die; A time to plant, and a time to pluck what is planted."* (Ecclesiastes 3:1-2 NKJV)

> *"And let us not grow weary while doing good, for in due season we shall reap if we do not lose heart."* (Galatians 6:9 NKJV)

There is a due season for your harvest. If you will not grow weary and keep obeying God and His commandments, you will reap much. God will implement His Word and honour it. He is not a respecter of persons and honours all who obey Him. Disobedience, however, will result in a poor harvest.

In the book of Malachi, God rebukes His people for not obeying Him, but even though He reproached them, He still told them He loved them.

> *"I have loved you,"* says the LORD. *"Yet you say, 'In what way have You loved us?'"* (Malachi 1:2 NKJV)

The Israelites began to get weary in their faith walk because they couldn't see any results.

> *"You also say, 'Oh, what a weariness! And you sneer at it,' says the LORD of hosts."* (Malachi 1:13 NKJV)

> *"You have wearied the LORD with your words; Yet you say, 'In what way have we wearied Him?' In that you say, 'everyone who does evil is good in the sight of the LORD, And He delights in them,' Or, 'Where is the God of justice?'"* (Malachi 2:17 NKJV)

In other words, they say,

"Look at all those sinners. It looks like they are doing pretty well. God is blessing them, but what about us? We've tried to live right, and what good has it done?"

The attitude of comparing the sinner and what he has with what you have, and then deciding it looks as if the sinner is better off, is stout against God.

> *"'Your words have been harsh against Me,' says the Lord, Yet you say, 'What have we spoken against You?' You have said, 'It is useless to serve God; What profit is it that we have kept His ordinance, And that we have walked as mourners Before the Lord of hosts?'"*
> (Malachi 3:13-14 NKJV)

People will say, "I had it better before I got saved." When people say these things, they speak against God, thereby playing right into the devil's hands. The devil tries to channel all the wealth into the sinner's hands to keep it out of our hands. He wants you to get weary and give up.

The Bible, however, reveals that wealthy people living in the world are just reservoirs of wealth for the saved. The Amplified Bible, Classic Edition says,

> *"and the wealth of the sinner [finds its way eventually] into the hands of the righteous, for whom it was laid up."*
> (Proverbs 13:22b)

This means that even when we make mistakes, even when we disobey God and fail to keep His commandments, all we must do is repent (turn away from the sin) and say, "Lord, I'm sorry, I repent, forgive me," and He will wipe our slate clean and treat us as though it never happened.

We have already seen that Jesus did not intend for His disciples to be poor. A vital point Jesus made to His disciples was that if they were faithful to the laws of God, they would receive a hundred-fold in material possessions during their lifetime. This critical point has been overlooked by many. Wealth and riches belong to the children of God; however, they are to be "received," not pursued.

I cannot emphasize enough that the cardinal law of God is giving. God is, by nature, a giver. God so loved that He gave - and we are to be just like Him. We are to be givers of ourselves. The fundamental characteristic of our lives should be to give. The Bible says a man's life does not consist of His possessions (Luke 12:15). The world has been deceived into measuring a man's worth by his material possessions. That is an inaccurate assessment. A man should be evaluated by how much he gives of himself.

Jesus issues a warning in the fourth chapter of Mark that once the Word is sown, satan comes immediately to take away the Word that was planted in a man's heart. He then lists satan's five major avenues: affliction, persecution, the cares of this world, the lusts of other things, and the deceitfulness of riches. If you are pursuing means, the devil has deceived you.

Here is the truth about giving and blessing: God does not need your money. It has nothing to do with you giving money to Him. He owns everything and doesn't need your money. The issue is twofold: it is about the condition of your heart - where your heart, there will be your treasure - and it is about God's economic system of blessing, which functions on giving.

> *"The best of all firstfruits of any kind, and every sacrifice of any kind from all your sacrifices, shall be the priest's; also, you shall give to the priest the first of your ground meal, to cause a blessing to rest on your house."* (Ezekiel 44:30 NKJV)

> *"Honour the Lord with your possessions, and with the firstfruits of all your increase; So your barns will be filled with plenty, and your vats will overflow with new wine."* (Proverbs 3:9-10 NKJV)

The point has repeatedly been made that we should give to God after we have returned our tithe to Him, but now that we understand giving, it is time to take a deeper look at whether we are even tithing properly! Is tithing a part of the Old or the New Covenant? In the next chapter, we dig even deeper into this vital area of God's economy, and you will see how having a rock-solid tithing base will significantly amplify your harvests from your giving. Let's take a look...

S.R. WATKINS

CHAPTER 13

ABRAHAM'S TITHE BEFORE THE LEVITICAL PRIESTHOOD

When discussing tithes and offerings, one of the fundamental questions typically asked is, "Where did tithing originate?" It is a good question. If you believe tithing originated with Moses and the Aaronic (Levitical) priesthood, the answer may surprise you.

In the following two chapters, I will show you profound spiritual truths about tithes and offerings from a time before the Levitical priesthood. To correctly understand how to tithe and present offerings in the New Testament, we need to know how tithing under the Levitical priesthood worked (under Moses) and look at a time long before that.

Did you know there is an example of a tithe before the Law of Moses? It is fascinating, I assure you. To understand this superior form of tithing, however, we need to look at what may be considered a crude, or even "primitive," form of tithing under the Levitical priesthood. No, that statement is not heretical; I will show a scripture that says the same thing. Let us dive in...

The Levitical Priesthood.

From Exodus 28:1, we clearly see God set apart Aaron and his sons to be priests to Himself so that they could represent the people of Israel. Aaron and his sons were of the House of Levi, hence the name Levitical priesthood:

> "Now take Aaron, your brother, and his sons with him, from among the children of Israel, that he may minister to Me as a priest, Aaron and Aaron's sons: Nadab, Abihu, Eleazar, and Ithamar."

Now let's note a few details about the Aaronic (Levitical) priesthood. I encourage you to pay close attention here, as I will contrast this priesthood with a better priesthood in the next chapter:

1. All priesthood members were descended from Aaron and his sons.
2. The priesthood was established upon law under the Mosaic Covenant.
3. According to Malachi 2:8, the occupation of the priesthood was to instruct the people in this Mosaic law.
4. Numbers 18:20 tells us that God did not allow the priests to own land.
5. Instead, in Numbers 18:21, God commands (makes it law) that the people bring a tenth of their income to support the Aaronic (Levitical) priesthood.
6. This tithe was transactional under Mosaic law - it was purely payment for services rendered. This is important to remember.
7. According to Hebrews 9:7, the sons of Aaron entered the Holy of Holies only once a year.

They dropped dead if they did not follow God's instructions to the letter on how to enter and exit the Holy of Holies.

8. Malachi 3:8-9 tells us that if an Israelite neglected to tithe, a curse fell upon them.

9. In Exodus 28:12, we see God sovereignly ordained the Levitical priesthood to minister exclusively to the nation of Israel.

10. The Levitical priesthood extended to no other nation (no Gentiles were under this covering).

11. According to Hebrews 9:6-7, one primary function of the priesthood was to present gifts and sacrifices to God on behalf of the Jewish people for the remission of sins.

12. Here we get to the critical points: Hebrews 8:6-7 tells us the Levitical priesthood was intended to be only temporary until a better covenant and priesthood was established.

13. According to Hebrews 7:23-24, the Levitical priests eventually died, ending their service. New priests were being born and raised into the priesthood all the time.

14. In Hebrews 8:4-5, we see the Levitical priesthood ministers from an Earthly model, meaning they serve as crude representations of, and were outside of the real examples from Heaven. Solomon's Temple in Jerusalem (on Earth) was the workplace of the Levitical priesthood.

15. Hebrews 7:28 tells us Levitical priests were fallible and limited by their human short-comings.

Now that we understand some details about the Levitical priesthood let's look at a time before this.

Before the Mosaic Tithe: Abram and Melchizedek.

Whenever God anoints and ordains a person, it is almost as if a spiritual bell is rung, signalling to both the angelic and the demonic that God has a call on this person's life. For the demonic, it is as though a spiritual target is painted on the person's back to interrupt their divine destiny. This is nothing to be afraid of, however - we grow by such trials.

In Genesis 12:1-3 (NIV) we see God place such a call on Abram, giving him a profound promise:

> *"The LORD had said to Abram, "Leave your country, your people and your father's household and go to the land I will show you. I will make you into a great nation and I will bless you; I will make your name great, and you will be a blessing. I will bless those who bless you, and whoever curses you I will curse; and all peoples on earth will be blest through you."*

In great faith, Abram obeyed God and left for Canaan, taking his nephew Lot with him. After that, a severe famine struck the land, so Abram and his grand caravan travelled to Egypt - which was still relatively fertile - until he could return on his mission to Canaan. When Abram reached Egypt, he faced a dilemma that had been bothering him, as we see in Genesis 12:10-20 (NIV),

> *"Now there was a famine in the land, and Abram went down to Egypt to live there for a while because the famine was severe. As he was about to enter Egypt, he said to his wife Sarai, "I know what a beautiful woman you are. When the Egyptians see you, they will say, 'This is his wife.' Then they will kill me but will let you live. Say you are my sister, so that I will be treated well for your sake and my life will be spared because of you."*

It happened precisely as Abram feared - when they reached Egypt, the Pharaoh's officials saw Sarai was beautiful, so she was quickly taken to Pharaoh's palace as a wife. They treated Abram well, believing (somewhat correctly) that he was Sarai's brother (her half-brother). Sarai must have been quite the knockout because they lavished gifts upon Abram - sheep, cattle, donkeys, camels, and male and female servants. If you think this is pretty messed up, you are correct.

God was obviously not too thrilled with this situation, considering the mother of the future nation of Israel had been added to an ungodly Pharaoh's haram. The Lord subsequently struck Pharaoh's house with severe plagues, which did not relent.

Eventually, Pharaoh realized he had been deceived, so he sent for Abram:

> "Then Pharaoh called Abram and said, "What is this that you have done to me? Why did you not tell me that she was your wife? Why did you say, 'She is my sister,' so that I took her as my wife? Now, then here is your wife; take her and go!" So Pharaoh commanded his men concerning him, and they escorted him on his way, with his wife and all that he had." (Genesis 12:18-20 NIV)

We often almost deify our spiritual forefathers, but it's easy to see Abram failed spectacularly here. His first mistake was running to and trusting in Egypt (incidentally, this becomes a recurring problem with his descendants). Abram then defiled his marriage by offering his wife to Pharaoh out of fear and even accepted gifts in reward! It was more than gifts - it was great wealth.

From this contaminated "wealth," Abram would have so many problems. To start, one of the female servants Pharaoh gave Abram was a girl named Hagar, from whom Ishmael was born. As Abram and Lot left Egypt and trekked into the Negev desert, the land was not fertile enough to sustain both caravans. Abram's and Lot's servants began to fight over their herd's grazing rights, and the quarrel became so sharp that Abram and Lot eventually decided they had to part ways to stop the fighting. Abram graciously allowed his nephew to choose which land he wanted, and Lot predictably chose the most fertile ground- the valley of the Jordan. Abram then settled in Canaan.

However, the problem with Lot settling in the valley of the Jordan was that the far edge of the valley ran into the city of Sodom. As we know, this was an evil city, the citizens of which were utterly unashamed and defiant to God in their evil. Of course, Lot camped right near the city. Keep paying attention because this is where it gets even more interesting.

To make a long story short, some neighbouring kings attack Sodom and Gomorrah, Lot is captured, and he and all his family, herds and wealth are carried off as the spoils of war. A servant escapes and tells Abram of Lot's plight. Abram gets two of his allies, gathers his fighting men, and goes after Lot's capturers.

Enter Melchizedek.

Abram ambushes his enemy by night and successfully frees Lot, his family, and his servants, and they recover all of Lot's wealth and take much more in spoils. While they journey back, the king of Sodom calls a meeting with Abram to address the people of Sodom, whom Abram has freed, and the wealth of Sodom he has captured from the king's enemies. The fascinating part is that out of the clear blue, a figure named Melchizedek enters the story:

> *"After Abram returned from defeating Kedorlaomer and the kings allied with him, the king of Sodom came out to meet him in the Valley of Shaveh (that is, the King's Valley). Then Melchizedek king of Salem (ancient Jerusalem) brought out bread and wine. He was priest of God Most High, and he blest Abram, saying, "Blessed be Abram by God Most High, Creator of heaven and earth. And praise be to God Most High, who delivered your enemies into your hand." Then Abram gave him a tenth of everything."* (Genesis 14:17-20 NIV)

Notice the passage says, "He was a priest of God Most High," and he was the king of Salem (meaning peace; it was also the ancient city of Jerusalem). Melchizedek brings out bread and wine (highly symbolic - we'll get to that), and he blest Abram. Abram then tithes a tenth of everything - the king of Sodom's captured wealth, and, I'm assuming, of Lot's wealth too. After this unusual meeting, we see the king of Sodom arrive, and in gratitude, he offers all the spoils of Sodom to Abram:

> *"The king of Sodom said to Abram, "Give me the people and keep the goods for yourself." But Abram said to the king of Sodom, "With raised hand, I have sworn an oath to the Lord, God Most High, Creator of heaven and earth, that I will accept nothing belonging to you, not even a thread or the strap of a sandal so that you will never be able to say, 'I made Abram rich.' I will accept nothing but what my men have eaten and the share that belongs to the men who went with me to Aner, Eshkol and Mamre. Let them have their share."*
> (Genesis 14:21-24 NIV)

We see from this scripture that Abram had finally learned his lesson. He would no longer accept ill-gotten wealth since he refuses the king of Sodom's offer. He also wants no one to mistake his coming prosperity as being given by an ungodly king. One must believe his meeting with Melchizedek, the priest of God Most High, and his subsequent blessing changed Abram.

Another problem was also addressed; much of Abram and Lot's wealth was gained from the Pharaoh and was thus tainted. Now remember I said Melchizedek's bread and wine were symbolic? Think about where else you've seen bread and wine; if you said, "At the Last Supper," you are correct! They were indeed Heavenly previews of redemption - symbolic of Jesus' body and blood; they thoroughly washed Abram's blessings clean. If Abram was wealthy before, "you ain't seen nothing yet." From here, Abram's wealth begins to increase dramatically.

So, who the heck is Melchizedek?

The short answer is we have no idea where Melchizedek came from, but out of several possibilities, one stands out as most probable:

In Hebrews 7:1-3 (NIV) Paul gives us some clues,

> *"This Melchizedek was king of Salem and priest of God Most High. He met Abraham returning from the defeat of the kings and blest him, and Abraham gave him a tenth of everything. First, the name Melchizedek means "king of righteousness"; then also, "king of Salem" means "king of peace." Without father or mother, without genealogy, without beginning of days or end of life, resembling the Son of God, he remains a priest forever."*

Notice the line,

"Without father or mother, without genealogy, without beginning of days or end of life, resembling the Son of God; he remains a priest forever."

As stated, Melchizedek had no father or mother, birth or death. Let us consider the possibilities:

First, could Melchizedek have been Adam reborn or sent back to Earth? Adam did not technically have a father and a mother, so he passed the first requirement. We know of Adam's beginning and his death, however. Also, consider that Melchizedek means "king of righteousness," Adam is infamous as the first man to transgress. Therefore, failing this second requirement, no - Adam definitely cannot be Melchizedek.

Some have supposed that Shem, Noah's son, could have been Melchizedek. It is possible he was alive in the time of Abram, but the Bible gives no indication of his life at that time (which would be expected), and he would have been ancient. More important, however, Shem, like Adam, has a beginning and an end. He has a mother and a recorded father. Therefore, no, Shem cannot be Melchizedek. This leads us to the fascinating remaining theory: Melchizedek was actually Jesus Christ Himself, presenting His Godhood to Abram in human form before He was born through a woman almost two thousand years later.

I understand this isn't easy to believe initially, but I assure you the theory is not heretical, and there are some convincing details. Let's take a look:

First, we must consider that Melchizedek brought bread and wine to the meeting. If these aren't the symbols of

Jesus' redemptive work on the cross, I have no idea what they could be.

Next, we must consider the name Melchizedek - "king of righteousness." The original Hebrew actually infers it means "King over the entire domain of righteousness." Also, Melchizedek was king of Salem, meaning peace, and the ancient city of Jerusalem. We know Jesus is the King of Jerusalem (Psalm 48:2).

Now this one is exciting; Hebrews 6:19-20 (NKJV) says,

> *"This hope we have as an anchor of the soul, both sure and steadfast, and which enters the Presence behind the veil, where the forerunner has entered for us, even Jesus, having become High Priest forever according to the Order of Melchizedek."*

This scripture ties Jesus directly to the Order of Melchizedek.

Finally, to fully persuade us, in John 8:56 (NKJV) rebuking the Pharisees, Jesus says,

> *"Your father Abraham rejoiced to see My day, and he saw it and was glad."*

How did Abram see Jesus' day, and what day did he see? Indeed, he saw the day of the crucifixion - the Last Supper, when Jesus broke bread and poured wine with His disciples as symbols of the work of redemption He was about to complete. These scriptures, especially the last, leave in my mind no doubt that Jesus Himself, embodied as Melchizedek, met Abram. Isn't that something?! It gets better. The real question is, "Why was this meeting between Abram and Melchizedek so important?"

The short answer is that this meeting was nothing but supernatural. After this meeting and Melchizedek's blessing, Abram was prepared to refuse the king of Sodom's offer. Remember, Abram went from giving his wife to Pharaoh to spare his own skin, and accepting much wealth in return, to refusing anything more than some food and drink from the spoils of war - only what it cost him and his men to recapture the king of Sodom's wealth and people. Just as Abram's faith was before the law of Moses, so Abram's tithe to Melchizedek was before the tithe of the law of Moses.

This makes tithing under the Order of Melchizedek a far superior form than what Malachi 3 teaches. Unfortunately, most churches teach from Malachi 3 today, which is based on Mosaic law. Subsequently, the heartfelt honour, reverence, and love behind Abram's tithe to Melchizedek are sadly overlooked. This needs to be remedied, which is one of the reasons for this chapter. I believe that understanding tithing according to the Order of Melchizedek will enlighten the worldwide body of Christ, break many chains, and result in a flood of prosperity and ministry expansion.

Hopefully, one thing is very clear from the material in this chapter Jesus is our present-day Melchizedek, under a new and better tithing example than the Mosaic law. And as Paul says in Galatians 3:29 (NIV),

> "If you belong to Christ, then you are Abraham's seed, and heirs according to the promise."

If we belong to Christ, and Jesus is the High Priest forever according to the Order of Melchizedek (specifically not the Levitical law), it should be easy to see that we should follow Abram's example by tithing in faith. We should often commune with our Lord and High Priest, breaking the bread of His body and drinking the wine of His blood.

Now, also note that the bread and wine that sanctified Abram's blessings enabled him to be exponentially more prosperous from that point on. This wealth also had no ungodly strings attached. These elements, symbolic of Christ's redemption and freedom from the law's curse (Galatians 3:13), released power for supernatural financial and material prosperity.

This can also be seen in 2 Corinthians 8:9 (NIV),

> *"For you know the grace of our Lord Jesus Christ, that though He was rich, yet for your sake He became poor, so that you through His poverty might become rich."*

This scripture is obviously not speaking about "spiritual poverty," so we could become "spiritually rich" because Jesus was never spiritually poor. He was the Anointed of God, the chosen One that is not spiritual poverty. No, this means He gave up His riches in glory in Heaven so that we could become prosperous for the work of the Kingdom.

The bottom line? Churches and businesses following the Order of Melchizedek will never suffer from poverty. Don't get me wrong, we are still supposed to tithe, but the question is, under what order are you tithing? The legalistic Levitical order or the Heavenly Order of Melchizedek?

As I've discussed above, one must know that it was practiced before the law to understand the origin of tithing and its place in the law. Hebrews 8:4-5 tells us clearly that the law is a crude shadow of Heavenly realities. We can infer that since Christ is the High Priest after the Order of

Melchizedek, and Abraham is the father of faith, tithing is an act of faith and transcends the old and new covenants. This means tithing should never be done out of legalistic obligation but of love and faith. We will examine this more, but when you tithe, I encourage you to pray this prayer in faith:

"Lord, it is Your will that Your Kingdom is established and prosper on this Earth. Since I have received salvation and the good word of the gospel, it is my pleasure to tithe to my local church, which does the work of the Kingdom. Of all you have given me, I am overjoyed to return at least 10 percent to You in faith and expectancy so that I can be blest according to Your Word and return even more next time. I have returned my tithe, and I now will make offerings to Your Kingdom for the same purposes."

Believe it or not, this was just an introduction to the Order of Melchizedek. Let us now take a deep dive into the astonishing meaning behind this great blessing from Jesus.

S.R. WATKINS

CHAPTER 14

THE ORDER OF MELCHIZEDEK

In the last chapter, we examined the Levitical priesthood and briefly examined how it was a crude or inferior type of the Order of Melchizedek. In this chapter, we will dive deeper into this Heavenly reality that belongs to us through Christ. I believe it will blow your mind, as it did mine.

I'm a straight shooter, as I imagine you've guessed by now, so I'll give you the bottom line first, and then we'll walk through it: The Order of Melchizedek is the highest priestly order God has established. Jesus is our modern-day Melchizedek, and His priesthood supersedes the Levitical priesthood drastically.

There is a lot more to this, but for brevity's sake, when Jesus died, He took His Holy, precious blood and poured it into the mercy seat as a peace offering for us. He offered this divine sacrifice to God almighty - His Heavenly Father. Subsequently, the veil separating the Holy of Holies in the temple was ripped in two the moment Jesus died. This symbolized the access granted to all believers into the Heavenly Holy of Holies forever. This access is given by Jesus to all who receive Him. After Jesus made this offering, He took His seat at God's right hand as our eternal High Priest in the Order of Melchizedek. That is a brief overview.

The truths I am about to share are so profound that they will literally change your life if applied, yet the problem is that most of the global Church today knows very little about the priesthood in the Order of Melchizedek. Because of this, they are either robbed of or don't claim the blessings that are rightfully theirs due to ignorance and false teaching on tithing. Why? One must understand that Jesus' priesthood in the Order of Melchizedek is based on faith, not law. This is important because Jesus' priesthood predates and supersedes the Mosaic laws of tithing and prosperity. When the believer understands the spiritual laws around these principles, it opens the door to financial abundance.

Galatians 3:13-14 (NKJV) says,

> "Christ has redeemed us from the curse of the law, having become a curse for us (for it is written, "Cursed is everyone who hangs on a tree"), that the blessing of Abraham might come upon the Gentiles in Christ Jesus, that we might receive the promise of the Spirit through faith."

From this great scripture, we can see Jesus redeemed us from the curse of the law, so having learned what we needed from the law, we could return to the blessings of Abraham (under the Order of Melchizedek).

Now, here is the exciting part: The unique aspect of the Order of Melchizedek is that, unlike the Levitical priesthood, the Order of Melchizedek is both a priestly ministry and a marketplace ministry. Hold on before you gather your rocks to throw; what do I mean? Remember

174

what I said in the last chapter, that Jesus is both King and High Priest? As King of Kings, His power transcends the temple's boundaries into the marketplace. What do I mean by the marketplace? "Kingdom businesses" can now operate in the secular marketplace yet reap Heavenly rewards. This includes all aspects of legitimate ministry, including souls and finances to support ministry and undertakings. I'll explain further in the next chapter. Let's look at an enthralling part of the Order of Melchizedek: our power and authority under this order...

Doc's Book Club: Here is a list of my favourite market place ministries books: anything written by Oz Hillman, Ernie Fougere and Rich Marshall; *"Christians in the Marketplace"* by Bill Hybels.

The Power of the Order of Melchizedek.

To understand the power of the Order of Melchizedek, let us take a look at how it contrasts to the list in the previous chapter, Tithing Under the Levitical Priesthood:

Tithing Under the Order of Melchizedek.

1. Our High Priest is Jesus our Messiah, and all believers have been made priests and kings in His likeness (Revelation 1:6).
2. The Order of Melchizedek was established upon faith under the Abrahamic covenant (Hebrews 7:9-10, Romans 4:16).
3. Jesus' current occupation as High Priest is to make intercession for us while Holy Spirit teaches us all things (Romans 8:34, John 14:26).
4. God has given us everything we need for ministry if we take the material resources (2 Peter 1:3).

5. Under the Order of Melchizedek, the tithe supports the work of the gospel, establishing the Kingdom of God. However, the gospel can also help labourers in ministry full-time (Acts 4:32 1 Corinthians 9:14).

6. The Order of Melchizedek tithe is not transactional but instead given in thanks for blessings and in faith for future blessings to further the work of the gospel (Luke 6:38, 2 Corinthians 8:2-4).

7. Jesus entered the Holy of Holies once and for all, and the job is complete. We now live by grace (we won't die for not following the law), through faith, under the Order of Melchizedek (Hebrews 9, Galatians 3:13).

8. Jesus redeemed us from the curse of the law; therefore, you are not cursed if you do not tithe. However, you are just not wise because you want to be able to receive blessings (Galatians 3:13).

9. The Order of Melchizedek extends to everyone who believes in Jesus Christ, Jew and Gentile alike - the Jew first and also to the Gentile (Romans 1:16).

10. Jesus presented Himself as the sacrificial Lamb once, for all people who will believe and receive (Hebrews 9:6-7, Hebrews 10:9-10).

11. The better, permanent covenant is here - the covenant of grace, yet it is founded on faith as Abram's example showed, predating the law and Mosaic covenant (Romans 4:16, Hebrews 7:22-25).

12. Jesus lives forever as our eternal High Priest (Hebrews 7:24).

13. Jesus presented Himself and His blood to the High Courts of Heaven, using the true Heavenly

objects (for example the mercy seat), of which Earthly examples are only crude representations (Hebrews 8:1-2, Hebrews 9).

14. Jesus is perfect, and flawlessly executed our redemption, making Him uniquely qualified to be High Priest, King of Kings, and Lord of Lords (2 Corinthians 5:21, 1 Peter 2:22).

This stuff is powerful, my friend! I strongly recommend contrasting this numbered list with the list in the previous chapter. If you take the time to study the scriptures I have provided in that list alone, you will be firmly convinced of the liberating power of Jesus as our High Priest under the Order of Melchizedek.

The Power of the Tithe Under the Order of Melchizedek.

Understanding sowing and reaping under the Order of Melchizedek will completely transform how the global Church receives the tithe. Perhaps more importantly, it will open the floodgates to the global Church for countless opportunities of financial super-abundance beyond the regular giving of tithes and offerings. Unlike the Levitical priesthood, the Church leadership under the Order of Melchizedek does not have to depend entirely on the people's tithes and offerings to sustain the ministry's work. Tithes and offerings are now just two of many streams of income God has made available to the New Testament Church.

First, let us reiterate point 6 from our list above: tithes are not transactional, meaning they are not a tax or payments for services rendered by Jesus. Such thinking is an affront to God. He is not our consultant nor a member of our staff. Our tithe is offered in love, humility, and loyalty in thanksgiving. It is never paid. Our High Priest is both God and King, Who, although He came as a servant, cannot be considered an employee. Why am I ranting about this? Have you ever heard the term "Pay your tithe?" I'm sure you have, and it illustrates an uninformed mindset on New Testament tithing under the Order of Melchizedek. Hopefully, you can now see that suggesting a tithe is "paid" to God is an affront to our great High Priest.

I made such a strong point for a reason. Think of it this way: we are mere stewards of everything our great High Priest and our Father have given us. ALL our finances already belong to God; therefore, He does not render services to us for payment. His salvation is a gift which we could never earn. What we return(tithes) and give(offerings) back to further His Kingdom should be from thanksgiving, and when given in faith and love by spiritual laws, we should reap even more to account for our stewardship. Makes sense?

Similarly, our shepherds and teachers live by the gospel - they are not "paid." We should support them if they work full time for the gospel, to lead us into the truths of God's Kingdom. We should remember to bless them in love for their devotion to expanding the Kingdom.

To be clear, out of our newfound freedom in grace and love, we choose to support God's Kingdom out of the finances He has given us, and indeed, it all belongs to Him anyway. The tithes and offerings we offer today under the Order of Melchizedek support the great High Priest's labourers in ministry (apostles, evangelists, prophets, pastors, teachers, etc.). This means we should never withhold our giving and support from our local church. If you love God and have gained salvation from someone's ministry (paid for by others), you should support the ministry.

That being said, please understand that you are not cursed if you do not support your local church. This corrupt thinking began from the incorrect application of Malachi 3:8-12 as a modern tithing model. In that passage, the prophet Malachi says that if you do not tithe, you are cursed with a curse for robbing God of tithes and offerings. Yet we know very well Jesus redeemed us from the curse of the law (Galatians 3:13). Plus, the Apostle John says in Revelation 22:3 (NKJV),

> *"And there shall be no more curse, but the throne of God and the Lamb shall be in it, and His servants shall serve Him."*

Our church leaders should never threaten new covenant believers living under the Order of Melchizedek with a curse if they do not tithe. This undermines the principles of faith and love in the new covenant spiritual laws of sowing and reaping.

Does this mean neglecting to support ministry will never affect us? Of course, it will. If we do not meet our High Priest in faith and adoration to return to Him what is genuinely His (to expand His Kingdom), how will we receive the bread and wine of the priestly Order of Melchizedek? You cannot receive what you are not present to take, right?

These elements represent the flow of God's revelation and the anointing of the sweet Holy Spirit. If you go long enough without spending time with your great High Priest and offering to Him a portion of what He has entrusted to you, the power of revelation and anointing will begin to decrease in your life.

If you still feel entitled not to support a ministry for any reason, ask yourself what gift you might give if you met your country's Prime Minister or President. A wise man or woman would know to take something very personal and carefully considered, something of value to entreat the minister of the highest office in the land. Your gift would demonstrate your value at such a meeting, right? You would present a gift if you wanted the PM or President to show you a favour. A gift also acknowledges the power of the leader. Most importantly, a gift is a show of thanksgiving on your part. Now contrast this idea to a tithing dogma that says getting more money is the primary purpose of tithing. It is ridiculous. We are dealing with the Kingdom of Almighty God! A theocracy. Getting more money by betting on the right ministries is a challenging hustle. No, it is about love, and like it or not, God loves you, and He is God-supreme ruler overall. Any doctrine focusing on giving to gain more money instead of giving to further almighty God's Kingdom out of pure love and thanksgiving is deeply unsound. It also demonstrates zero knowledge of God's spiritual laws under the Order of Melchizedek. I caution you not to fill your mind with such ideas.

The Church and the Order of Melchizedek.

I mentioned before that under the Order of Melchizedek; the church is now free to operate in both the marketplace and through tithes and offerings of the local congregation. Let us look at this more in-depth now. I am saying that church shepherds (and sheep) are not limited to reaching only those who come to church.

I believe a huge global revival is approaching, some of the fruit of which will be God's handiwork in the marketplace. Recently, I heard a prominent intercessor/prophet from the

USA say that a vast revival would start in Western Canada and then move south into the western USA states. This coincides with a prophetic Word that my brother heard over 35 years ago; that two cities in North America would have revivals; Calgary, Alberta, and Portland, Oregon. * Mark my words; it will be a supernatural move of God in the lives, businesses and creative inventions of those Christ-followers who skillfully operate under the Order of Melchizedek. Like many of our forefathers and mothers, these men and women will flip the world's economic markets right-side up by becoming unprecedented influencers and bastions of wealth for the Gospel. (Note: Prophetic Words are not for sure what will happen; it is not fortune-telling. Whether a Word comes to pass depends upon the person the Word is intended for and whether they "make" it happen. For example, if a prophet says he sees you operating on patients in Africa, I guess it will not happen unless you go to medical school)!

Also, the reality is that most of those desperately needing Christ are found in the marketplace; the places most of us work every day. Sadly, many church leaders are ignorant of the Order of Melchizedek and try to function under the law-bound Levitical priestly rules. This means many shepherds strictly limit their provision for Kingdom work to tithes and offerings. Besides this being in opposition to the new covenant laws of abundance, this burdens the sheep tremendously.

Many of these church leaders unwittingly rely on men for their provision. They even change their teachings and messages based on the church's financial situation. This obsolete mindset mugs pastors into the blessings they

(* We recently saw revival begin in Asbury College in Kentucky, USA and then move worldwide...)

could receive if they just opened their doors to entrepreneurial opportunities for their church members.

Further, since the Order of Melchizedek is both marketplace and ministry, all believers in Christ find themselves directly in active ministry. While we consider evangelists, prophets, pastors and teachers as working "full-time" in ministry, we are all called to the consistent work of the ministry under the Great Commission (Matthew 28:16-20). (Note EVERY Christian is in full-time ministry)!

What is already happening is that Holy Spirit-inspired men and women will storm the secular business markets with Godly ideas and inventions, the profits of which will support ministry on an unprecedented level. This is the power the Order of Melchizedek unleashes.

The Spiritual Authority of the Order of Melchizedek.

In this section, I will recap a few things I have already shown, but they lead to a greater revelation that will bless you. We know the Order of Melchizedek, in contrast to the temporary, man-driven Levitical priesthood, is a Priesthood that lasts forever (Hebrews 7:3, Psalm 110:4). Let's now take a look at the kingship and authority of Melchizedek. Hebrews 7:1-2 (NKJV) says,

> *"For this Melchizedek, King of Salem, priest of the Highest God, who met Abraham returning from the slaughter of the kings and blest him, to whom also Abraham gave a tenth part of all, first being translated "king of righteousness," and then also King of Salem, meaning "King of peace."*

From this foreshadowing, we can see that the Order of Melchizedek is based upon the righteousness of Jesus, its High Priest, Who became our eternal place of peace since. In this permanent, Heavenly priestly order, Jesus Christ reigns worthy of all the glory and the honour as King and High Priest. Contrasting to the Levitical priesthood, the high priest was merely a priest of God and nothing more. He had no office nor anointing of a king, and he only presented offerings of animal sacrifices to God in temporary atonement for sin. The Levitical priest had no governing authority over the Jewish people.

Under the Order of Melchizedek, Jesus operates not only under the eternal anointing of the High Priest but He is anointed as King of Kings as well. Because of His authority in kingship, the increase in power is exponential rather than a sum of the two parts. This means Jesus' power and the anointing available in the Order of Melchizedek are infinitely more powerful than the Levitical priesthood for many reasons.

What this means for us is that when we submit to the priestly Order of Melchizedek, we become partakers of the divine, royal authority delegated by Jesus (Luke 10:19). Furthermore, in Matthew 18:18 (NKJV) Jesus says,

"Assuredly, I say to you, whatever you bind on earth will be bound in heaven, and whatever you loose on earth will be loosed in heaven."

The authority (power) delegated by Jesus in these verses was unprecedented. Today, with the knowledge and practice of these truths, we can wipe out the devil's works and expand God's Kingdom like wildfire.

Moreover, the Order of Melchizedek is enforced by a mighty heavenly host of angels, yet even these angels are subject to our Christ-delegated authority. Hebrews 1:6-7 (NKJV) tells us:

"But when He again brings the firstborn into the world, He says: "Let all the angels of God worship Him." And of the angels He says: "Who makes His angels spirits And His ministers a flame of fire.""

The Levitical priesthood had no such astounding benefit. Still, many believers need to learn about their unfathomable power under this new covenant and priestly order. Jesus' message began with twelve men and spread rapidly throughout the world. They healed, cast out devils, performed many signs and wonders, and even raised people from the dead. This was all done using knowledge of the authority given to us under the kingly and priestly Order of Melchizedek. Even so, many Christians understand that Jesus has this authority but don't know they have it. Consider that Jesus said we would do even greater works than He did when we operate in the divine laws of the Order of Melchizedek (John 4:12).

Faith is the Foundation of the Order of Melchizedek.

In the previous chapter, I mentioned this truth several times, and now we will dig into it in deeper detail. Faith is the spiritual currency of the Order of Melchizedek. Hebrews 11:6 (NKJV) says,

"But without faith, it is impossible to please Him, for he who comes to God must believe that He is and that He is a rewarder of those who diligently seek Him."

Every country has its own legal tender. It would be best to convert your currency into theirs when buying anything from a foreign country. The values of currencies also fluctuate, with some being stronger than others. As we now know, the Order of Melchizedek is a regal (kingly) order, and therefore, it has its spiritual currency, which does not fluctuate but is instead infinitely powerful. The currency of this all-powerful order is the wealthiest and most powerful currency in eternity.

Like any currency, the Order of Melchizedek's cash allows those within its Kingdom and Priesthood to acquire and trade in its divine economy. Believers can claim or reap anything needed: funding for ministry, freedom from demonic oppression, healing, strength, peace, and more. They can also sow seeds of church, healing, love, peace, joy, finances, and more. As long as you use the spiritual currency of the Order of Melchizedek, you can believe anything according to God's Word.

Yet note that without the currency of faith, you cannot please God. He also cannot reward anyone unless they come by faith. Believe it or not, this was true even under the Levitical law. Although the law presented a crude model of Heavenly examples of righteousness, one had to obey the law in faith to be rewarded by God. If anyone tried to please God using the so-called currency of the law under the Levitical priesthood without faith, trying to rely on their own works, God was not impressed, and their effort was not honoured (Psalm 69:30-31, Psalm 50:13-15, 1 Samuel 15:22-24).

You have to use faith to please God, but what is faith really? Hebrews 11:1 (NKJV) says,

"Now faith is the substance of things hoped for, the evidence of things not seen."

So how do we grow in this faith?

How to Grow in the Order of Melchizedek.

You must spend time with your High Priest. Just as Abraham met with Melchizedek and partook in the bread and wine, you must spend time in a relationship with God to understand your power under the Order of Melchizedek. One way to best dwell under this divine order is to develop an ear for His voice as you spend time with your Lord. In John 10:27, (NKJV) Jesus said,

"My sheep hear My voice, and I know them, and they follow Me."

When we neglect our quality time with Him, we become desensitized to His voice and fail to follow Him.

Next, you need teaching. This book is a good start, but the absence of quality teaching in the church on this subject is why many Christians do not walk in spiritual and, therefore, financial victory. Hosea 4:6 (NKJV) says,

"My people are destroyed for lack of knowledge."

Don't be destroyed. Get some knowledge. Seek sound teaching that resonates with your spirit and is affirmed by the Word of God and the Holy Spirit."

You are what you eat. As you are taught, you must progress from drinking spiritual milk (baby concepts) to eating spiritual meat (advanced concepts, often reached only through obedience and practice of what you have learned). Sadly, many church leaders preach "ear-tickling" messages while preceding the truth in love. The sheep will follow where these pastors (who have become chiefly motivational speakers with "feel-good messages") lead. Unfortunately, the sheep never grow in the power that belongs to them.

Make sure you are getting quality spiritual nutrition. This means more than a snack on a Sunday morning. You need daily food. Be sure to get your bread and wine every single week.

Summary

How can this teaching help you today? I'll tell you… give to the Kingdom of God in love and thanksgiving under the Order of Melchizedek. Never give out of fear. This means do not give under fear of shame, force, tax, obligation, curse, or anything else not born of love. Anything that is not of love and faith is sin (Galatians 5:6, Romans 4:23). When you give, it should be in loving obedience to God so you can work His will in your life with all provision, righteous stewardship, divine authority, and power.

Ask yourself, "Am I prospering? Do I have more than enough to give to works of the ministry or undertake ministry myself?" If the answer is no, you are not operating in the laws of the Order of Melchizedek. You need to be obedient in returning your tithes and giving your offerings, but your attitude and motivation should be that of love and ministry support. When you do that, you will begin to see a dramatic change.

When you focus on the Great Commission and the individual calling God gave you, everything will begin to line up. If you are not actively a danger to the works of darkness, you are probably not active enough. It would be best if you upped the ante. Aside from the financial blessings and power available, you must step into the spiritual authority Jesus died to give you. YOU have the power. Nobody is going to do it for you. You need to get moving, and the primary way to start is by supporting the expansion of God's Kingdom.

Have you healed the sick lately? Cast out any demons? Raised the dead? Mark 16:17 says those signs follow those operating under the Order of Melchizedek. The literal text says, "them that believe," but believe in what? In Jesus? He is a High Priest according to the Order of Melchizedek, so these signs will follow those who believe in, and operate in, this divine order of Jesus. If these signs are not following you, are you indeed a believer? I think you are, but the depth of your belief needs to improve. Then you will see change.

I encourage you to consistently meet with your High Priest and return your tithe. Start there and trust Him to provide enough so you can begin to produce even more. Refrain from withholding your tithe out of concern about how it is being used. If you are being fed at church, you need to tithe. When you begin to do so out of love and thanksgiving to God, brace yourself! You will be blest going in and out (Deuteronomy 28:6). You will have all the necessary resources to pursue God's calling. This may take you to the marketplace, where He will significantly empower you to be a wealth-generator for His kingdom. The wiser you are as a steward, the more He will entrust to you. Then you will have your part in fulfilling the Great Commission, which is to go into the world and make disciples of all men for your great High Priest.

That was fun. Now that you understand the power of the Order of Melchizedek let us take an even more enthralling look at how the laws of sowing and reaping work in this spiritual currency of faith. You're going to love this!

CHAPTER 15

THE LAW OF SOWING AND REAPING
PART 1

When God created the heavens, the Earth, and everything in them, He created everything to function within His established principles and laws. Consequently, just as the natural world operates within physical laws, like the laws of gravity and aerodynamics, it also works within a set of spiritual rules. One of those laws encompasses both the spiritual and physical - the law of seedtime and harvest. There is something supernatural about the fact that a farmer can plant a grain of wheat into the ground, water it, and with some heat, sunshine and a little time, out of the earth grows a wheat stock with many more new grains of wheat on it. Although we may wonder, it is simply a miracle of God's perfectly designed creation.

When we align ourselves with God's physical world and His supernatural world, it follows that blessings will flow in our lives. God created the world as He did to bless us, leading us to worship Him. It is only due to the fall of man that we must contend with obstacles in the way of the tremendous spiritual law of seedtime and harvest. The good news is that once God's principles of prosperity are applied, combined with the spiritual direction of seedtime and harvest, we cannot help but reap a harvest. We must learn how.

For example, consider Genesis 8:22 (NKJV),

> *"While the earth remains,*
> *Seedtime and harvest,*
> *Cold and heat,*
> *Winter and summer,*
> *And day and night*
> *Shall not cease."*

This scripture tells us that the law of seedtime and harvest will operate as long as the Earth exists. Five valuable principles regarding the law of sowing and reaping need to be understood and applied. I will shed some light on the first principle in the rest of this chapter.

Spiritual Laws Never Change.

As long as the Earth remains, there will be seedtime and harvest, day and night, summer and winter. We cannot change this, so we adjust and learn to work with it to our advantage. This is because we are dealing with a law God put into motion.

When something is consistent and never changes, it is called a law. A law is defined as a general principle to which everything applicable must conform, and God tells us in Genesis 8:22 that seedtime and harvest are spiritual laws by Him. A New Testament reflection of this law is Galatians 6:7 (NKJV),

> *"Do not be deceived, God is not mocked; for whatever a man sows, that he will also reap..."*

192

This is my favourite scripture because it summarizes everything life is about. Everything we have today is the result of what we did yesterday. Even the very fact that you exist is because of something God did before you were born.

Everything affecting your life, whether positive or negative, is the harvest of seeds sown into your life by either you or others. Furthermore, reaping what you sow is an everyday occurrence. When you walk down the street with a smile on your face, people will smile back at you. March down the road and be miserable, and you'll quickly find people will respond the same way. You can choose to live a healthy lifestyle, or you can choose to be a couch potato and watch your health decline. Either way, you will reap what you sow, as this law applies to everything.

To further prove my point, look at 2 Corinthians 9:6 (NKJV),

> *"But this I say: He who sows sparingly will also reap sparingly, and he who sows bountifully will also reap bountifully."*

We plant seeds all the time into our own lives and the lives of those around us. We do this with our thoughts, our words, and our actions. We are, therefore, all sowers, and when God tells us in Mark 4:14 (NKJV),

> *"The sower sows the word,"*

He is comparing words with seeds. Therefore, we can say every word we speak is a seed. Our heart is the ground where these seeds are planted, so if the soil is good, the seeds will take root and grow to produce good fruit. You can plant good seeds from the Word of God in that ground or bad seeds of doubt and unbelief. Planting bad seeds in the bottom of your heart will produce a crop of misery, sickness, poverty, lack, and want.

Jesus explains this concept clearly to the religious leaders of His day without mincing words. Look at Matthew 12:34-37 (NKJV),

> "*Brood of vipers! How can you, being evil, speak good things? For out of the abundance of the heart the mouth speaks. A good man out of the good treasure of his heart brings forth good things, and an evil man out of the evil treasure brings forth evil things. But I say to you that for every idle word men may speak, they will give account of it in the day of judgment. For by your words you will be justified, and by your words you will be condemned.*"

Let me give you an example of what this scripture is telling us. I know a woman who became a paraplegic after being involved in a severe car crash. I remember her saying, "I am going to be in this wheelchair for the rest of my life, so you had better get used to it!" I tried to introduce her to the concept of healing, but she wanted nothing to do with it. Consequently, she reaped what she sowed and is still in her wheelchair to the day of this writing, even though the crash occurred in the mid-1990's. Nothing in her life has changed; sadly, it never will until she changes how she uses her words.

It is also essential to understand that our eyes and ears are gateways to our hearts. Anything negative we hear is planted in our hearts and has the potential to take root. Darkness can fill us if our eyes are not focused on God's Word. In contrast, if we focus on God's Word, His light will prevent any darkness from taking root in our hearts, and our entire being will be filled with His light. Whatever we listen to and adhere to will produce fruit in our lives, good or bad.

If we are unsatisfied with our lives or unhappy with our circumstances, we cannot blame anyone but ourselves. We are the ones planting the seeds in our hearts. If we don't want tomatoes in our garden, we don't plant tomato seeds. If we don't wish to defeat, we must quit planting seeds of failure.

Doc's Book Club: Read *"The Principle of the Path"* by Andy Stanley.

Proverbs 23:7 (KJV) tells us,

"as a man thinketh in his heart so is he..."

Our hearts are spiritual production centres where our seeds will germinate and grow. They become a reality as we think about the words we hear and meditate on them. We become what we believe and dwell on, and the seeds we sow in our hearts will eventually reap a harvest.

Sowing seeds of hatred and strife will reap hatred and strife and always be around you. On the other hand, if you sow seeds of love and kindness, that is what you will reap. This is proven in the following scriptures:

"Those who plow iniquity, And sow trouble shall reap the same." (Job 4:8 NKJV)

"Sow for yourselves in righteousness; Reap in mercy." (Hosea 10:12 KJV)

In these verses, God explains the law of seedtime and harvest - if you want good things in your life, you must sow good seeds.

Of course, this is easier said than done. The world has taught us to fail, be sick, and go broke. We have been taught how to live in misery, fail in marriage, fail in business, and for the most part, we have been diligent students. How do we now reap a different harvest from what has been sown into us all our life? Can we change a harvest of misery and defeat? Absolutely. Jesus tells us in Matthew 19:26 (NIV),

> *"with God all things are possible."*

How do we make the change and unlearn what we have been taught? The answer, as usual, is found in God's Word,

> *"And do not be conformed to this world, but be transformed by the renewing of your mind, that you may prove what is that good and acceptable and perfect will of God."* (Romans 12:2 NKJV)

Now we know we need to renew our mind, but what does that mean, and how do we do it? Again, we look to the Bible for guidance,

> *"Be anxious for nothing, but in everything by prayer and supplication, with thanksgiving, let your requests be made known to God; and the peace of God, which surpasses all understanding, will guard your hearts and minds through Christ Jesus. Finally, brethren, whatever things are true, whatever things are noble, whatever things are just, whatever things are pure, whatever things are lovely, whatever things are of good report, if*

there is any virtue and if there is anything praiseworthy - meditate on these things. The things which you learned and received and heard and saw in me, these do, and the God of peace will be with you." (Philippians 4:6-9 NKJV)

Read these verses repeatedly and ponder what they mean. Study them until they sink in. These scriptures tell us we must be transformed from our old thinking by renewing our minds. This means changing the way we think. How do we do that? By thinking about and meditating upon things that are true, noble, just, pure, and whatever is lovely, virtuous, and praiseworthy. Discard any negative seeds sown in your direction, and replace them with truth, goodness, and purity. Once your thinking has been renewed, your words and actions will follow.

A friend saw a particular job advertised once, and it just seemed to have his name all over it! It was precisely what he was qualified for and looking for, and it just seemed to be a perfect fit. He really wanted the job, so before he applied, he followed the principles of God's laws:

1. He fasted and prayed about it for ten days to ensure he was doing the right thing.
2. He spent time with the Lord, talking about the job and listening for His response about whether he should apply.
3. He claimed the job as his and oversaw his words regarding the job, the company, and the interview.
4. Halfway through the fast, he received two "downloads" about the business and its future direction. In short, God gave him a complete vision statement for the company.

5. He applied for the position and included the vision statement God gave him in his application letter and resume.
6. He knew this had to be about God, not him, so he continued praying and seeking the Lord.

Some things had to be done naturally, too. He bought a new suit, created a dynamite resume, and polished his interview skills.

Now at this point, you are probably guessing that he got the job. Well, he didn't and didn't do anything "wrong." All the steps he took were correct. However, sometimes other people might make mistakes; in this case, I think the company did because they hired the wrong guy! God cannot overcome other people's decisions - right or wrong. The Bible tells us to watch our words. Proverbs 18:20-21 (NKJV) says,

> "A man's stomach shall be satisfied from the fruit of his mouth; From the produce of his lips he shall be filled. Death and life are in the power of the tongue, and those who love it will eat its fruit."

(Note to my story: my friend did get a job and it was better than the one he had wanted! God was still leading him; in a better way that he had thought.)

The Bible tells us to:

> "Put away from thee a froward mouth, and perverse lips put far from thee." (Proverbs 4:24 KJV)

A froward mouth is an uncontrolled mouth not under God's Word's conviction. Learn to speak the Words of God in every situation, and the harvest that begins to grow in your life will be one of joy, peace, health, happiness, and prosperity.

The same principles of seedtime and harvest also apply to money, and the Bible states that money is like seed and the giving of finances is like sowing. Again, consider 2 Corinthians 9:6 (NKJV),

"But this I say: He who sows sparingly will also reap sparingly, and he who sows bountifully will also reap bountifully."

Now what if you don't have any financial seed to sow? The answer to that question is also found in the Bible:

"For God is the one who provides seed for the farmer and then bread to eat. In the same way, he will provide and increase your resources and then produce a great harvest of generosity in you." (2 Corinthians 9:10 NLT)

Several times, I have heard a story describing how Kenneth Copeland began his ministry. He was a student at Oral Roberts University in Tulsa, Oklahoma, and one time during a class break, he attended a seminar where the speaker was Kenneth E. Hagin. Pastor Hagin introduced the concept of seedtime and harvest - a notion Kenneth Copeland had never heard before. Pastor Hagin also spoke about partnering with him and asked the people attending if they would like to plant a seed in his ministry.

Kenneth Copeland wanted to partner with Pastor Hagin and plant a seed into his ministry but didn't have as much as two cents on him. He only thing that he had to give away was the pencil the usher had handed to him along with the offering envelopes! Having no money, Kenneth Copeland put the pencil in the offering envelope as his seed offering. Before the end of the day, a stranger gave Kenneth a ten-dollar bill! God supplies seed to the sower, even if it is just a pencil!

This story happened in 1967; ten dollars was a lot back then. That was the very start of Kenneth Copeland Ministries. Now, a little more than fifty years later, Kenneth Copeland Ministries has five international offices, with over five hundred people working at the head office in Fort Worth, Texas. The ministry has its own airport, hangar, several ministry aircraft, and TV and recording studios, and it all started with a pencil, using the powerfully profound law of seedtime and harvest. The entire ministry is debt free.

You recognize how seeds are planted in your heart by how you think and speak is essential to apply the law of seed-time and harvest in your life. The following chapter will cover the following four valuable principles in sowing and reaping.

CHAPTER 16

THE LAW OF SOWING AND REAPING
PART 2

God's Word tells us we should renew our minds and transform our old way of thinking so our behaviour will change. This is because our actions and intentions are often what hinders our harvest. A farmer doesn't just scatter seeds everywhere and hope they will grow into a good harvest. He is careful and intentional about which seeds he plants, where he plants them, and how he sows them. He prepares the ground adequately, ensuring he uses good seeds for the specific crop he wants, then carefully plants them in fertile soil. After that, he doesn't sigh and hope for a harvest; he expects a harvest from what he has sown.

The previous chapter explained the first principle of sowing and reaping - that seedtime and harvest is a spiritual law by which we live every day - what we sow; we will reap. This chapter will cover three principles of how, when, and where to sow for your desired harvest.

From point one in the last chapter, we move on to point two:

Give Cheerfully (Spiritual Laws Never Change).

We know that if we give something, we should give it cheerfully, but we have been taught to hold onto our possessions and store them up for the future. How do we cheerfully give away what we have worked hard to earn? To be able to give cheerfully, we need to change how we view giving and renew our thoughts about it. Look at it this way; when we give a family member or friend a gift that we know they want or need, that feeling of anticipated pleasure, waiting to see the joy on their face when they open the gift, makes giving them a pleasant experience. In the same way, we can provide to God cheerfully by envisioning the joy He feels at our obedience to Him in our giving,

"So let each one give as he purposes in his heart, not grudgingly or of necessity; for God loves a cheerful giver." (2 Corinthians 9:7 NKJV)

Giving for the Gospel's sake is planting seeds in the Kingdom of God, and this is another reason to give cheerfully. When a farmer is in his field planting his seeds, he has joy on the inside of him because he knows he will receive a harvest many times greater than what he has planted. He has fun because he expects a return on what he has sown. When you sow your finances, do you expect a harvest? You should because God says He will multiply the seed sown (2 Corinthians 9:10).

People say, "You need to give till it hurts." This is not a statement based on scripture because giving should be a joyful experience. If it is not, then don't do it. Do not give until it hurts; give until it is not joyful anymore. Can you be positive in giving ten dollars? Twenty dollars? How about a hundred? When deciding what to give, keep increasing the amount until it's not joyful anymore. A five-dollar seed offering might be all one person can afford or all that they have faith to believe for. For another person, it might be a hundred dollars and for another, thousands of dollars. Make sure you give joyfully; when it is no longer joyful, you know you have reached your maximum.

Once your seed has been planted, exercise faith and stand on the Word because you never know in what form your harvest will arrive. God sometimes has strange and unusual ways of supplying harvests to people. The following stories are two examples of this...

I once heard a minister relate a story about a man who was laid off from his job at an automobile manufacturing plant. Despite extensive efforts to get other work, he remained unsuccessful and became financially desperate. While attending a church convention, the man heard one of the speakers teach on a subject he had never heard before, seedtime and harvest. At this point, the man was down to the last five-dollar bill in his wallet. In faith, he took that five-dollar bill and put it into the offering envelope. He praised God for it, released it, exercised his faith, and declared it an abundant harvest.

A short time later, while tinkering with the transfer case on an SUV, he remembered this particular major car company had experienced problems with the design of this specific model. Consequently, the transfer case on those models wore out too soon. He prayed for inspiration and received from God what I like to call a "download" about the working of this transfer case. He approached the manufacturer and showed them the design he had put onto paper by then. They were so impressed that they bought the design from him and gave him a royalty on this new "leading edge" technology. He became very wealthy and continued to support the preacher he had heard speak that night about seedtime and harvest, only instead of planting five-dollar seeds, he was planting seeds of thousands of dollars.

The second story involves a young woman who faithfully attended church, tithing as she should and generously planting seeds by giving where she could. She was nevertheless experiencing difficulties in her career and finances. Regardless of her circumstances, she faithfully stood on the Word and trusted God to work it out. One day while on a commercial flight, she was sitting alone in a row of seats when a pair of bare feet protruded past her chair and came to rest on one of the armrests alongside her! She was shocked at the impropriety and knew no one would believe her when she told them. She whipped out her smartphone, recorded a video of the unusual behaviour, and then posted it on her Facebook page. Her friends found the video highly amusing and shared it with their friends, who sent it to their friends until someone contacted her and offered her a royalty if she allowed him to take it viral. She agreed to this and made a lot of money from the video! Who would have thought? God certainly does have a sense of humour! Never forget that God has endless ways of getting money to you!

This principle is at work in every facet of life. Words, thoughts, actions, and money are all seeds. Ideas are seeds; one idea inspired by God can change your life. Thoughts from the devil are seeds trying to overcome the Word of God. You stand in the strategic position of being the only one who can determine the outcome of your life by the seeds you allow to enter your heart.

Consider Your Ways.

Everything we do revolves around the law of seedtime and harvest - our words, our thoughts, our finances. The principles surrounding seedtime and harvest are discussed repeatedly throughout the Old and New Testaments. Just as a farmer deliberates on planting for the correct harvest, we should consider our motives for giving.

> *"Now therefore, thus says the LORD of hosts: "Consider your ways! You have sown much, and bring in little; You eat, but do not have enough; You drink, but you are not filled with drink; You clothe yourselves, but no one is warm; And he who earns wages, earns wages to put into a bag with holes. Thus says the LORD of hosts: Consider your ways!"* (Haggai 1:5-7 NKJV)

If you are sowing seeds according to God's Word and have not been reaping the abundant harvest that God promises, God says you should consider your ways. Take an inventory of your life and determine what is hindering your harvest. Sowing and reaping include tending and protecting your harvest while you wait for it. Unforgiveness in your life is like worms eating the roots; in the same way, the weeds of pride will choke your harvest.

> *"Therefore, if you bring your gift to the altar, and there remember that your brother has something against you, leave your gift there before the altar, and go your way. First be reconciled to your brother, and then come and offer your gift."* (Matthew 5: 23-24 NKJV)

In the passage above, Jesus refers to unforgiveness and pride affecting your offering. Note: He says, "if... your brother has something against you..." not, "if you have something against your brother." It takes humility to attempt reconciliation when you may not even be in the wrong. Be sure you are not harbouring unforgiveness in the soil of your heart and try to make right with anyone who might have anything against you. Then pray the words of David,

> *"Search me, O God, and know my heart: try me, and know my thoughts: And see if there be any wicked way in me, and lead me in the way everlasting."* (Psalm 139:23-24, KJV)

Live like You Expect a Harvest.

Do you expect the law of gravity to work when you jump off a cliff? Well, the law of seed time and harvest is no different. Granted, physical laws happen whether we believe or understand them, but we must activate spiritual laws. Even though a farmer knows it is hard, labouring work planting for a harvest, and even though he knows there is much tilling, weeding, and fertilizing ahead of him, his joy comes from expecting a harvest when the time is right. He knows the law of seedtime and harvest, so there is joy in planting the seed. The law of sowing and reaping is not a "get-rich-quick" scheme or an overnight success formula that you can apply and then live any way you want. Receiving blessings results from a lifestyle of seed-time and harvest, to which you must be committed, or it will not work for you.

The laws of God work together - one is designed to affect the other. You cannot pick out one thing, ignore the rest, and expect it all to work. Just as with the physical law of flying, there is the law of lift, the law of drag, and the law of thrust. You will only get off the ground if you apply those laws properly. Once you make it off the ground, if you do something to interfere with those laws, such as reduce the thrust by turning the engines off, you negate that law. Another direction comes into manifestation immediately - the law of gravity!

Sow Correctly - Don't Just Give It Away.

The vast majority of us work hard to obtain the money we have, so we must use it wisely. Besides, everything belongs to God anyway, so we should not be careless. God wants us to be wise stewards of the financial seed He provides us. Just as the farmer does not sow on rocky ground, we need to be sure the ground where we plant our financial seed is fertile soil.

For example, before I sow into any ministry or organization, I take the time to learn about them. As a rule, I only sow into Christian organizations and find out what kind of ministry work they do. I investigate what their administrative expenses are compared to their revenue, and I want to see the fruit of that ministry. Then I pray and ask the Lord what I should do.

An important point that may seem obvious but must be mentioned is not consuming your seed. Some people do that! They go and spend it instead of planting it. Without seed, there is no harvest.

Follow this formula for seedtime and harvest:

- Make sure you are sowing into good soil.
- Sow cheerfully.
- Water your seed with praise and thanksgiving.
- Evaluate your life and examine your motives.
- Expect a harvest.
- Don't consume your seed!

Finally, as with everything in life, keep going if you are asking the Lord and not receiving any answers. It might be a time to self-evaluate and assess your relationship with God. Look at correcting any sin in your life. It also may be a time for you to fast and pray. Whatever it takes, ensure you are in His will when planting your seeds.

Review

1. Seedtime and harvest is forever
2. Give cheerfully
3. Examine yourself
4. Live like you expect a harvest
5. Sow correctly - don't give it away
6. And don't consume your seed!

CHAPTER 17

A STUDY OF SUCCESS AND WEALTH
PART 1

Having determined that sowing and reaping is an unchanging spiritual law put into place by God and having also examined the regulation of seedtime and harvest, we can conclude that if we live a lifestyle of planting good seeds, we will enjoy a life of reaping good crops. However, This raises a question of whether we are ready for the harvest: "Have we prepared for prosperity?"

Large sums of money in the wrong hands can ruin a person, and meeting our needs does not benefit the Church or those in need of God's message of salvation. How do we use our harvest to advance the Kingdom and avoid slipping into destruction? In the following two chapters, we will analyze the potential pitfalls of wealth, investigate the behaviour of a wealthy believer, and examine the steps toward Godly wealth.

Part 1: Wealth Versus Prosperity.

"Wealth" is the ability to obtain what is immediately required. "Prosperity" is having enough provision to complete God's instructions.

Questioning whether we are ready for our harvest or prepared for prosperity is an unusual question. Still, many people must learn to manage abundant financial blessings. Statistics show that money is rarely adequately managed when a person receives a significant amount in some windfall - like a sudden inheritance or lottery winnings.

Jesus taught us in Luke 12:48 (NKJV),

> *"to whom much is given, from him much will be required."*

What would God require of someone who has "much" money? God expects proper stewardship of anyone He has blest with financial abundance. Why does God expect this? As with everything in life, the money belongs to God. If God has blest a person with substantial amounts of money, then what is "required" of them is Godly management of those finances.

Good stewardship includes.

  Diligent tithing
  Firstfruits offerings
  Giving alms
  Seed planting
  Investing the funds wisely

We have explored four of the five points above, and God also expects us to grow the finances He provides through intelligent and informed investment. To illustrate this, Jesus uses the Parable of the Bags of Gold in Matthew 25:14-30 (NIV).

The Parable of the Bags of Gold.

"Again, it will be like a man going on a journey, who called his servants and entrusted his wealth to them. To one he gave five bags of gold, to another two bags, and to another one bag, each according to his ability. Then he went on his journey. The man who had received five bags of gold went at once and put his money to work and gained five bags more. So also, the one with two bags of gold gained two more. But the man who had received one bag went off, dug a hole in the ground, and hid his master's money.

After a long time, the master of those servants returned and settled accounts with them. The man who had received five bags of gold brought the other five. 'Master,' he said, 'you entrusted me with five bags of gold. See, I have gained five more.' His master replied, 'Well done, good and faithful servant! You have been faithful with a few things; I will put you in charge of many things. Come and share your master's happiness!' The man with two bags of gold also came. 'Master,' he said, 'you entrusted me with two bags of gold; see, I have gained two more.' His master replied, 'Well done, good and faithful servant! You have been faithful with a few things; I will put you in charge of many things. Come and share your master's happiness!'

Then the man who had received one bag of gold came. 'Master,' he said, 'I knew that you are a hard man, harvesting where you have not sown and gathering where you have not scattered seed. So I was afraid and went out and hid your gold in the ground. See, here is what belongs to you.' His master replied, 'You wicked, lazy servant! So, you knew that I harvest where I have not sown and gather where I have not scattered seed?

211

*Well then, you should have put my money on deposit
with the bankers, so that when I returned I would have
received it back with interest.*

*So take the bag of gold from him and give it to the one
who has ten bags. For whoever has will be given more,
and they will have an abundance. Whoever does not
have, even what they have will be taken from them. And
throw that worthless servant outside, into the darkness,
where there will be weeping and gnashing of teeth."*

Apparent in this parable is that Jesus was concerned about
properly investing the funds we are provided with. He
understands that an excellent investor will take an element
of informed and calculated risk and be a good steward of
money overall. I sometimes wonder if people don't receive
a complete harvest because God knows that they may not
manage the money wisely if they receive a large harvest.
Often, large sums of money in people's hands can do more
harm than good, resulting in recklessness, even to the point
of destroying their own lives.

Our life consists of a series of tests * God places before us,
and as we pass each test (assuming we do pass), another
follows. This continues throughout our lives and is
required as part of the working out of our salvation
(Philippians 2:12-13). If we fail any of these tests, we do not
advance and remain in the same position until we pass it.
Tragically, many people in this world, including Christians,
do not pass these tests of life. Often, they are stifled in one
area and never move past it. For some, that failed test is
the handling of money.

* Doc's Book Club: Read *"Life is a Test: Hope in a Confusing World - A Daily Devotional"* by S. R. Watkins, Ph.D
(Volumes 1, 2 and soon to be 3)!

Years ago, when I lived in Canmore, Alberta, there was a family in our church who were very poor. One day a person called the church pastor and told him he wanted to donate a van to this family. The pastor was delighted to receive such an amazing alms gift for the family and arranged to receive the van and take it to them. When the pastor delivered the gift to the needy family, the father went outside to receive the van, and his first comment to the pastor was, "it has a crack in the window." The father's ungrateful attitude continued during the subsequent conversation, which surprised and disappointed the pastor. Furthermore, the family did not look after that van in terms of maintenance; it was never washed or kept clean. This is an example of a poorly managed gift, and as I watched this family over the years, they never escaped their poverty.

Also evident from the parable above is Jesus' opposition to lousy investing. Managing money requires some financial education, which many people do not realize. Over 50 percent of the population of first-world countries have too much debt. This means they also live from one paycheque to the next, do not have sufficient savings, and are vulnerable to the "ebbs and flows" of the Babylonian system of finance in which the world operates. We live in a world where people cannot differentiate between "needs" and "wants." Needing food and clothes and wanting the latest smartphone are two entirely different issues.

God is not opposed to wealth; He is opposed to the sin of covetousness. Being wealthy is to have a full supply and abundant provision for His work. This is confirmed in His Word:

"And God is able to bless you abundantly, so that in all things at all times, having all that you need, you will abound in every good work." (2 Corinthians, 9:8 NIV)

The question is, how would you react if put in charge of a lot of money? Have you proven yourself a good steward over what God has blest you with so far in life? Have you been trustworthy with what has been entrusted to you? Have you passed or failed the financial test? There is often, however, a sharp contrast between God's economic system and His covenant people concerning the handling of wealth. "Rich" is not a bad word; it is a biblical word meaning to accumulate resources, grow them, and become wealthy. The key to biblical wealth is how it is handled, which is clearly defined in Scripture.

Proverbs 1:32 (KJV) says,

"the prosperity of fools shall destroy them."

Proverbs 28:10 (KJV) says,

"the upright shall have good things in possession."

Proverbs 10:22 (NKJV) says,

"The blessing of the Lord makes one rich, and He adds no sorrow with it."

Proverbs 13:11 (AMPC) says,

"Wealth [not earned but] won in haste (authors note - like a lottery win) *or unjustly or from the production of things for vain or detrimental use [such riches] will dwindle away, but he who gathers little by little will increase [his riches]."*

An important point to note in these verses is that the rich should not trust in their riches but rather in God. It requires renewing your mind in this area; the more you prosper, the more you will have to deal with it. It requires judging your inner attitude and faith every day to make sure you depend on God and not on what you have in the bank. That shouldn't scare you - you need to make a strong determination to do it and then stick to it.

Given the lesson in Proverbs 13:11 above, why people buy lottery tickets has always baffled me. I see nothing wrong with buying a ticket from a boy at the local Peewee hockey league who is going door-to-door selling raffle tickets as a fundraiser for his club. This is not about winning; it's about supporting the local league and encouraging children to learn the value of work and "doing their bit" to support their club. I will also gladly buy an annual ticket to the local STARS ambulance lottery and one for the Foothills Hospital in Calgary. I don't buy them hoping to rely on the windfall for some financial relief, but I see it as an annual charitable donation to these two wonderful organizations. I do, however, see buying government (or otherwise) funded commercial lotteries in the hopes of winning as a gross waste of money. Statisticians tell us there is a greater chance of being hit by lightning than winning a lottery! That is not my genuine concern; the more significant issue is that these people put more faith in lotteries than in the Word of God! (Note: 72% of those who receive substantial wins have no original capital left within five to seven years).

God's Prosperity versus the World's Prosperity.

Relying on the world's view of prosperity has its down-falls. By the world's definition, prosperity is very limited in its scope - it only offers financial ability and power. The world admits it cannot overcome poverty, sickness, spiritual lack, or social ills. On the other hand, true prosperity is the ability to use God's power to meet the needs of humanity in any realm. God's power is the only authority that covers the entire spectrum of human existence.

The difference between the world's way and God's way is clear:

1. Worldly wealth is all about self; true prosperity, obeying God, and serving others.
2. The world's motivation for acquisition is accumulation; true prosperity is motivation for expansion and distribution of wealth where needed.
3. The world's wealthy use people to get things. Prosperity utilizes things to love people.

As Christians, our aim should be to become experts at managing money the Kingdom way. God is looking for people He can trust, people who will biblically manage wealth once they have it in their hands.

In 1 Timothy 6:17-19 (NKJV) Paul gives instructions to the rich,

> "Command those who are rich in this present age not to be haughty, nor to trust in uncertain riches but in the living God, who gives us richly all things to enjoy. Let them do good, that they be rich in good works, ready to give, willing to share, storing up for themselves a good foundation for the time to come, that they may lay hold on eternal life."

The Message translation says it this way,

> *"Tell those rich in this world's wealth to quit being so full of themselves and so obsessed with money, which is here today and gone tomorrow. Tell them to go after God, who piles on all the riches we could ever manage to do good, to be rich in helping others, to be extravagantly generous. If they do that, they'll build a treasury that will last, gaining life that is truly life."*

This scripture does not tell the rich to get rid of everything they have because God doesn't want people to have things. It doesn't ask us to keep one set of clothes, move into a cabin in the hills, and be humble. Doing that takes you out of the position to bless others.

A few years ago, I was on a backcountry trail ride with a group of Christians, and a discussion surrounding finances arose. Our group leader said he and his wife were quite content earning $40,000 a year, and they didn't see a need to make any more. That may sound pious, but what about all the giving he is not doing because he doesn't have it to give? I was delighted to hear he could live on $40,000 a year, but what about giving more money to the rest of the world? Earn more, give more. Simple stuff...

The goal of every Christian should be to aim for incredible financial blessings so that they can be significant financial blessings to others. Let me word it another way - the goal of every Christian should be to become a multi-millionaire! Think about what size your tithe would be! Think about the size of the first fruit offerings, the seed offerings, and the alms offerings! Every church mortgage in the world would be paid off in a week. The gospel may be free, but it takes money to preach it, and more preaching and salvations come with more money.

I am not suggesting that Christians need to keep their nose to the grindstone, working three jobs a week to become a millionaire. That is not what I mean. What every Christian should do is find out what their calling is. Using spiritual gift tests is one way of doing this. I think every Christian must find out who and what they are in terms of their anointing and spiritual gifts (Note: Peter Wagner is known as "the father of Spiritual Gifts," as he was the one who first wrote and popularized it. He has several excellent books you can buy and read about the subject).

God has given some people the gift of entrepreneurship/leadership/administration to create money for the Kingdom. Those gifts may only be for a select few, but that does not mean Christians with other callings and gifts are excused from managing their money correctly. Every Christian should become a good steward of God's financial resources and do what they are called to do to build the Kingdom of God, using their gifts and financial resources.

Compare the following scriptures confirming that prosperity results from doing and living in God's way.

"The poor plead for mercy, but the rich answer harshly." (Proverbs 18:23 NIV)

"But when you had eaten and were satisfied, you became proud and forgot me." (Hosea 13:6 NLT)

"With your wisdom and understanding you have amassed great wealth - gold and silver for your treasuries. Yes, your wisdom has made you very rich, and the riches have made you very proud." (Ezekiel 28:4-5 NLT)

"The wiser you are, the more worries you have; the more you know, the more it hurts." (Ecclesiastes 1:18 GNT)

"Workers may or may not have enough to eat, but at least they can get a good night's sleep. The rich, however, have so much that they stay awake worrying." (Ecclesiastes 5:12 GNT)

"Whoever loves money never has enough; whoever loves wealth is never satisfied with their income. This too is meaningless. As goods increase, so do those who consume them. And what benefit are they to the owners except to feast their eyes on them?" (Ecclesiastes 5:10-11 NIV)

"This is what the Lord says: Don't let the wise boast in their wisdom, or the powerful boast in their power, or the rich boast in the riches. For those who wish to boast should boast in this alone: that they truly know Me and understand that I am the Lord who demonstrates unfailing love and who brings justice and righteousness to the earth and that I delight in these things. I, the Lord have spoken." (Jeremiah 9:23-24 NLT)

Compare the previous scriptures to these:

"True humility and fear of the Lord leads to riches, honour, and long life." (Proverbs 22:4 NLT)

"Behold that which I have seen: it is good and comely for one to eat and to drink, and to enjoy the good of all his labour that he taketh under the sun all the days of his life, which God giveth him: for it is his portion. Every man also to whom God hath given riches and wealth, and hath given him power to eat thereof, and to take his portion, and to rejoice in his labour; this is the gift of God." (Ecclesiastes 5:18-19 KJV)

Own Wealth - Don't Let Wealth Own You.

Some scriptures above illustrate that it is possible to pass the poverty test but fail the prosperity test. Your needs are met, and you receive great abundance, but your heart will grow cold towards God if you do not keep His Word first place in your life. We must be vigilant against being taken with the things that have been added to us. They could be things like cars, planes, houses, land - whatever you like. We have to walk circumspectly (Eph. 5:15) to walk in prosperity - we have to keep putting God first in our life.

Don't let riches make you lose sight of the lessons learned in God's Word. Be open to God's guidance each day. There is a lot to be learned from Zacchaeus' response to Jesus in the passage below,

> "Then Jesus entered and passed through Jericho. Now behold, there was a man named Zacchaeus who was a chief tax collector, and he was rich. And he sought to see who Jesus was, but could not because of the crowd, for he was of short stature. So, he ran ahead and climbed up into a sycamore tree to see Him, for He was going to pass that way. And when Jesus came to the place, He looked up and saw him, and said to him, 'Zacchaeus, make haste and come down, for today I must stay at your house.'"

> So he made haste and came down, and received Him joyfully. But when they saw it, they all complained, saying, "He has gone to be a guest with a man who is a sinner.

> Then Zacchaeus stood and said to the Lord, "Look, Lord, I give half of my goods to the poor; and if I have taken anything from anyone by false accusation, I restore fourfold."

And Jesus said to him, "Today salvation has come to this house, because he also is a son of Abraham; for the Son of Man has come to seek and to save that which was lost." (Luke 19:1-10 NKJV)

When all your needs are met, remember who met them. Remember, it was God who gave you the wealth. Always bear one thing in mind: wealth can come quickly and go fast. Examples of this are the many entertainers or athletes who suddenly start making more money than they know what to do with. Not being born-again, Spirit-filled people and living in a dark world, they will not give any of it to God or the Church. Instead, they will provide it to over-priced stores for luxury consumer goods, possibly even a drug dealer, or many other avenues of immorality. Financially, they have the world on a string, but the world is all they have, so their money drives them into ruin.

When immoral people have money, they do evil things with it, leading to death - sadly, often at an early age. You might ask why a celebrity would throw his or her life away. The reason is that they don't know what else to do with it because they are living in the kingdom of darkness.

"But people who long to be rich fall into temptation and are trapped by many foolish and harmful desires that plunge them into ruin and destruction." (1 Timothy 6:9 NLT)

Whether money is good or bad depends upon who has it and how it is used. Righteous people use their money for good things and are blest abundantly. Now let us look at how wealthy believers live their lives and what we can learn from them.

S.R. WATKINS

CHAPTER 18

A STUDY OF WEALTH AND SUCCESS
PART 2

When people are operating in the law of sowing and reaping, they often wonder why God is seemingly not blessing them. The reality is that they frequently do not recognize His blessings when He is blessing them. In this lesson following Part 1 in the previous chapter, let us instead consider what wealth and being blest really mean and whether we are, in fact, wealthy and blest without realizing it. What do rich believers look like, and how do they behave?

Part 2: The Profile of the Wealthy Believer.

See if you can pick up any aspects of your life in the following Psalm,

> *"Praise the LORD. Blessed is the man who fears the LORD, who finds great delight in his commands. His children will be mighty in the land; the generation of the upright will be blest. Wealth and riches are in his house, and his righteousness endures forever.*

*Even in darkness light dawns for the upright, for the
gracious and compassionate and righteous man. Good
will come to him who is generous and lends freely, who
conducts his affairs with justice. Surely he will never be
shaken; a righteous man will be remembered forever. He
will have no fear of bad news; his heart is steadfast,
trusting in the LORD. His heart is secure, he will have
no fear; in the end he will look in triumph on his foes.
He has scattered abroad his gifts to the poor, his
righteousness endures forever; his horn will be lifted high
in honour. The wicked man will see and be vexed, he will
gnash his teeth and waste away; the longings of the
wicked will come to nothing."* (Psalm 112)

Does this Psalm describe you? If it does not, it should,
because this is a description of a wealthy believer:

Verse 1: The believer is blest because he honours God and
His Word. The words "bless" or "blessed" mean "to
empower," and in this case, they mean empowered to
prosper. Again, understand you are blest to be a blessing.
Verse 2: His children are blest because of his giving. Are
you giving? First returning tithes, then firstfruits, then seed
offerings and alms.
Verse 3: Wealth and riches are in his house. Is there any
question about whether you are to be rich?
Verse 4: Is gracious and full of compassion.
Verse 5: He displays favour and lends to others.
Verses 6-8: His heart is established and is not moved
during adverse economic times.
Verse 9: He is a giver. He reaches out to the poor, and he is
constantly advancing.
Verse 10: He resists the devil, and the devil flees!

I guess that ninety percent of people in this world live in
their soul, meaning they live in a way pleasing to their five

senses instead of living as directed by their spirit. We are to live by our spirit, through our soul. Note: The Psalm above tells us,

> "Blessed is the man who fears the LORD, who finds great delight in his commands."

Living to please your natural senses over the commands of the Lord will cause you to fail repeatedly. Have you ever failed repeatedly? Have you made lots of money in your life and lost it? This was not an accident; it was the result of your choices. Your failures will keep refining you, so the next time you make money, you will look after it and manage it better for the Kingdom. This knowledge should bring you joy in the future.

God wants us to be blest, but our choices and behaviours can hinder our blessings. Below are some comparative behaviours between wealthy and poor people:

1. Seventy percent of wealthy people eat less than 300 calories of junk food per day versus ninety-seven percent of poor people, who eat more than 300 calories of junk food per day.
2. Twenty-three percent of wealthy people gamble versus fifty-two percent of poor people who gamble.
3. Eighty percent of wealthy people are focused on accomplishing some single goal versus only twelve percent of the poor who focus on accomplishing a single goal.
4. Seventy-six percent of the wealthy exercise aerobically four days a week versus twenty-three percent of the poor who exercise in this way.

5. Sixty-three percent of the wealthy listen to audio books during their commute to work versus five percent of poor people who do the same.

6. Eighty-one percent of the wealthy maintain a to-do list versus nineteen percent of the poor who maintain the same list.

7. Sixty-three percent of wealthy parents encourage their children to read two or more non-fiction books a month versus only three percent of the poor.

8. Seventy percent of wealthy parents encourage their children to volunteer ten hours or more a month versus three percent of the poor who do this.

9. Eighty percent of the wealthy make calls to wish people a happy birthday versus eleven percent of the poor.

10. Sixty-seven percent of the wealthy write down their goals versus seventeen percent of the poor.

11. Eighty-eight percent of the wealthy read thirty minutes or more each day for education or career reasons versus two percent of the poor who do the same.

12. Six percent of the wealthy say what is on their mind versus sixty-nine percent of the poor.

13. Seventy-nine percent of the wealthy network five hours or more each month versus sixteen percent of the poor.

14. Sixty-seven percent of the wealthy watch one hour or less of TV every day versus twenty-three percent of poor people.

15. Six percent of the wealthy watch reality TV versus seventy-eight percent of the poor.

16. Forty-four percent of the wealthy wake up three hours before work starts versus three percent of the poor.

17. Seventy-four percent of the wealthy teach good daily success habits to their children versus one percent of the poor.
18. Eighty-four percent of the wealthy believe good habits create opportunity versus four percent of the poor. (Ninety-six percent of the poor think success has to do with "luck.")
19. Eighty-six percent of the wealthy believe in life-long educational self-improvement versus five percent of the poor.
20. Eighty-six percent of the wealthy love to read versus twenty-six percent of the poor.
21. Bonus statistic, and the most important-ninety percent of wealthy Christians pray every day.

(Reference: Rich Habits Institute.)

Are you doing "wealthy things" or "poor things?"

Seven Ways to Walk as a Wealthy Believer.

I understand it is difficult to retrain yourself from a child-hood of indoctrination of poor habits and likely decades of continuing these habits and mindsets as an adult. Even once we are born again and have begun renewing our minds, our busy and challenging lives can sometimes distract our walk with God, causing us to lose focus and direction. Jesus never said that life would be easy. Below is a seven-point guide to help you walk as a wealthy believer:

1. Focus on the Lord, and He will be with you.

   The Bible says,

"He sends rain on the just and the unjust."
(Matthew 5:45 NKJV)

which explains why tithing and giving works for the unsaved as well as believers. This is true, but to be truly blest, you must be born again and know Jesus as your Lord and personal saviour (John 3:3). In addition, every attempt must be made to keep His commandments (John 14:15) and live a Holy life, separated from the world's way.

"...all have sinned and fall short of the glory of God,"
(Romans 3:23 NKJV)

Therefore, confess your sins to Him, repenting (turning away) from them, and ask God for His forgiveness. God is faithful and just to forgive you. If you stay totally focused on Jesus and walk in the Spirit you will not want sin in the first place.

2. Know God's ways and how He operates.

"Wisdom is the principal thing; Therefore, get wisdom. And in all your getting, get understanding."
(Proverbs 4:7 NKJV)

A good place to obtain wisdom is from the wisest man who ever lived, so read at least one chapter of the Book of Proverbs every day. It is interesting to note that there are 31 of them; i.e. one per day for a month.

"Where there is no vision, the people perish."
(Proverbs 29:18 KJV)

3. You must renew your mind and conform your thoughts to God's Word.

   "Do not conform to the pattern of this world, but be transformed by the renewing of your mind. Then you will be able to test and approve what God's will is - his good, pleasing and perfect will." (Romans 12:2 NIV)

   "For though we walk in the flesh, we do not war according to the flesh. (For the weapons of our warfare are not carnal but mighty in God for pulling down strongholds;) casting down arguments and every high thing that exalts itself against the knowledge of God, bringing every thought into captivity to the obedience of Christ." (2 Corinthians 10:3-5 KJV)

4. Begin to confess words of faith and declare the promises of God. Decree Godly prosperity over your life.

   "And since we have the same spirit of faith, according to what is written. I believed and therefore I spoke, we also believe and therefore speak."
   (2 Corinthians 4:13 KJV)

5. Meditate on the Word.

   "Keep this Book of the Law always on your lips; meditate on it day and night, so that you may be careful to do everything written in it. Then you will be prosperous and successful." (Joshua 1:8 NIV)

6. Begin the process of seedtime and harvest in your life. Today!

7. Stay consistent and committed to what you started:

"But we have this treasure in earthen vessels, that the excellence of the power may be of God and not of us. We are hard-pressed on every side, yet not crushed; we are perplexed, but not in despair; persecuted, but not forsaken; struck down, but not destroyed - always carrying about in the body the dying of the Lord Jesus, that the life of Jesus also may be manifested in our body." (2 Corinthians 4:7-10 NKJV)

Are You Blest?

We have established that God wants us to be blest, and that being rich to assist others in spreading His gospel is part of God's plan for us. Why then do so many Christians not "feel" blest? I think the problem lies with understanding the definition of the words. The term is relative to each person's situation: a mother in Africa may feel blest to have enough food for her family for the day, and a father in Asia may be considered rich because he owns a twenty-year-old car. Let us never confuse envy with lack. Just because we do not have what our flesh desires, does not mean we are not blest.

To test whether we are blest, let us compare Canada and the USA to the rest of the World:

1. Do you have clean water? The next time you uncap a bottle of water or pour a drink from the tap, remember that one in eight people in the world (1 billion people) lack access to clean water. Many millions of women around the world spend several hours a day collecting water. When you take a five-minute shower, you use more water than a typical family in a developing country uses in an entire day.

2. Do you have a bathroom? About 40 percent of the world's population (3.2 billion people) do not have toilets. Lack of sanitation facilities guarantees the spread of disease and is a major reason why more than two million people die annually of diarrhea (80 percent of the more than 90 million people in Pakistan do not have the daily use of a flushing toilet - how many do you have in your house)?

3. How's your electricity? The power in your house might be interrupted briefly three times a year because of storms, but 2 billion people - a quarter of humanity - live without any electricity.

4. Do you have a secure roof over your head? 1.4 billion people live in slums or shantytowns. This is almost one-sixth of the world's population. Of this total, 640 million children live without adequate shelter; they live in cardboard boxes, tin-roofed shacks, one-room mud huts or filthy, crowded tenements. This is not exclusive to the developing world - in Canada and the USA combined, there are between 2.3 to 2.5 million people classified as homeless.

5. Is there food on your table? In Canada, and particularly in the USA, we are battling an obesity epidemic. Yet according to UNICEF, 22,000 children die each day due to poverty. Approximately 790 million people in the developing world are chronically undernourished, and almost 28 percent of all children in developing countries are estimated to be underweight or stunted.

6. Do you have a stove? In developing countries, some 2.5 billion people use wood, charcoal, or animal dung to meet their energy needs for cooking. In sub-Saharan Africa, more than 80 percent of the population depends on these crude, traditional means for cooking, as do over half of the populations of India and China. The really sad part is indoor air pollution, resulting from the use of solid fuels, claims the lives of 1.5 million people each year. More than half of these lives are children below the age of five years old.

7. Do you have regular income? You may have had to take a pay cut during the last recession, but keep in mind at least 80 percent of humanity lives on less than $10 a day. The world's average income is about $7,000 a year. Still, only about 19 percent of the world's population live in countries with per capita incomes at least this high.

8. Did you go to school? Nearly a billion people entered the twenty-first century unable to read a book or sign their name. Enrollment data shows about seventy-two million children of primary school age in the developing world were not in school in 2005 (and 57 percent of them were girls).

9. Are you generally healthy? People from Canada and the USA face illness like people in other nations - and more than thirteen million people from Canada and the USA are battling cancer in any given year, but many of us have access to health care. In the developing world, more than 2.2 million children die each year because they are not immunized. An estimated forty million people in developing countries are living with HIV/AIDS. Every year there are 350 - 500 million cases of malaria, with one million fatalities - mostly in Africa.

10. Are you free to worship God? More than 400 Christians die for their faith every day around the world, and most of these believers suffer in Islamic countries. The top hot spot for Christian persecution according to Open Doors International, however, is the atheist regime of North Korea.

Below is a simple illustration of the world population breakdown. Say we could shrink the Earth's population to a village of precisely one hundred people, with all the existing human ratios remaining the same, there would be:
• 57 Asians
• 21 Europeans
• 14 North, Central, and South America's
• 8 Africans
• 52 females
• 48 males
• 70 non-whites
• 30 whites
• 70 non-Christians
• 30 Christians
• 98 heterosexual
• 2 homosexuals
• 80 substandard housing
• 30 illiterate
• 50 malnourished
• 1 near death
• 1 near birth
• 1 college educated
• 1 computer owner
• 6 people would possess 59 percent of the entire world's wealth, and all 6 would be from the USA and Canada

Further "food for thought," in case you still doubt whether you are blest or not:

• If you woke this morning with more health than illness, you are more blest than the one million people around the world, who will die this week from sickness.

• If you have never experienced the danger of battle, the loneliness of imprisonment, the agony of torture, or the pangs of starvation, you are ahead of 500 million people in the world.

• If you are able to attend a Christian church service without fear of harassment, arrest, torture or death, you are more blest than three billion people in the world.

• If you have food in the refrigerator, clothes on your back, a roof over your head, and a place to sleep, you are richer than 70 percent of people on Earth.

• If you have some money in the bank, cash in your wallet, and spare change in a dish somewhere, you are among the top 8 percent of the world's wealthy.

• If your parents are still alive and still married, you are very rare, even in Canada and the USA.

• Reading this book means you are more blest than over two billion people in the world, who cannot read at all.

(Reference www.globalissues.org).

By now we can clearly see the word "poverty" is a relative term. In Canada and the USA, there are about thirty-five million people living in poverty. This level of poverty, however, is completely different from the level of poverty experienced in other countries. In our culture, over half of the poor own their own homes, and 10 percent of them live in homes worth more than $300,000. Over 70 percent of our poor own their own car, and 30 percent own two cars; 98 percent own a colour television set, and 50 percent own two. I am sure people in third world countries would jump at the chance to be "poor" in our countries.

Review

1. Wealth is the ability to obtain what is immediately required. Prosperity is having enough
   provision to complete God's instructions.
2. Worldly wealth is about serving self.
3. True prosperity is about serving God.

S.R. WATKINS

CHAPTER 19

A STUDY OF WEALTH AND SUCCESS
PART 3

While it is essential for every believer to learn how to work with money, managing finances is not everyone's specialty or gift. If you are one of those who are unsure of how best to steward the resources God supplies you, rest assured that the basics of what you need to know are in His Word. Below are ten things about money to keep in mind:

1. Do not love money, and certainly do not worry about it.

> *"Therefore, I say to you, do not worry about your life, what you will eat or what you will drink; nor about your body, what you will put on. Is not life more than food and the body more than clothing?"* (Matthew 6:25 NKJV)

The devil wants you to worry about your finances, so your trust will move from God to the world's Babylonian system. He knows if you follow God diligently and honour Him in all your ways, if you love Him and live your life for Him, your Father will prosper and bless you.

> *"Blessed shall you be when you come in, and blessed shall you be when you go out."* (Deuteronomy 28:6 NKJV)

2. Work with excellence in all you do.

> *"And whatever you do, do it heartily, as to the Lord and not to men." (Colossians 3:23 NKJV)*

When you work with all your might unto God, He is your ultimate boss. It does not matter if your natural boss is a jerk and does not appreciate your contribution to the business, God is over him, and He knows your heart and sees what you do. He sees your diligence, motivation, integrity, and honesty. Your Father sees it all, and He will bless the fruit of your hands.

> *"And the LORD will make you the head and not the tail; you shall be above only, and not be beneath, if you heed the commandments of the LORD your God, which I command you today, and are careful to observe them."* (Deuteronomy 28:13 NKJV)

3. Know the purpose of money.

> *"And you shall remember the Lord your God, for it is He who gives you power to get wealth, that He may establish His covenant which He swore to your fathers, as it is this day."* (Deuteronomy 8:18 NKJV)

It is not about you, as Rick Warren says in his best-selling book, *"The Purpose Driven Life."* It is about what you can do with money to serve and extend God's Kingdom.

4. Recognize it is God's money.

Remember, God is the source of all we have. It comes from Him, and He has a much bigger purpose for the money He supplies than we realize when we receive it. He wants to multiply that money, but if you do not honour Him or are stingy or caught up idolizing money, He will not bless you with more because those attitudes put you on the road to destruction. If you are heading to ruin, God will not assist you by giving you more.

5. Be a cheerful and generous giver to God and to those in need around you.

> *"So let each one give as he purposes in his heart, not grudgingly or of necessity; for God loves a cheerful giver."* (2 Corinthians 9:7 NKJV)

6. Give into the right soil.

There are various types of soil into which seeds can fall or be planted. Jesus points this out in the Parable of the Sower in Matthew 13. He also points out that not all soil is good for growth. Always ensure the soil into which you plant is good soil to receive a good harvest.

7. Understand the seasons.

We need to be aware that there are going to be seasons of famine and seasons of plenty. We see this reflected in scripture and need to understand that a time of plenty is preparation for famine. Joseph prepared for the coming famine when God blest Egypt with great abundance for seven years (Genesis 41:54). Isaac sowed during famine, *"and reaped in the same year a hundredfold."* (Genesis 26:12 NKJV)

If you have planted in a season of famine, are prospering, and can be trusted to manage correctly what you have, you will gain even more. Exercise a spirit of excellence during this time, and God will cause you to prosper when the world fails financially.

8. Prosper where you have planted.

Work towards prospering in your current position. Stop complaining about your circumstances or playing the "if only" game. Plant in good soil and start to prosper where you are.

9. Have faith in God to ask for BIG things.

Our God, the creator of the universe, is not small. He is

> "*able to do immeasurably more than all we ask or imagine.*" (Ephesians 3:20 NIV)

> "*Eye has not seen, nor ear heard, nor have entered into the heart of man the things which God has prepared for those who love Him.*" (1 Corinthians 2:9 NKJV)

10. Seek wisdom.

We all make mistakes but do not let these mistakes stop you from pressing into the goal. Seek wisdom on how to fight the good fight of faith.

> "*Wisdom is the principal thing; therefore, get wisdom. And with all your getting, get understanding.*"
> (Proverbs 4:7 NKJV)

Study the Word, take relevant courses, and read books - learn what you do not know, and then put this knowledge into action. Keep a good set of books, including reading books on budgeting and planning, to help you obtain the understanding you need. I recommend the Crown Ministries programs.

Review

1. The Lord must be with you and you with Him.
2. Study His Word.
3. Confess words of faith over your family and yourself.
4. Start practicing seedtime and harvest - beyond the tithe.
5. Stay consistent and do not waver! Keep planting seeds!

S.R. WATKINS

CHAPTER 20

THIRTY-ONE WAYS TO HAVE THE WINDOWS OF HEAVEN OPENED UPON YOUR LIFE.

In the past nineteen chapters of this book, we have corrected some religious notions regarding prosperity and clarified why God wants us, His children, to prosper. We investigated the biblical principles of wealth and success and how to use our wealth to further God's Kingdom. The role of tithing in God's economy was examined, and we explored tithing under the priestly Order of Melchizedek and why this is far superior to tithing under the Law of Moses. The law of seedtime and harvest was presented, and attitudes hindering the harvest were outlined. In conclusion, this chapter will review these principles and look at how to open the windows of Heaven to pour blessings upon your life.

1. Tithing Is a Scriptural Requirement, Not a Preferred Option.

Many people consider tithing to be an Old Testament law, saying it does not apply to us under the New Covenant. Jesus makes it clear in Matthew 5:17, however, that He did not come to abolish the law, but rather to fulfill it. In Matthew 23:23, Jesus also plainly states that we should tithe. There need be no debate on the matter.

"And concerning the tithe of the herd or the flock, of whatever passes under the rod, the tenth one shall be holy to the LORD." (Leviticus 27:32 NKJV)

"A tithe of everything from the land, whether grain from the soil or fruit from the trees, belongs to the LORD; it is holy to the LORD." (Leviticus 27:30 NIV)

"Then Melchizedek King of Salem brought out bread and wine; he was the priest of God Most High. And he blest him and said: Blessed be Abram of God Most High, Possessor of heaven and earth; And blessed be God Most High, Who has delivered your enemies into your hand. And he gave him a tithe of all." (Genesis 14:18-20 NKJV)

"What sorrow awaits you teachers of religious law and you Pharisees. Hypocrites! For you are careful to tithe even the tiniest income from your herb gardens, but you ignore the more important aspects of the law-justice, mercy, and faith. You should tithe, yes, but do not neglect the more important things." (Matthew 23:23 NLT)

Excuses for not tithing are self-defeating:

"I'll start tithing when I have some money." - You will never have enough to tithe until you start tithing!
"I can't afford to tithe." - You never will unless you do. Please understand that withholding your tithe is like putting bars on the windows of Heaven over your life.

This is the bottom line: Tithing is a commandment from God, not an available option.
   a. The 90 percent left of your income will super-naturally go further when you tithe.

b. Failing to tithe removes the foundation for increased blessing.

c. Tithing is an act of worship - we do not "give" our tithe to God, we return it to Him.

Why do we experience such blessings when we return 10 percent of our income to God? It is certainly not because He needs the money. Tithing is a powerful way to plug into God's plan and support His work on Earth. The combined local congregations - making up the larger Church - provide the funds to support ministries and outreaches to build up the Body of Christ, minister to the poor, support missions, sponsor spreading the gospel via radio or television, and contribute towards providing a living for pastors in ministry. I believe people should tithe to their local church where they are cared for, which is the base for all other outreaches.

2. Offerings Bring Multiple Blessings.

Our offerings (planting seeds) not only bless us but also benefit many others, most of whom we are unaware. Imagine having so much money that you tithe 10 percent, live on 10 percent, and offer 80 percent of your income. What impact would it have on the Church and, ultimately, spreading the gospel to the rest of the world?

3. Align Your Priorities with God and His Word.

God knows we have physical requirements, but we all too often first seek our needs to be met in the physical world, and then tend to our spiritual needs. Jesus instructed us in Matthew 6:33 (NKJV),

"But seek first the kingdom of God and His right-eousness, and all these things shall be added to you."

Your priorities should look like this:

    a. Your relationship with God: spend time determining His will for your life.

    b. Your family: your responsibility to your spouse first, then your children.

    c. Others: your responsibility to your ministry, job, and others you encounter daily.

    d. Yourself: your responsibility to maintain your spiritual and physical health.

When you get your priorities right, everything falls into place.

4. Keep Double-Mindedness Out.

After deciding to be obedient to God and follow His instructions, stick by your decision! Double-mindedness means you can't make decisions or you return to your decisions, and change them. An example of double-mindedness is inconsistent tithing, which displays erratic faith and a lack of wisdom, as explained in the verse below:

> *"But let him ask in faith, with no doubting, for he who doubts is like a wave of the sea driven and tossed by the wind. For let not that man suppose that he will receive anything from the Lord; he is a double-minded man, unstable in all his ways."* (James 1:6-8 NKJV)

5. Attitude Makes Offerings Acceptable to God.

Giving clothes with holes in them to the poor offends God and is an unacceptable offering. In Malachi 1:10 (NLT), God tells us He will not accept worthless offerings. If your giving is affected by the shortages in your life instead of God's supply, you are giving from what you do not have instead of blessing God for what He has already provided. Instead, let a heart of gratitude for what God has done for you motivate your offerings. Instead of considering the shortages in your life as a negative, believe them as the next thing your mighty God will overcome. With this mentality, your shortage will become a target for destruction instead of the limiting source of your giving.

When deciding on how much to give after your tithe, don't dwell on what you do not have. Let your gratitude for what God has already done guide your offerings. Never let a fear of lack determine what you will give.

6. Be Righteous in All Your Ways.

God wants us to be faithful and attentive even to the little things in life so that He can bless us with more (Luke 19:17). We need to prove ourselves as good and faithful stewards of what He gives us because to whom much is given much is required (Luke 12:48).

7. Do Not Fear.

"Fear not" is mentioned more than 450 times in the Bible, which confirms that God doesn't want us to have fear in our lives. Fear is the devil's "faith," and it works to our destruction. This is echoed in Job's words after satan took everything from him and infected his body with boils:

> *"For the thing I greatly feared has come upon me, and what I dreaded has happened to me."* (Job 3:25 NKJV)

Scripture tells us that when we walk with God, there is no need for fear:

"For God has not given us a spirit of fear, but of power and of love and of a sound mind." (2 Timothy 1:7 NKJV)

"But when Jesus heard it, He answered him, saying, "Do not be afraid; only believe, and she will be made well." (Luke 8:50 NKJV)

Many fears plague people every day, but for every fear, the Bible has an answer. I encourage you to study these scriptures yourself:

Fear of Death	Hebrews 2:14-15
Fear of Man	Proverbs 29:25
Fear of Failure	Romans 8:37-39
Fear of Rejection	John 6:37
Fear of Sickness	Isaiah 53:5, 1 Peter 2:24
Fear of Insufficiency	2 Peter 1:3

8. Live by Faith.

Having been saved by faith (Romans 10:9), it makes sense we should continue to live by faith,

"The just shall live by faith." (Romans 1:17b NKJV)

After deciding to be obedient to God and follow His instructions, stick by your decision! What does it mean to live by faith, and how do we do it? The Bible tells us that unto every man, a measure of faith is given (Romans 12:3), so we all have faith. We increase our confidence by hearing the Word of God (Romans 10:17), and we express faith by walking in love (Galatians 5:6b). Hebrews 11:6 tells us that if we are not living by faith, we are not pleasing God, and Romans 14:23 confirms this by saying that whatever is not of faith is sin.

Therefore, we are to grab hold of the promises of God, stand on them, confess them, believe them, and exercise our faith, which is to

"call those things that be not as though they were."
(Romans 4:17 KJV)

Hebrews 11:1 (KJV) tells us,

"Now faith is the substance of things hoped for, the evidence of things not seen."

In the following verse, Jesus asked the men whether they believed He was able to do what they asked, and then acted on the faith they displayed:

"And when He had come into the house, the blind men came to Him. And Jesus said to them, "Do you believe that I am able to do this?" They said to Him, "Yes, Lord." Then He touched their eyes, saying, "According to your faith let it be to you." (Matthew 9:28-29 NKJV)

You receive the measure of faith once you are saved, then it becomes vital for you to study God's Word so that your faith can be increased.

9. You Must Believe to Receive.

One of the most powerful forces in the world is unbelief. Even Jesus couldn't work where there was unbelief,
"Now He did not do many mighty works there because of their unbelief." (Matthew 13:58, NKJV)

Doubt occurs when you allow fear to take hold of your mind instead of trusting in God. Fearful and unbelieving thoughts, placed into your mind by the enemy, need to be

249

rejected and replaced with instances of where God has come through for you in the past. Recalling these times will remind you that God will do it again.

> *"Casting down arguments and every high thing that exalts itself against the knowledge of God, bringing every thought into captivity to the obedience of Christ."* (2 Corinthians 10:5 NKJV)

In Mark 9:23 (NKJV), Jesus explained the importance of believing God's promises in difficult situations, saying, "If you can believe, all things are possible to him who believes."

10. Have Godly Desires.

Whose desires do you spend your time trying to fulfil? Are you chasing your desires, or are they the Lord's? God makes it clear in the following scripture that you must commit yourself to Him and delight yourself in His ways before you receive the desires of your heart:

> *"Delight yourself also in the LORD, And He shall give you the desires of your heart. Commit your way to the LORD Trust also in Him, And He shall bring it to pass."* (Psalm 37:4-5 NKJV)

The desire to acquire money should come from a place of trust in God and a will to use it in His service. Money is merely a tool to get the work of God accomplished. Jesus equated the desire for worldly possessions and riches with idolatry when he said:

> *"No one can serve two masters; for either he will hate the one and love the other, or else he will be loyal to the*

one and despise the other. *You cannot serve God and mammon."* (Matthew 6:24 NKJV)

11. Don't Look Back.

Having a fascination with former sins holds people back from progressing in their Christian walk, often without them realizing it. Our past is all too frequently the devil's playground, and it prevents us from growing in our relationship with God. Jesus warns us about this in scripture:

> *"But Jesus said to him, 'No one, having put his hand to the plow, and looking back, is fit for the kingdom of God.'"* (Luke 9:62 NKJV)

When we choose to follow Jesus and ask His forgiveness for our past sins, we must believe He has forgiven us as His Word says, and then we must forgive ourselves. We must choose to leave the past behind and look ahead to what God has planned for us, as Paul urges in the following verse:

> *"Brethren, I do not count myself to have apprehended; but one thing I do, forgetting those things which are behind and reaching forward to those things which are ahead."* (Philippians 3:13 NKJV)

12. Prevent Marital Conflict.

Men, do you sometimes feel God is not hearing your prayers? It may be that the fulfillment of your prayers is being obstructed by the way you treat your wife. Are you honouring her and treating her with compassionate understanding? The Bible is clear on how to treat your wife:

> *"Husbands, likewise, dwell with them with under-standing, giving honour to the wife, as to the weaker vessel, and as being heirs together of the grace of life, that your prayers may not be hindered."* (1 Peter 3:7 NKJV)

Jesus set the standard on how to love and cherish a wife and following His example will improve your relationship with your wife and with God:

> *"Husbands, love your wives, just as Christ also loved the church and gave Himself for her."* (Ephesians 5:25 NKJV)

Here is a note to all the men reading this book. Statistically, 80% of the church's intercessors are women. Why? I don't know, but I can guess. They hear from God better than men do because they don't have their pride and egos in the way. Men, listen up! When your wife speaks, there is a good chance it is God. Shut up and listen (and women, don't abuse your gift, or He will take it away from you).

13. Avoid Strife.

Strife and conflict of any kind are unhealthy for your Christian walk. When we pray for peace, we must be prepared to be peacemakers in all situations.

> *"If it is possible, as much as depends on you, live peace-ably with all men."* (Romans 12:18 NKJV)

Striving to serve God means we must also be gentle with those around us:

> *"And a servant of the Lord must not quarrel but be gentle to all, able to teach, patient."* (2 Timothy 2:24, NKJV)

14. Honour Your Man of God.

It is your pastor if you are unclear about who your man of God is! Your man of God is the second most important person in your spiritual life after Jesus. If that is not the case, find a new church. God's Word tells us anyone teaching the Word is worthy of double honour (1 Timothy 5:17). This sentiment is echoed throughout the Bible:

> *"Behold, I have given the children of Levi all the tithes in Israel as an inheritance in return for the work which they perform."* (Numbers 18:21 NKJV)

> *"Let the elders who rule well be counted worthy of double honour, especially those who labour in the word and doctrine. For the Scripture says, "You shall not muzzle an ox while it treads out the grain," and, "The labourer is worthy of his wages."* (1 Timothy 5:17-18 NKJV)

As church members, we should be going out of our way to bless our pastor and his spouse as much as possible. Let's be obedient to God's Word and give them double the honour.

15. We Are Commanded to Work.

God's intention was always for us to work. When God told Adam to *"Subdue the Earth"* in Genesis 1:28, He knew it would take some effort and work for this to happen. Verse 15 of the next chapter tells us,

> *"Then the Lord God took the man and put him in the garden of Eden to tend and keep it."* (Genesis 2:15 NKJV)

To "tend and keep" the garden meant a lot of work. Proverbs warns,

> *"The soul of a lazy man desires, and has nothing; But the soul of the diligent shall be made rich."* (Proverbs 13:4 NKJV)

Paul frequently chose not to accept support from the churches he planted, even though he could have; rather working with his hands while he ministered to the people, saying:

> *"For even when we were with you, we commanded you this: If anyone will not work, neither shall he eat..."* (2 Thessalonians 3:10 NKJV)

Be a good worker and work hard because though you may think you are working for your employer, you are ultimately working for God. You work to increase your giving and not work to make a living. You don't work for your living because God supplies all your needs according to his riches in glory (Philippians 4:19).

If you are an employer, you probably know the verse in Colossians 3:23-24 well, which tells Christian employees they should work hard to serve their employer as if they are doing it for the Lord. I agree with this, but it works both ways. The emphasis is on the employer to set an example of caring for people, especially for young employees who may be in their first full-time working position. Setting a Christian example is vital to the businessman's success and is pleasing to God. If God has given you the responsibility of employing people, you should pay your staff well. Malachi 3:5 says that God will swiftly judge those who oppress people about their wages.

16. Be Patient - Don't Get Discouraged.

When you sow your seed, the harvest is often not instantly received, but you must take your stand and believe you have received what God's Word promises. Go on about your business, patiently waiting for your harvest to come. Do not waver. Stand without doubting; your harvest will come when you have faithfully stood. James 1:3-4 (NKJV) says,

> *"Knowing that the testing of your faith produces patience. But let patience have its perfect work, that you may be perfect and complete, lacking nothing."*

17. Be Careful What You Think.

A well-known but often ignored proverb is,

> *"For as he thinks in his heart, so is he."* (Proverbs 23:7 NKJV)

Factual knowledge is obtained from the visible world around us. The visible world, though, is temporary and subject to constant change. God says,

> *"For I am the Lord, I do not change."* (Malachi 3:6 NKJV)

Only be influenced by faith knowledge. The basis of faith-knowledge is what the Bible tells you God has promised. When you believe what God says over what your circumstances reflect, the miracles of God can freely flow through the open doors of Heaven.

> *"So, Jesus answered and said to them, "Have faith in God. For assuredly, I say to you, whoever says to this*

mountain, 'Be removed and be cast into the sea,' and does not doubt in his heart, but believes that those things he says will be done, he will have whatever he says. Therefore, I say to you, whatever things you ask when you pray, believe that you receive them, and you will have them." (Mark 11:22-24 NKJV)

The conquering of your thought life will guard your heart against things rising against the Word of God. Our life is what our thoughts make it. Change your thoughts, and you can change your world.

18. Be Careful How You Speak.

One of the biggest mistakes we make is how we use the words we speak. The Bible tells us life is in the power of the tongue:

"Death and life are in the power of the tongue, and those who love it will eat its fruit." (Proverbs 18:21 NKJV)

We can speak life or death over people and situations, so we need to carefully consider what we say in our day-to-day lives:

"A wholesome tongue is a tree of life, but perverseness in it breaks the spirit." (Proverbs 15:4 NKJV)

The words you speak will have consequences for those they are spoken over, as well as in your own life. Jesus warns us of this:

"For by your words you will be justified, and by your words you will be condemned." (Matthew 12:37 NKJV)

256

19. Pay Your Vows.

Don't make a pledge in haste or in the joy of the moment, because not fulfilling that pledge is a sin against God.

> *"When you make a vow to the LORD your God, you shall not delay to pay it; for the LORD your God will surely require it of you, and it would be sin to you. But if you abstain from vowing, it shall not be sin to you. That which has gone from your lips you shall keep and perform, for you voluntarily vowed to the LORD your God what you have promised with your mouth."* (Deuteronomy 23:21-23 NKJV)

In Ecclesiastes 5:5 (NKJV) we are told,

> *"Better not to vow than to vow and not pay."*

A vow is a pledge or promises to someone. If you have made a hasty pledge or vow and could not pay it, you can correct the unpaid vow by honouring the commitment and adding 20 percent to the total, as Leviticus 27:13 tells us.

20. Steward Faithfully What You Have Received.

In Matthew 25:14-30, Jesus relates a parable about the proper use of the talents you have received and warns us to be fruitful with our talents, or they could be taken away. We may think our ability to obtain wealth comes from within us, but God says our earning power comes from Him:

> *"And you shall remember the LORD your God, for it is He who gives you power to get wealth, that He may establish His covenant which He swore to your fathers, as it is this day."* (Deuteronomy 8:18 KJV)

From these passages we can see God has given us the power to get wealth so that we can be His faithful stewards. Is the money you earn yours to fund your lifestyle or does it belong to God to fund His harvest?

21. Discern, Not Deceive the Lord's Body.

The word "discern" means recognizing and giving proper place to something. God's Word cautions us to examine ourselves, so as to avoid judgment before partaking in communion:

> "Therefore, whoever eats this bread or drinks this cup of the Lord in an unworthy manner will be guilty of the body and blood of the Lord. But let a man examine himself, and so let him eat of the bread and drink of the cup. For he who eats and drinks in an unworthy manner eats and drinks judgment to himself, not discerning the Lord's body." (1 Corinthians 11:27-29 NKJV)

In 1 Corinthians 10:16-17 (NKJV), Paul explains that because believers all partake in the communion of the body of Christ, we,

> though many, are one bread and one body; for we all partake of that one bread."

We must, therefore, treat the Church - the Body of Christ - with the same discernment as with the body and blood of Jesus, not deceiving ourselves or each other.

22. Don't Love Money.

We all know the verse in 1 Timothy 6:10 (NKJV) that tells us, *"the love of money is the root of all kinds of evil,"*

and we are aware of the evil things people will do for money, but we seldom consider our desire for wealth as evil. I encourage you to examine your motives to ensure your accumulation of capital does not stem from doubt in God's supply. When we save and invest, are we good stewards so we can give to the Kingdom of God or store up for a "rainy day?" Does that rainy day reflect our doubt about God's supply? Or could it be greed or laziness? Jesus put it this way:

> *Then He spoke a parable to them, saying: "The ground of a certain rich man yielded plentifully. And he thought within himself, saying, 'What shall I do, since I have no room to store my crops?' So, he said, 'I will do this: I will pull down my barns and build greater, and there I will store all my crops and my goods. And I will say to my soul, "Soul, you have many goods laid up for many years; take your ease; eat, drink, and be merry."' But God said to him, 'Fool! This night your soul will be required of you; then whose will those things be which you have provided?' "So is he who lays up treasure for himself, and is not rich toward God."* (Luke 12:16-21 NKJV)

There is nothing wrong with having money, as long as it doesn't have you!

> *"For what will it profit a man if he gains the whole world, and loses his own soul?"* (Mark 8:36 NKJV)

23. Stay out of Debt.

To be good stewards of what God has provided us with we need to learn about money management, and then combine that knowledge with what the Bible teaches. Proverbs 22:7 (ESV) reveals the basic truth,

"the borrower is the slave of the lender."

If you must buy on credit (for example, a home for your family), make sure the item's value can cover the debt if sold. Never buy what you can't afford by spending what you haven't earned yet.

24. Avoid the Curse of Poverty by Teaching Your Children Biblical Economics.

Our society trains our children to live in debt. To reiterate a point from an earlier chapter, let me just run down a small list again of the debt-oriented lives to which we expose our children each day:

1. They live in houses with a thirty-year mortgage.
2. They wear clothes purchased with credit cards.
3. Those same clothes are washed in washing machines purchased on monthly payment plans.
4. They study from mortgaged computers.
5. They watch mortgaged televisions.
6. They sleep on mortgaged beds.
7. They are born into a family up to its eyeballs in debt.
8. They live eighteen to twenty-five years in this debt-ridden environment.
9. When they are old enough to drive, we usually co-sign a bank loan to purchase their first automobile.

By so doing, we launch them into their own ocean of debt, never to be debt free again.

25. Give to the Poor.

The following verses seem to suggest that giving to the poor is like depositing into a heavenly bank account:

"Blessed is he who considers the poor; The LORD will deliver him in time of trouble." (Psalm 41:1 NKJV)

"He who has pity on the poor lends to the LORD, And He will pay back what he has given." (Proverbs 19:17)

26. Shun Religious Tradition.

Religion is one of the worst things that ever happened to the body of Christ. Billy Graham used the example of a vaccination to demonstrate how religion keeps people from a relationship with God. When we receive a vaccination for measles, we are, in the real sense of the word, receiving a watered-down version of that actual disease. This is because a little "taste" of the measles germ is enough to activate the white corpuscles in your body, which then recognize the germ and know how to find and resist it in the future. Dr. Graham's point was that we get inoculated with just enough religion to keep us from a real and personal connection with Jesus Christ. Religion is a false obedience to God, and Jesus told the Pharisees and scribes exactly this when He said,

"Thus, you have made the commandment of God of no effect by your tradition." (Matthew 15:6b KJV)

The two main kinds of religious traditions are:

1. Ceremonial
2. Traditional interpretation of God's Word, which include:

- Watering down the Word, so as not to offend anyone.
- "You never know what God will do" - The Bible tells us exactly what God will do.
- "The Lord giveth and the Lord taketh away" - God rebuked Job for saying this.
- "Healing has passed away" - The Book of Acts has never ended, so we are living in the same Holy Spirit power today.
- "A rich man can't get into Heaven" - Nowhere does the Word of God say this.

Church denominations are often the ones that teach and keep these traditions. An aunt of mine, who had made an altar cloth for her church, became offended over the fact that the altar guild was not using the cloth correctly, as she believed they should. She was so upset because her religious tradition had been offended that she stopped going to church!

Doc's Book Club: Read *"Pagan Christianity?"* by Frank Viola.

27. Receive God's Blessings Gracefully.

We must recognize when God is blessing us through someone else, because it is often our pride that wants to refuse help from others. Learn to simply say, "Thank you," not "Oh, you shouldn't have!" False humility isn't humility at all.

262

28. Gain Understanding.

Jesus said that with whatever means you have when you give, your ability to receive will be either expanded or limited.

> *"If anyone has ears to hear, let him hear." Then He said to them, "Take heed what you hear. With the same measure you use, it will be measured to you; and to you who hear, more will be given. For whoever has, to him more will be given; but whoever does not have, even what he has will be taken away from him." Mark 4:23-25 (NKJV)*

Included in this is your understanding. If you understand little, you will receive little. If you understand much, you will receive much. The more you know, the more you can receive. Perhaps God is not pouring part of the end-time harvest into your hands because you cannot manage what you have, and you have little understanding of what to do with the blessing He wants to pour into your hands. In other words, He is waiting for you to "get it together."

In the parable of The Sower, Jesus said,

> *"When anyone hears the word of the kingdom, and does not understand it, then the wicked one comes and snatches away what was sown in his heart. This is he who received seed by the wayside." (Matthew 13:19 NKJV)*

Jesus continues in verse 23 by saying,

> *"But he who received seed on the good ground is he who hears the word and understands it, who indeed bears fruit and produces: some a hundredfold, some sixty, some thirty." (Matthew 13:23 NKJV)*

In Proverbs, we read the importance of gaining under-standing in our lives:

> *"Get wisdom! Get understanding! Do not forget, nor turn away from the words of my mouth. Do not forsake her, and she will preserve you; Love her, and she will keep you. Wisdom is the principal thing; Therefore, get wisdom. And in all your getting, get understanding."* (Proverbs. 4:5-7 NKJV)

29. Don't Hide Sins - Confess and Repent.

Regarding his prayers, the psalmist says,

> *"If I regard iniquity in my heart, The Lord will not hear."* (Psalm 66:18 NKJV)

As believers and followers of Jesus, we are called to be a light to the world. We cannot sin in secret because God knows everything (1 John 3:20). You may fool others for a short while, but your life will soon reflect the evidence of your ways. What is raging in our society today is online pornography - yes, even amongst Christians. I mean, why not? Watch it, and a quick-click on your mouse, and it all disappears, right? No, Holy Spirit knows all about it. It can and often does become an addiction, and then the cracks in a person's personality start with the lying, then the sin of shame and regret, anger... I know of a pastor in Texas whose full-time ministry is to counsel and deliver pastors from pornography addiction. (yes, you read that correctly - pastors)!

> *"He who covers his sins will not prosper, but whoever confesses and forsakes them will have mercy."* (Proverbs 28:13 NKJV)

30. Don't Raise Money - Release it.

Christians often ask, "What would Jesus do?" I wonder why they ask this because they usually don't do it when they find out! Nowhere in the Bible does it tell us Jesus raised funds for His ministry. When He needed money, He trusted God and once even had His disciple catch a fish, which produced a coin for Him (Matthew 17:27).

Instead of following in His footsteps and using our faith, we arrange Bingo nights, White Elephant sales, chicken dinners, TV appeals, and whatever else we can think of, all to keep the church doors open. There is no faith in raising money in this way. The problem is that churches depend on these fundraising events instead of trusting God to meet their needs. If every Christian tithed, there would not be any fundraising. So, what would Jesus do? I can tell you what He did - He tithed and trusted God.

I know of a Christian-based organization specializing in summer horse camps and other outdoor activities. They do not tithe, and they struggle to keep the doors open every year. They grovel for money year-round, underpay their staff (read Malachi chapter 3 to see what happens when you do that), and in December, they email a plea for money. Over the winter, they host a "pie auction," where people are lured with food and entertainment bids and pay hundreds of dollars for a home-baked pie. This is all done, of course, with the justification that "it is for a good cause." Why do people have to be entertained before they give? And they only will if they get a tax receipt. Sounds peachy. But there is nothing scriptural about it! Jesus never raised money, so why should we? If I oversaw this outfit, I would do this:

1. Tithe to other camps and churches (and the only reason they don't is either ignorance, fear or both).
2. Pay their staff a decent and honest wage.
3. Live by faith, not fear.
4. Have regular events not filled with entertainment and other "fundraising" deals but have an excellent "barn burning" worship and dinner, with testimonies, healings/deliverances and an altar set-up so that people could come forth and plant their financial seeds in good soil. Why do the givers feel they need to get something? How about just praising the Lord and giving???

31. Unbelief.

People frequently confuse unbelief with lack of faith. When a man asked Jesus to heal his son,

> *"Jesus said to him, 'If you can believe, all things are possible to him who believes.' The man replied, 'Lord, I believe; help my unbelief!'"* (Mark 9:24 NKJV)

The difference between belief and unbelief is trust in whether God is able and willing to provide what we ask. The man asking Jesus to heal his son had no doubt Jesus could heal his son; his unbelief arose in whether he believed Jesus was willing to heal his son.

We may subconsciously feel God would be unwilling to answer our prayers for many reasons. Some of these may include feeling unworthy of God's consideration or believing that what we ask is too small in God's grand scheme of things to warrant His attention. Reject these unbiblical ideas and refuse evil imaginations. Refuse to accept sickness when believing for healing. Don't receive thoughts of financial failure when you believe in God for your promised position. God

> *"is able to do exceedingly abundantly above all that we ask or think, according to the power that works in us."* (Ephesians 3:20 NKJV)

Conclusion

Well, you made it to the end of my book, for which I am sincerely grateful. You pushed through the "bulldozing," I pray Holy Spirit helped you gain some new revelation from what I presented. Although I am straightforward, please believe this book was written in love from a lifetime of practice to help free the Church and, by extension, the world (when they are saved) from the demonic grip of poverty.

God wants you free. Free to never lack. Free to bless others. Free to spread the gospel. This is your ultimate reason to understand biblical economics. Please re-read this book, using it as a manual. Practice the biblical knowledge you have learned here - I promise it will change your life. As necessary, share a copy with a friend or loved one struggling in poverty. Some people may be resistant, but they will give the truth a chance when someone is desperate enough.

> *"Beloved, I pray that you may prosper in all things and be in health, just as your soul prospers."* (3 John 2:2 NKJV)

I hope and pray that this book will completely change people's lives, as the information in it completely changed me. What you have read through these pages has taken me over 30 years to learn. Two things prevent people from having any level of spiritual, emotional, physical and financial success in life:

1. wisdom - (i.e., the "know-how" to do it, which comes from the Bible)
2. discipline - the ability to carry it out once you have learned it.

Life is not easy, and there is no free ticket for anyone. However, I do know one thing; life is a lot easier when you can use the power of the Word of God to change your life. Years ago, an unsaved person debated with me whether heaven and hell existed. I responded, "If there is no God or Heaven and I am wrong, and consequently I have wasted my life. If I am right, you, sir, have wasted eternity." That made him stop and think! Are you a gambling man? I'm not....

You have finished the book; now what?

Have you ever heard of the "Pareto Principle?" You probably know it better as the 80/20 rule. It was named after its founder, the Italian economist Vilfredo Pareto, in 1895. He noticed that people in society seemed to divide naturally into what he called the "vital few," or the top 20 percent in terms of money and influence, and the "trivial many," or the bottom 80 percent.

In terms of this book and the study guide, the 80/20 rule translates into this: 80% of the readers (or students in my seminars) will say, "Gee, this is interesting information."

Only 20% of the readers/students will take the information, study it and make the necessary changes in their lives.

My question to you, dear reader, is which group you will be in? The 80% or the 20%? Wouldn't it be amazing if those two numbers could be reversed? How about 80% of you take this information and revolutionize your life? Then go and teach it to others. Well, it is up to you... What will you do?

Drop me an email and give me your testimony.

Blessings, and Happy Trails,

Dr. S. R. Watkins

Note: I teach this entire book in 12 hours. If you or your church will like to sponsor one of these seminars, connect with me through my website. I do not charge for teaching the course but request two love offerings be taken for my ministry (we all have expenses in life)! You can charge for the seminar or host for free as a church. You or your church must agree to pay my travel, food and accommodation expenses. Generally, I teach 3 hours Friday night, all day Saturday, and then give a message at your Sunday service if you desire. I am also available for individual financial consulting, and there is no charge for it, as I am not a certified financial planner and, therefore, not licensed to charge a fee. I also consult with church boards as well. My contact information is on the website.

Additionally, I teach a variety of different courses, I consult to churches and charities as well. All this information is on my website. www.newstartministries.ca

S.R. WATKINS

EPILOGUE - MY STORY

HOW I GOT FROM WHERE I WAS TO WHERE I AM.

I was born and raised in the Anglican Church, coming from a long heritage of Anglicans on both sides of my family. I remember starting Sunday school at St. Mark's Anglican Church in Calgary at age four. "Growing" through the ranks, I followed the Anglican tradition and was confirmed at age 16. By 20, I was like many young people of that generation; I didn't know if there was a God, and I certainly did not live what would be called a "Christian lifestyle."

In January 1981, when my brother experienced a massive personal crisis, he connected with our former and retired priest from our family church, who directed him to a book by Rev. Dennis Bennett called *"Nine O'clock in the Morning"* (in reference to Acts 2). The book relates to the "discovery" of the charismatic movement that Rev. Bennett had as an Anglican. The book had quite an effect on my brother, so much so that he gave me a copy and insisted that I read it. I was utterly dumbfounded when I heard things like "praying in tongues, laying on of hands, people getting healed," etc. Despite warming the pew in the Anglican church for most of my life, I had never heard of such things. How could I have missed all of this? Further, was all this "charismatic stuff" actual or fake?

Being a rednecked Albertan, doing a "snow job" on me wasn't easy!

I remember spending hours at the library conducting research (long before the internet)! and reading every book I could get my hands on. Then in August 1981, Billy Graham hosted one of his crusades at McMahon Stadium in Calgary. Having just graduated from business school, I was unemployed, primarily due to the infamous NEP (National Energy Policy) brought in by Pierre Trudeau, which destroyed the economy of Alberta (and now his son is repeating that, but that is another book)! With time on my hands, I decided to volunteer at the Crusades and was assigned to work at the book table.

At the training sessions, we were told that when Dr. Graham "gives the invitation," that would be our queue to leave our seats and be prepared to return and work at the book table. I remember thinking to myself, "invitation to what? Lunch?" I had no clue.... (but I was smart enough not to open my big mouth and let everybody else know how ignorant I was...)

Dr. Graham concluded his message on the first night with the same earth-shattering questions he often asked. "Do you know Jesus? You may be a church member, you may be in the choir, you may have taught Sunday school, or you may be confirmed (that one hit home)! Still, suppose you have never decided to ask Jesus into your heart. In that case, you are not saved." I was housesitting for some friends at the time. After that first night, I didn't sleep a wink. How could it possibly be that I had spent 16 years of my life in the church and was not, "born again?" It was not worth the risk when I contemplated that if Dr. Graham was right, I was going straight to hell! Needless to say, the next night, I skipped working at the book table and went forward after the "invitation." (and BTW, there was no lunch!)

Like many people, I expected a considerable emotional experience with bells and whistles. Nothing like that happened - and usually doesn't for most people, as becoming born-again is not an emotional experience but a spiritual one. Within two months of this event, my brother and I bought a small business, and I moved to Banff, Alberta, in October to take possession of it. I returned to the Anglican Church there because that was all I knew. Unfortunately, the spiritually dead experiences that I had in my previous church life continued for several years. I grew a little bit, but not much.

In 1992, the priest of our church in Banff brought in some out-of-town speakers who hosted a "Life in the Spirit conference." I am indebted to brothers Ron and Ken Fabbi of Lethbridge, Alberta, for teaching that course, as it changed my life. Looking back, I realize how incredibly ignorant my new wife and I were about anything to do with Holy Spirit. Around that time, my brother gave me a VHS tape with a message called, *"Hey, That's My Harvest,"* preached by a Cajun from Louisiana named Jesse Duplantis. I had never heard of this guy, nor had I ever heard of a message like that! I was so cynical and red-necked that after watching it, I thought, "Just another one of those TV evangelists trying to get my money." I asked my brother who this "con man" was, and he replied, "Oh, he's connected with Kenneth Copeland." "Who's he?" I asked. "He's a preacher from Texas and is having a convention in Anaheim in July."

I had been married only a few months, and as Charles Capps would say, "We were so poor we couldn't pay attention." - and ignorant too! I was incredibly frustrated over things I was starting to hear about faith, prosperity, healing, and deliverance. How did I know nothing about these things, and what were they about? In July 1992, we pulled out our credit cards and flew to Anaheim, California, for a six-day "Kenneth Copeland West Coast Believers Convention."

On the first day, we walked into the auditorium and saw people jumping up and down to the music, throwing their hands in the air and acting pretty bizarre! We do not do that in the Anglican Church! I questioned my sanity because I remember saying, "I don't like attending our church services that are one hour long, so how am I going to survive six days of this!" Kenneth Copeland said, "Turn around to two or three people, shake their hand, and tell them that you love them in the Lord." You've got to be kidding, me??!!

I survived until Jerry Savelle came out to speak and said, "Turn around to two or three people, hug them, and tell them that you love them in the Lord!" I turned to my wife and said, "Rapture! Now!" I honestly thought I would die inside and decided there was no way I was turning around and hugging anybody! However, I forgot one thing; we were not sitting in the front row, and there was a row of people in front of us! The next thing I knew, a big lady turned around, wanting to hug me! I think she probably saw the fear of God in my eyes and face and so graciously put her hand out, and we shook hands. I don't even think I said a word; I was shocked. I managed to get back at Jerry Savelle, though; every time he came out to speak, I just coincidentally had to go to the washroom, so I missed the hugging orgy; and that's where I was spiritually in July 1992.

By the end of the convention, my wife and I were putting our hands in the air, joining in the worship, and we sat back and watched complete miracles taking place. We saw people get out of wheelchairs and walk; we heard testimonies of people being healed of AIDS; we heard testimonies of people getting out of financial difficulty through the laws of seedtime and harvest - in short, our lives were completely changed. By the end of the week, we were in tears about having to go home!

It has been quite a roller coaster of growth and development since then. We outgrew the Anglican Church and drove to Calgary every Sunday for two years to attend Victory Churches International. Every Sunday, we would buy the cassette tape of the previous Sunday's message and play it back on our 1.5 hour drive home. We were so hungry! We attended three more Believers Conventions, and I think I've watched probably seven or eight in the last 30 years, but now, of course, we can watch them live, stream-fed on my computer (you've got to love all this technology)! Over time, we were introduced to other ministries such as Kenneth Hagin, Keith Moore, Benny Hinn, Joyce Meyer, Derek Prince, Reinhard Bonnke, and many others. Repeatedly, I have gone on a bit of a witch hunt, checking these ministries, speaking to their staff, putting the Word of God to the test in my life, etc. Being a businessman, I was interested in the so-called "prosperity message,"- a name I do not like because it is not a "message;" it's the Word of God - and eventually, I was asked to teach a course at the charismatic Anglican church we were attending in the Town of Okotoks, Alberta.

For the next six years, I attended conferences at Word of Life Church in Red Deer, Alberta, where I met a man who would eventually become my spiritual father and mentor,

Dr. C. Peter Wagner. He taught a two-day seminar every year after the three-day conference, and I attended every one. Peter had retired from Fuller Seminary and started his school, Wagner Leadership Institute, now Wagner University. It was a chance for laypeople like myself, who had careers and couldn't go to seminary, to advance their education in the Word of God. It was correspondence, which accommodated my schedule of being self-employed. I started at the bottom and earned an Associate Certificate, and then 11 years later, I completed my Bachelor, Master, and Doctorate of Practical Ministry (aka Apostolic Leadership). I cannot begin to tell you the learning curve I experienced! One of my legacies with Peter is that I was the last person he graduated at a Wagner University convocation before he passed away (with a name like "Watkins," I am usually the last guy on the list). I can't tell you how much I miss him; I am very much indebted to Peter and his wife, Doris.

Along the way, I learned a great deal about spiritual warfare and forgiveness. I spent ten years studying inner healing and deliverance with the most credible people in the world at the International Society of Deliverance Ministers (started by Peter Wagner and his wife, Doris - www.isdm.org). I have had several deliverance sessions and have been set free of the generational sins and curses plaguing my family. In Peter's classes, he often made mention of Chuck Pierce and Robert Heidler. Finally, one day I asked Peter, "Who are these people?" He told me, and I have been connected with The Global Spheres Center, in Corinth, Texas, for over 20 years, watching their services live via the internet every Sunday. I have attended MANY of their conferences and usually fly down there once or twice a year - www.gloryofzion.org. Dr. Robert Heidler has taught me more than anyone else in my life. I regard Robert as the most outstanding teacher in the body of Christ today. His wife, Linda, has been a tremendous personal support to my family and me, and she is a solid teacher in her own right. I have learned all about the rise of the Messianic Church, the Apostolic Church, God's calendar, alignment with the Holy Spirit, etc., and I am still learning every Sunday morning...

When I first started attending Glory of Zion, I thought the people and their services were a bit "kooky." Still, I soon learned that my red-necked attitude was coming out again (technically, is it called a "spirit of religion"- rampant in today's church). It seems human nature that we tend to criticize what we don't understand, so rather than do that, I studied the scriptures and found the exact opposite. Glory of Zion is a "cutting-edge" church and does everything "by the book" - The Book of Acts. Chuck and his brother, Keith, have taught me about prophecy, thank you! The music/dance there has taught me all about worship (thank you, Elaine, John, James, Leanne, Maggie, Justin, Darren, and the team). The incredible staff, including Ann, Anita, Carol, Bill, Cindy, Tyler, Janice, Barbara (both of them)!, Lisa, Austin, Sandra, Lane, Klancy, Donna, Chad, Susan, Odilia and a host of other people that I don't know, have changed my life. Thanks, everyone!

In 2015, I had two prophetic words directing me to write a book. I knew what I was supposed to do: take my biblical economics course and turn it into a book. I kept putting it off for years because I didn't want to do it. I knew that writing a book would be an enormous amount of work. However, when I lost out on a teaching position because I didn't have a Ph.D., I started researching on the internet to get one with my existing credentials. I found three options and settled on The Christian Bible Institute & Seminary in

Houston, Texas. For that reason, I have written this book (not to mention that I am finally being obedient)!

In March 2018, I made my second ministry trip to Rwanda, where I hosted two three-day conferences exclusively for pastors and then taught at Sunday services. I then met my daughter in Israel, where we went on a 10-day bus tour, which was quite life-changing. Since then, I have been involved with Compassion Canada and sponsor six children in Rwanda. In April 2019, I was invited to join the Canadian Coalition of Apostolic Leaders, which automatically gave me membership into the International Coalition of Apostolic Leaders based in Fort Worth, Texas. I attended my first meeting there in October 2019, and it was indeed a transforming experience. Thank you, Dr. Phil Nordin!

In January 2020, the Lord told me to start a publishing business/ministry to produce more books. Then during covid, He told me to write a daily devotional, and when it was printed, I wrote yet another one (volume 2). I have ten posters called "The Christian Manifesto Series," and a secular business book is also "in the works." as well as a book for young people called "Prayer Pilot." I have no shortage of projects! Watch at some future date for these products on either www.newstartministries.ca.

In January 2025, I will embark on a four-month (God willing) around-the-world working excursion, including a month of teaching/missions in Rwanda. There are over one million orphans in Rwanda, and I use donated funds to buy clothes and live goats for them. If you wish to support this venture, please go to my website. (www.newstartministries.ca)

So now what? Do I think I know it all? NO! The biggest thing I learned about studying the Bible is that the more you learn, the more you realize how much you don't know, and you must keep studying. Some days I think I haven't even scratched the surface...

Suggested Reading

Be in Health - Dr. Henry Wright
The Believer's Authority - Kenneth Hagin
Battlefield of the Mind - Joyce Meyer
Blessing or Curse - Derek Prince
The Blessing - Kenneth Copeland
Change Agent - Os Hillman
Deceived; Who Me? - Craig Hill
Failing Forward - John C. Maxwell
Five Wealth Secrets 96% of Us Don't Know - Craig Hill
The Apostolic Church Arising - Dr. Robert Heidler and Dr. Chuck Pierce
Hello Tomorrow - Dr. Cindy Trimm
How to Reach Your Life Goals - Dr. Peter Daniels
Living Your Strengths - Donald O. Clifton
Managing God's Mutual Funds - Kenneth Copeland
The Millionaire Mind - Thomas J. Stanley & William D. Danko
The Prayer of Jabez - Bruce Wilkinson
Humility - Andrew Murray
Set Yourself Free - Dr. Robert Heidler
Power in Praise - Merlin Carothers
Put Your Dream to the Test - John Maxwell
Principle of the Path - Andy Stanley
The Purpose Driven Life - Rick Warren
The Awesome Power of Blessing - Richard Brunton
The Messianic Church Arising: Restoring the Church to our Covenant Roots.- Dr. Robert Heidler

The Secrets of the Secret Place - Bob Sorge
Receive Your Healing and Reclaim Your Health - Cal Pierce
The Tongue - A Creative Force - Charles Capps
Wealth, Riches and Money - Craig Hill & Earl Pitts
Wild at Heart - John Eldridge
The Invisible War; what every believer needs to know about satan, demons, and spiritual warfare - Chip Ingram
The 15 Invaluable Laws of Growth - John Maxwell
What's Behind the Ink? - Dr. Bill Sudduth
So Free! - Dr. Bill Sudduth
Victorious Eschatology - Harold R. Eberle
I Give You Authority - Charles Kraft
Deliverance; Rescuing God's People - Pat Legako and Cindy Gribble
God@Work - Rich Marshall
Faith@Work Movement - Os Hillman
Discover Your Spiritual Gifts - Dr. Peter Wagner
Rome's Anathemas - Dr. Selwyn Stevens
Releasing Heaven on Earth - Rev. Dr. Alistair Petrie
Pagan Christianity? - Frank Viola

(Note: I update this list periodically on my website).

I highly recommend any books written by:
Dr. Charles Pierce, Dr. Robert Heidler, Kenneth and/or Gloria Copeland, Dr. Jerry Savelle, Craig Hill, Rev. Dr. Jesse Duplantis, Dr. C. Peter Wagner, Dr. Selwyn Stevens, Barbara Wentroble, Rev. Dr. Alistair Petrie, Kenneth Hagin, John Avanzini, Derek Prince, Cal Pierce, Ron Kendall, John Maxwell, Dr. Joseph Mattera, John Polis, Rich Marshall, Harold R. Eberle, Andy Stanley, Charles Stanley, Frank Viola, Keith Moore, Dr. Che Ahn, John Bevere, Drs. Russ and/or Mave Moyer, Robert Henderson, Cindy Jacobs, Joyce Myer, Os Hillman, Isaac Pitre, Dennis Peacocke, Dr. Chuck Pierce and Dr. Henry Wright.

Shopping and Seminars!

Posters:
Available from New Start Ministries for download.
www.newstartministries.ca

Books:
Available from Amazon, Indigo/Chapters, Barnes & Noble,
or order from your favourite bookstore via Ingram Sparks.

1. *"Biblical Economics 101; Living Under God's Financial
Blessing."*
2. *"Life is a Test: Hope in a Confusing World. Volume One"*
3. *"Life is a Test: Hope in a Confusing World. Volume Two"*
4. *"Life is a Test"* volume three will be pinted in 2024.

Teaching, Seminars and Consulting:
Invite Dr. Watkins to your church, conference or business
event!

Pastors, would you and your church like to sponsor a
seminar and have Dr. Watkins teach? Consult with you and
your board? Then book a Biblical Economics 101 weekend.
This seminar is perfect for those who wish to:

• Get out of unnecessary debt.
• Build kingdom wealth.
• Break free from a scarcity and poverty mentality?
• Break the mindset that to be a good Christian, you must
be broke and poor.
• Destroy the lie that if we love God, we must commit to a
life of poverty.
• Learn how wealth and a heart for Jesus go hand-in-hand
and are not mutually exclusive.
• Understand finances through the laws of seedtime and
harvest and how tithing can change your finances.

Learn about:

- False Ideas about Money
- The Purpose of Money
- Does God want you to be Blest? (yes, and out of debt too)!
- God's Economy
- A Study of Wealth and Success
- The Way to Prosperity

The schedule for a Biblical Economics 101 weekend is usually 3 hours Friday night, all day Saturday (12 hours worth of teaching)! and then he can give a message at your Sunday service if you desire. Dr. Watkins can come a few days early or stay a few days after the seminar for individual financial consulting, free of charge.

Dr. Watkins does not charge for teaching his courses, but requests two love offerings be taken for his ministry. As a church, you can charge for the seminar or host it for free.

Additional Teaching Courses:

- Spiritual Gifts (including an individual survey for participants)
- Operating in the Courts of Heaven
- Healing
- Deliverance
- Spiritual Mapping and Cleansing of the Land

For a complete updated list, go to:
www.newstartministries.ca

info@newstartministries.ca

Life is a test...

Hope in a Confusing World

A Daily Devotional
Volume 1

from the author of
"Biblical Economics 101: Living Under God's Financial Blessing"

S. R. Watkins

Life is a test...

Hope in a Confusing World

A Daily Devotional
Volume 2

S. R. Watkins

Another 365 Days of Inspiration, Wisdom and Comfort!

THE BLESSING

In the **NAME** of **JESUS,** I bless you with the **PROMISES** of **GOD**, which are **YES** and **AMEN.** I pray the **HOLY SPIRIT** will make you **HEALTHY** and **STRONG** in **BODY, MIND** and **SPIRIT** and move you in **FAITH** and **EXPECTANCY.**

May **GOD'S ANGELS** be with you to **PROTECT** and **KEEP YOU.**

GOD BLESS YOU WITH:

- **ABILITY, ABUNDANCE**, and an assurance of **HIS LOVE** and **GRACE**
- **CLEAR DIRECTION** and a **CONTROLLED** and **DISCIPLINED LIFE**
- **COURAGE** and **CREATIVITY**
- **SPIRITUAL PERCEPTION** of **HIS TRUTH**
- **GREAT FAITH, HIS FAVOUR** and **MAN'S**
- **GOOD HEALTH** and a **GOOD (AND GODLY) SPOUSE**
- **HANDS** to **BLESS OTHERS**
- **HAPPINESS, FULFILLMENT, CONTENTMENT, HOPE**, and a **GOOD OUTLOOK ON LIFE**
- **A LISTENING EAR, LONG LIFE** and an **OBEDIENT HEART TO THE SPIRIT OF GOD**
- **HIS PEACE, PLEASANT SPEECH,** and a **PLEASANT PERSONALITY**
- **PROMOTION, PROTECTION, PROVISION, SAFETY** and **STRENGTH**
- **FINANCIAL SUCCESS**
- **TRUST AND WISDOM**

AND MAY GOD BLESS YOU WITH:

Goodness and mercy following you all the days of your life, that you might dwell in the house of the Lord forever.

The Lord bless you and keep you.
The Lord makes His face shine upon you and be gracious to you.
The Lord turns His face towards you and gives you peace.

I bless you in the Name of the Father, the Son, and the Holy Spirit. **AMEN.**

What is

FAITH?

Having been saved by **FAITH**, *"If you declare with your mouth, "Jesus is Lord," and believe in your heart that God raised him from the dead, you will be saved."* (Rom. 10:9) It makes sense that we should continue to live by **FAITH**, *"The righteous shall live by faith."* (Rom. 1:17b) What does it mean to live by **FAITH**, though, and how do we do it? The Bible tells us, *"by the* **FAITH** *God has distributed to each of you"* (Rom. 12:3) so we all have **FAITH**. We increase our **FAITH** by hearing the Word of God. Consequently, *"***FAITH** *comes from hearing the message, and the message is heard through the word about Christ."* (Rom. 10:17), and we express **FAITH** by walking in love, *"The only thing that counts is* **FAITH** *expressing itself through love."* (Gal. 5:6) Hebrews 11:6 tells us that if we are not living by **FAITH**, we are not pleasing God, *"And without* **FAITH**, *it is impossible to please God,"* and Rom. 14:23 confirms this by saying that *"everything that does not come from* **FAITH** *is sin."*

Therefore, we are to grab hold of the promises of God, stand on them, confess them, believe them, and exercise our **FAITH**, which is to *"calls into being things that were not."* (Rom. 4:17) Hebrews 11:1 tells us, *"Now* **FAITH** *is confidence in what we hope for and assurance about what we do not see."* In Matthew, *"When he had gone indoors, the blind men came to him, and he asked them, 'Do you believe that I am able to do this?' 'Yes, Lord,' they replied. Then he touched their eyes and said, 'According to your* **FAITH** *let it be done to you;' Their sight was restored."* (Matt. 9:28-29) Finally, we build our **FAITH** by praying in the Holy Spirit, *"by building yourselves up in your most holy* **FAITH** *and praying in the Holy Spirit."* (Jude 20)

Scripture quotations identified NIV are from the Holy Bible, New International Version®. NIV®.

Copyright© 1973, 1978, 1984, 2011 by Biblical, Inc.TM Used by permission of Zondervan. All rights reserved worldwide. www.zondervan.com.

The "Faith" Poster is part of the Christian Manifesto Poster series. Produced in Calgary, Alberta, Canada, by New Start Ministries Ltd. These posters are available for sale from: www.newstartministries.ca COPYRIGHT 2022.

The Fruit of the
SPIRIT

There is a difference between Spiritual Gifts and Spiritual Fruit. Gifts are precisely that; a gift that God gives believers, and they are exactly that, Gifts, not loans with conditions for they are irrevocable (Rom. 11:29). Even if we don't use them or misuse them, we still have them. (The "Gifts of the Spirit" Poster is available as part of this poster series.)

There are 9 Spiritual Fruits that are more like characters of behaviour. Love is listed first, which is then part of the other eight, which are different ways in which love manifests itself.

- Joy is love rejoicing.
- Peace is love resting.
- Long-suffering is love forbearing.
- Kindness is love serving others.
- Goodness is love seeking the best for others.
- Faithfulness is love keeping its promises.
- Gentleness is love ministering to the hurt and pain of others.
- Self-control is love in control.

What is your **Mission** Impossible? *(1)

A mission is a vision given and powered by God through impartation.

The spiritual replication of Jesus into you is the goal of your life.*(2) Any other goal is secondary at best and harmful at worst. God built you to be His Spiritual being and for you to live out your life from His Spirit in you, rather than from within your soul.*(3)

Your mission (should you be willing to accept it) is the biggest gift that God can give you. It will be all life-consuming and give you the clarity to know what your life is all about. When God gives you your mission (ask Him; He will tell you*(4),then preparation will be next:

· What will you have to do to fill the mission?
· What character, knowledge and discipline will you have to do to develop the mission?

Problems are not from a lack of discipline but rather a lack of vision.*(5) If discipline is an issue, you have not received God's full impartation. Using your faith,*(6) God will give you the plans*(7) resources*(8) and energy(9) to accomplish His mission for you.

Be guaranteed that you will be hit with obstacles*(10). God's barbells build spiritual muscle. Sin in you, others and satan creates the barriers you must go through to transform you into being Christ-like. Human soulish will won't work, as it leaves you tired, angry, hurt and bitter.

God → Vision → Mission → Obstacles → Transformation → Goal Achieved

Question: Are you willing to give up your life to another being (God) and lose it so that you can find it*(11) by Him working through you to accomplish the mission you're trying to find?*(12)

*1. Mathew 19:26 *4. John 10:27 *7. Proverbs 8:12 *10. 2 Corinthians 4:8-9
*2. John 3:13 *5. Proverbs 29:18 *8. Deuteronomy 8:18 *11. Mathew 10:39
*3. Romans 8 *6. Hebrews 11:1,6 *9. Galatians 6:9 *12. Luke 19:17; 1 Corinthians 9:24

This is your **LIFE**.

The one that God gave you. Find out what He has called you to do, and do it (think it will be something you like and that you are good at. If in doubt, ask Him.) If you don't like something in the world, then...

Be an agent of change.

If you don't have enough time, shut off your phone, computer, and TV and plant your money into His Kingdom to help preach the Gospel (it isn't your money anyway). If you are looking for the love of your life, stop. You will find them when you start doing what God has called you to do. Jesus loves you, and that is all that matters. Meditate on His Word, do His Word and live His Word. Yes...

It really is that simple.

Emotions are great, but keep them under His control. Look after your body; it is the temple of the Holy Spirit. Open your heart, life and money to people and let your light shine by doing good works. Live by God's faith. Help others to build their dreams and in doing so, you will build your own. Then you can...

Travel & help.

It really is the best education in the world, and you will find your life if you lose it by doing the works of God. Life is not about finding yourself but rather about creating yourself in the image of Jesus and making the world a better place when you leave than when you arrived. The world does not owe you anything. You owe the world everything. Don't talk about your rights. Fulfill your duties and responsibilities. Don't protest, pray. Because...

Life is short.

Billions of people are hungry, cold, poor, sick, hurt, at war, and going to hell because you haven't helped them and told them about Jesus. After all, your real calling in life is to go out and make disciples of all men. It is not about you. So...

What are you waiting for?

The "This is your Life" Poster is part of the Christian Manifesto Poster Series. Produced in Calgary, Alberta, Canada, by New Start Ministries Ltd. These posters are available for sale from: www.newstartministries.ca Copyright 2022

S.R. WATKINS

MONEY.

What God says about

There are over 2480 scriptures that refer to money or stewardship. The words "rich" or "riches" are in the Bible 186 times. "Money" is in the Bible 114 times. Jesus spoke more about money and stewardship than any other subject. The purpose of money is to build up the Kingdom of God (Deuteronomy 8:18) so that the great commission can be fulfilled. (The gospel is free – it just takes money to preach it.)

Jesus was born rich into royalty and said we were to be like Him. The Magi's gifts were worth $400 million in today's dollars.* Jesus owned a house (John 1:38-39), paid taxes (Matthew 17:24), was on the lecture circuit at age 12 (Luke 2:47), ran a business with his dad, had a treasurer, had a staff of 12 and later 72 (Luke 10:17), had people giving financial support to His ministry (Luke 8:2-3), wore designer clothes (John 19:23-24), and became poor once in His life for us on the cross (2 Corinthians 8:9). His first miracle was one of luxury in a setting of wealth (John 2: 1-8) and He had the skills to supply lunch for 5,000 men and their families (John 6:7).

Success is the ability to endure pain; wealth is the ability to obtain what is immediately required,* and prosperity is having enough provision to complete God's instructions.

Money may not bring happiness, but it brings more joy than poverty ever did! Tithing is not a method of getting money from you but a method of getting money to you.

Money is the answer to everything. (Ecclesiastes 10:19b)

Poverty is not a financial problem. It is a spiritual one – a curse (Deuteronomy 28: 1). Worldly wealth is all about financial accumulation for self. True prosperity is all about economic expansion for God, who wants you to use it for distribution to others.

Meditate on the Word, and you will be prosperous (Joshua 1:8).

The greatest tragedy of human existence is not knowing what you don't know. Now you know...

So what are you going to do about it?

The "Money" Poster is part of the Christian Manifesto Poster series. Produced in Calgary, Alberta, Canada, by New Start Ministries Ltd. These posters are available for sale from: www.newstartministries.ca COPYRIGHT 2022 (*Dr. Peter J. Daniels with permission).

290

How to be RICH God's way

Tithe 10% of your gross income to your local church. It is not yours or yours to keep. Plant financial seeds into His Kingdom through alms to the poor (like missions), and firstfruits to your church and other ministries. Use cash (not credit or debit cards) as much as possible (when you see money slipping out of your fingers, you will think twice about spending it.) Pay credit card balances immediately when they are due.

Reduce your consumer spending. Learn how to be thrifty and economical in your shopping. Buy used as much as possible.

Pay down the mortgage on your house, which should have a basement suite or some rental income to it. Payments should be weekly, starting on Monday.

Get a retirement plan started when you are 18. Invest wisely in solid "blue-chip, dividend-paying stocks."

Establish an education fund for your children. When they reach college age, they buy a house with the education fund in their name. They get rent-paying roommates to pay the mortgage and pay their own tuition.

Buy term life insurance to care for your loved ones.

Save 10% of your gross income for emergencies. If there is something that you want to buy, learn to save for it by putting 20% of your money away to save for significant expenditures.

Get all the education that you can to get a good, well-paying job with excellent benefits and be a good employee.

Establish a trust fund for your grandchildren.

Start this plan when you are 18, and by retirement, you will be a millionaire.

What **Spiritual Gifts** has God given you?

1. **Administration** - The Gift of Administration is the exceptional power that God gives to Christians to clearly understand the immediate and long-range goals of a particular unit of the Body of Christ and devise and execute effective plans to accomplish those goals. (Luke 14:28-30 • Acts 6:1-7 • Acts 27:11 • 1 Corinthians 12:28 • Titus 1:5)

2. **Apostle** - The Gift of Apostle is the exceptional power that God gives to Christians to assume and exercise divinely imparted authority to establish the foundational government of an assigned sphere of ministry within the Church by setting things in order. (Luke 6:12-13 • 1 Corinthians 12:28 • Ephesians 2:20 • Ephesians 4:11-13)

3. **Celibacy** - The Gift of Celibacy is the exceptional power that God gives to Christians to remain single and enjoy it, to be unmarried and not suffer undue sexual temptations. (Matthew 19:10-12 • 1 Corinthians 7:7-9)

4. **Craftsman** - The Gift of Craftsman is the exceptional power that God gives to Christians to design and craft items based on an inherent skill given by God to create objects to glorify God. (Exodus 28:3 • Exodus 28:28 • Exodus 35:10 • Exodus 35:35 • Exodus 36:4)

5. **Deliverance** - The Gift of Deliverance is the exceptional power that God gives to Christians to cast out demons and evil spirits. (Acts 8:5-8, 16:16-18 • Matthew 12:22-32 • Luke 10:12-20)

6. **Discerning of Spirits** - The Gift of Discerning of spirits is the exceptional power that God gives to Christians to know whether certain behaviour purported to be of a divine reality divine, human or satanic. (Matthew 16:21-23 • Acts 5:1-11 • Acts 16:16-18 • 1 Corinthians 12:10 • 1 John 4:1-6)

7. **Evangelist** - The Gift of Evangelist is the exceptional power that God gives to Christians to share the gospel with non-believers in such a way that they become disciples and responsible members of the Body of Christ. (Acts 8:5-6 • Acts 8:26-40 • Acts 14:21 • Ephesians 4:11-13 • 2 Timothy 4:5)

8. **Exhortation** - The Gift of Exhortation is the exceptional power that God gives to Christians to minister words of comfort, consolation, encouragement to other members of the Body in such a way that they feel helped and healed. (Acts 14:22 • Romans 12:8 • 1 Timothy 4:13 • Hebrews 10:25)

9. **Faith** - The Gift of Faith is the exceptional power that God gives to Christians to discern with extraordinary confidence the will and purposes of God. (Acts 11:22-24 • Romans 4:18-21 • 1 Corinthians 12:9 • Hebrews 11)

10. **Giving** - The Gift of Giving is the exceptional power that God gives to Christians to contribute their material resources to the work of the Lord liberally and cheerfully beyond the tithes and offerings expected of all believers. (Mark 12:41-44 • Romans12:8 • 2 Corinthians 8:1-7 • 2 Corinthians 9:2-8)

11. **Healing** - The Gift of Healing is the exceptional power that God gives to Christians to serve as human intermediaries through whom it pleases God to cure illness and restore health apart from the use of natural means. (Acts 3:1-10 • Acts 5:12-16 • Acts 9:32-35 • Acts 28:7-10 • 1 Corinthians 12:9, 28)

12. **Helps** - The Gift of Helps is the exceptional power that God gives to Christians to invest the talents they have in the lives of other members of the body thus enabling those others to increase the effectiveness of their own spiritual gifts. (Mark 15:40-41 • Luke 8:2-3 • Acts 9:36 • Romans 16:1-2 • 1 Corinthians 12:28)

13. **Hospitality** - The Gift of Hospitality is the exceptional power that God gives to Christians to provide an open house and warm welcome to those in need of food and lodging. (Acts 16:14-15 • Romans 12:9-13 • Romans 16:23 • Hebrews 13:1-2 • 1 Peter 4:9)

14. **Intercession** - The Gift of Intercession is the exceptional power that God gives to Christians to pray for extended periods of time frequently and get specific answers to their prayers, to a degree much greater than that which is expected of the average Christian. (Colossians 1:9-12 • Colossians 4:12-13 • 1 Timothy 2:1-2 • James 5:14-16 • Luke 22:41-44 • 1 Timothy 2:1-2)

15. **Interpretation** - The Gift of Interpretation is the exceptional power God gives Christians to make known in the vernacular the message of another person who speaks in tongues. (1 Corinthians 12:10, 30 • 1 Corinthians 14:13 • 1 Corinthians 14:26-28)

16. **Knowledge** - The Gift of Knowledge is the exceptional power that God gives to Christians to discover, accumulate, analyze, and clarify information and ideas pertinent to the body's well-being. (Acts 5:1-11 • 1 Corinthians 2:14 • 1 Corinthians 12:8 • 2 Corinthians 11:6 • Colossians 2:2-3)

17. **Leadership** - The Gift of Leadership is the exceptional power that God gives to Christians to set goals for the future and to communicate these goals to others in such a way that they voluntarily and harmoniously work together to accomplish these goals for the glory of God. (Luke 9:51 • Romans 12:8 • 1 Timothy 5:17 • Hebrews 13:7, 17)

18. **Mercy** - The Gift of Mercy is the exceptional power that God gives to Christians to feel genuine empathy and compassion for individuals who suffer distressing physical, mental or emotional problems and to translate that compassion into cheerfully done deeds that reflect Christ's love and alleviate the suffering. (Matthew 20:29-34 • Mark 9:41 • Luke 10:33-35 • Acts 11:28-30 • Acts 16:33-34)

19. **Miracles** - The Gift of Miracles is the exceptional power that God gives to Christians to serve as human intermediaries through whom it pleases God to perform powerful acts that observers perceive to have altered the ordinary course of nature. (Acts 9:36-42 • Acts 19:11-20 • Acts 20:7-12 • Romans 15:17-19 • 1 Corinthians 12:8-10, 28-29)

20. **Missionary** - The Gift of Missionary is the exceptional power that God gives to Christians to minister whatever other spiritual gifts they have in a second culture. (Acts 8:4 • Acts 13:2-3 • Acts 22:21 • Romans 10:15 • 1 Corinthians 9:19-23 • Ephesians 3:6-8)

21. **Musician** - The Gift of Musician is the exceptional power that God gives to Christians to play an instrument and/or create and/or perform compositions and/or communicate by song, music that inspires others and offers praise and worship to God. (1 Chronicles 16:41-42 • 2 Chronicles 5:12-13 • Psalm 150 • Deuteronomy 31:19-22, 30-32:44)

22. **Pastor** - The Gift of Pastor is the exceptional power that God gives to Christians to assume long-term responsibility for the spiritual welfare of a group of believers. (John 10:1-18 • Ephesians 4:11-13 • 1 Timothy 3:1-7 • 1 Peter 5:1-3)

23. **Poverty** - The Gift of Poverty is the exceptional power that God gives to Christians to renounce material comfort and luxury and adopt a personal lifestyle equivalent to those living at the poverty level in order to serve God more effectively. (Acts 2:44-45 • Acts 4:34-37 • 1 Corinthians 13:1-3 • 2 Corinthians 6:10 • 2 Corinthians 8:9)

24. **Preaching** - The Gift of Preaching is the exceptional power that God gives to Christians to minister by proclaiming publicly (or through writing) the Word of God to instigate teaching, revelation, wisdom and understanding. (Acts 16:24-26 • Acts 20:20-21 • 1 Corinthians 9:16 • Ephesians 3:1-7)

25. **Prophecy** - The Gift of Prophecy is the exceptional power that God gives to Christians to receive and communicate a message of God to His people through a divinely anointed utterance. (Luke 7:26 • Acts 15:32 • Acts 21:9-11 • 1 Corinthians 12:10, 28 • 1 Corinthians 14:3 • Ephesians 4:11-13)

26. **Service** - The Gift of Service is the exceptional power that God gives to Christians to identify the unmet needs involved in a task related to God's work and make use of available resources to meet those needs and help accomplish the desired results. (Acts 6:1-7 • Romans 12:7 • Galatians 6:2, 10 • 2 Timothy 1:16-18 • Titus 3:14)

27. **Teaching** - The Gift of Teaching is the exceptional power that God gives to Christians to communicate information relevant to the health and ministry of the Body and its members in such a way that others will learn and understand. (Acts 18:24-28 • Acts 20:20-21 • 1 Corinthians 12:28 • Ephesians 4:11-13)

28. **Tongues** - The Gift of Tongues is the exceptional power that God gives to Christians to speak in a language they have never learned and/or to receive and communicate an immediate message of God to His people through a divinely anointed utterance in a language they never learned. (Acts 2:1-13 • Acts 10:44-46 • Acts 19:1-7 • 1 Corinthians 12:10, 28 • 1 Corinthians 14:13-19)

29. **Wisdom** - The Gift of Wisdom is the exceptional power that God gives to Christians to apply the mind of the Holy Spirit in such a way as to receive insight into how given knowledge may best be applied to specific needs arising in the Body of Christ. (Acts 6:3, 10 • 1 Corinthians 2:1-13 • 1 Corinthians 12:8 • James 1:5-6 • 2 Peter 3:15-16)

30. **Worship Leader** - The Gift of Leading worship is the exceptional power that God gives to Christians to accurately discern the heart of God for a particular public worship service, to draw others into an intimate experience with God during the worship time and to allow the Holy Spirit to change directions. (1 Samuel16:23 • 1 Chronicles 9:33 • 2 Chronicles 5:12-14)

Spiritual Gift Classifcations within the Five-Fold Ministry

Apostle	**Prophet**	**Evangelist**	**Teacher**	**Pastor**
Apostle	Prophecy	Evangelist	Teacher	Pastor
Leadership	Discernment	Faith	Wisdom	Administration
Giving	Exhortation	Miracles	Knowledge	Hospitality
Celibacy	Intercessor	Healing	Mercy	Service & Help
	Tongues & Interpretations	Missionary	Preaching	Worship Leader
	Musician	Deliverance		Poverty (voluntary)
				Craftsman

The "Spiritual Gifts" Poster is part of the Christian Manifesto Poster series. Produced in Calgary, Alberta, Canada, by New Start Ministries Ltd.
These posters are available for sale from: www.newstartministries.ca COPYRIGHT 2022

The Ten Stages in the Life of a Christian

ENTREPRENEUR

1. **I THOUGHT IT** – God gives you the vision, and you have a flash of euphoric inspiration. (Prov. 8:12)

2. **I CAUGHT IT** – You start to get excited about the vision but make the mistake of telling your family and friends, and they tell you that you are crazy and that your idea will never work. (Proverbs 29:18)

3. **I BOUGHT IT** – You consider the cost of the vision, pay the price and get nothing but discouragement, but you decide to live by faith. (Romans 1:17; Galatians 3:17)

4. **I SOUGHT IT** – Nobody can talk you out of it, but despite that, you lose money and begin to second guess yourself. Then you remember that God is bigger. (Philippians 4:13)

5. **I FOUGHT IT** – To keep from "losing it" while others are mocking you. You want to quit. (Psalm 27:14)

6. **I WAS FRAUGHT WITH FEAR** – but I persevered. (Isaiah 41:10)

7. **I GOT IT** – YOU MEET WITH SUCCESS! You actually possess the dream and are glad you paid the price. (I Samuel 18:14)

8. **I HAD AN ONSLAUGHT** – Suddenly, everyone wants to be your "best friend," and your family completely supports you. (Ezekiel 16:14) So,

9. **I TAUGHT IT** – You pass it on to the next generation. (Matthew 5:19)

10. **I HAVE AN AFTERTHOUGHT** – and realize that God was with me all the time. (Deuteronomy 31:6b)

WEALTH.

Jesus was beyond

Without the obligations of managing/owning a vineyard, Jesus turned water into wine, and it wasn't even His water! Not just wine, but "the best wine," without even paying for it! (John 2:10)

As an inside trader in the fishing industry, He had prior knowledge in respect to the location and volume of catch that would make any futures trader on the New York Stock Exchange a millionaire in 30 days. (John 21:6)

Of the twelve businessmen He dined with on one occasion, Jesus could predict which one could not be trusted, right down to the time that the betrayal took place (Matthew 26:21), as well as which of the twelve would deny Him, even after publicly confirming a vote of confidence in favour of Jesus' leadership. (Matthew 26:34) Any executive demonstrating such insight into people's character as Jesus possessed could easily demand a "mega salary" to chair the board meetings of any multinational conglomerate corporation and they would be so willingly pay.

When it came to paying taxes, He was able to extinguish His liability simply by having a fish pay the tax for Him! (Matthew 17:27)

He could heal the incurable diseases of His day with just a touch, and no medical costs. (Luke 5:13)

When He wanted to travel into town, without so much as a phone call, He had a donkey waiting that He had never bred, never fed, never stabled, or ever trained, and He never had to worry about parking when He arrived at His destination! He received a voluntary "red carpet" reception. (Matthew 21:7)

If "knowledge is wealth," Jesus tops the list again, as the intellectuals of His day marveled at His knowledge. (Luke 20:26; John 7: 14-15)

His Father owns the largest cattle ranch on the planet (Psalm 50:10), the whole Earth itself and everything in it. (Psalm 24:1)

Jesus' house contains many mansions, and the road on the main street in His neighborhood is constructed with gold. (Rev. 21:21)

He was able to multiply assets exponentially! In the case of the feeding of the 5,000 men, if we conclude that one person would have eaten half a loaf of bread and one fish, then Jesus' "food fund" showed a capital growth rate of 50,000% per day (bread) and over 250,000% per day (fish).

Jesus was a trend dresser, so much so that after His death, rather than cut up His coat and divide it four ways as a souvenir, the soldiers decided to draw straws for this trophy and keep the quality seamless garment as one piece. (John 19:23-24)

His burial was that reserved for the very, very rich. In this case, the mega rich merchant Joseph, from the town of Arimathea, owned the tomb that Jesus was buried in, so He didn't even have to pay a dime for the tomb! (Matthew 27:60)

Jesus was beyond wealth, because you clearly can't give what you haven't got, and you can't lead from behind, so when Jesus' Father promised to give wealth, He could only do so if He first possessed wealth (Ecclesiastis 5:19). You would, therefore, not be surprised to discover that this same Jesus was able to teach His wealth techniques to the "apprentices" that followed Him and do the things that He did with His power, which He and we could also do – and even greater things! (Deuteronomy 8:18; John 14:12)

Jesus was clearly beyond wealth!

(and He is willing to teach it to us. Are you willing to learn it?)

The "Wealth" Poster is part of the The Christian Life Manifesto Series. Produced in Calgary, Alberta, Canada by New Start Ministries Ltd. Written by Dr. Peter J. Daniels and re-printed with permission. www.newstartministries.ca COPYRIGHT 2022

The Christian Life
COMMANDMENTS

1. Be humble. (I Peter 5: 6-7)
1. Be humble. (I Peter 5: 6-7)
2. Live by faith. (Romans 1:17)
3. Give to the poor. (Proverbs 19:17)
4. Listen more, and talk less. (James 1:19)
5. Be kind to unkind people. (Ephesians 4:32)
6. Know when to keep quiet. (Proverbs 15: 1-2)
7. Confess your mistakes and sins. (I John 1:9)
8. Life is not fair; get used to it. (Ephesians 9:11)
9. Strive for excellence, not perfection. (Titus 3:8)
10. Be on time. Don't make excuses. (Philippians 2:14)
11. Don't worry about anything. Trust God. (Matthew 6:25-27)
12. Stop blaming others for your circumstances. (Romans 2:1)
13. Bless someone when they cut you off in line. (Luke 16:27)
14. Cultivate good manners, including table manners. (Titus 3:2)
15. Love God and your neighbor as yourself. (Mark 12:30-31)
16. Tithe 10% of your gross income to your church. (Malachi 3:10)
17. Change your circumstances with positive confessions. (Matthew 12:37)
18. Exercise and take care of your temple of the Holy Spirit every day. (3 John 1:2)
19. Return what you borrow in better shape than when you borrowed it. (2 Kings 6:5)
20. Take time daily to be alone with God, and learn to hear His voice. (John 10:27-28)
21. Learn from the past. Plan for the future, and live in the present. (Deuteronomy 4:9)
22. Do something nice anonymously. God knows about it; no one else has to. (Matthew 6:4)
23. When you travel, learn everything about the country you are going to. (2 Timothy 2:15)
24. The entire world can change if people would humble, pray, seek and turn to God. (II Chronicles 7:14)
25. Meditate on the Word daily. "This Book of the Law shall not depart from your mouth, but you shall meditate on it day and night, so that you may be careful to do according to all that is written in it. For then you will make your way prosperous, and then you will have good success." (Joshua 1:8 ESV)

GOD By Design

By Design:

- You were created before the earth was. (Eph. 1:4, Jer.1:5)
- You were created in His image. (Gen. 1:27)
- You were created to worship. (Is. 43:21) If it's not God you are worshiping, then it will be some other thing or narcissistic endeavour; it is God's nature for you to worship.
- You were created to do good works. (Eph. 2:10)
- You were created to connect with Him; depend on Him moment by moment. (Acts 17:28)
- You were created to live in an "earth suit" here on this planet for a limited time to bring heaven into the earth (Matt. 6:10), and in doing so, your job is to go out into the world and make disciples of all men. (Matt. 28:19)
- You are to continue this life as soul and spirit only in eternal heaven (paradise) with God. However, God gives you freedom, and that freedom is the ability to "choose" as to whether you live for Him now and with Him later. (Deut. 30:19, Jos. 24:15)

Starting Life and Living it to the Fullest.

Years ago, an article in our local newspaper about a community building under construction to help the "bored youth." I wrote the following letter to the editor.

To our "bored youth." Here are some suggestions to help you with your problem: rake the lawn, plant a garden, paint the fence, clean the garage, wash the car, make some repairs around the house, learn to cook, sew, paint, build, or any of dozens of other hobbies; shovel the snow for a senior, give help to a pastor or priest, tutor someone, read to the blind, visit the sick or the senior's centre, coach a minor-league, become a Brownie or Scout Leader, learn to play a musical instrument, go to church, work on volunteer organizations, help a disabled person, go buy the groceries for people who are "shut ins," help your parents and a teacher, do your homework, start a fund raiser for a charity, register for a continuing education course, participate in any of dozens of recreational activities that are in abundance in our community, get involved in politics, get a job, start your own business, surf the net and learn something, babysit, and if all else fails go to the library and read a non-fiction book! (note: a man I know started mowing lawns when he was 14. Here it is years later, and he has 35 staff.)

Your parents do not owe you entertainment, your community does not owe you recreational facilities, and the world does not owe you anything. On the contrary, you owe the world something - your time, energy, gifts, talents, and money so that no one will be at war, in poverty, sick or lonely again. Life is about making the world a better place when you leave than when you arrived. Don't be a protester; grow up and be an agent of change...

Billions of people are, cold, poor, sick, hurt, hungry, or at war because you haven't helped them. Life is not about you. So, what are you bored about and what are you waiting for?

Made in the USA
Columbia, SC
25 August 2024

41128794R00176